Turning | Points
IN WORLD HISTORY

The Scientific Revolution

Mitchell Young, *Book Editor*

Bruce Glassman, *Vice President*
Bonnie Szumski, *Publisher*
Helen Cothran, *Managing Editor*

GREENHAVEN PRESS
An imprint of Thomson Gale, a part of The Thomson Corporation

THOMSON

GALE

509
SCI

Detroit • New York • San Francisco • San Diego • New Haven, Conn.
Waterville, Maine • London • Munich

© 2006 Thomson Gale, a part of The Thomson Corporation.

Thomson and Star Logo are trademarks and Gale and Greenhaven Press are registered trademarks used herein under license.

For more information, contact
Greenhaven Press
27500 Drake Rd.
Farmington Hills, MI 48331-3535
Or you can visit our Internet site at http://www.gale.com

Cover credit: © Giraudon/Art Resource, NY
Library of Congress, 12, 62, 76

LIBRARY OF CONGRESS CATALOGING-IN-PUBLICATION DATA

Young, Mitchell.
    The scientific revolution / Mitchell Young, book editor.
        p. cm. — (Turning points in world history)
    Includes bibliographical references and index.
    ISBN 0-7377-2987-2 (lib. : alk. paper)
        1. Science—History. I. Title. II. Turning points (Greenhaven Press)
    Q125.Y676 2006
    509—dc22
                                                                2005040268

Printed in the United States of America

Contents

The "Father of Chemistry," Robert Boyle, was one of the first great experimenters. His chemistry experiments set a standard of excellence for future laboratory scientists.

Chapter 4: The Legacy of Science

investigation as a means of gaining true insight into
nature.

Foreword

Certain past events stand out as pivotal, as having effects and outcomes that change the course of history. These events are often referred to as turning points. Historian Louis L. Snyder provides this useful definition:

> A turning point in history is an event, happening, or stage which thrusts the course of historical development into a different direction. By definition a turning point is a great event, but it is even more—a great event with the explosive impact of altering the trend of man's life on the planet.

History's turning points have taken many forms. Some were single, brief, and shattering events with immediate and obvious impact. The invasion of Britain by William the Conqueror in 1066, for example, swiftly transformed that land's political and social institutions and paved the way for the rise of the modern English nation. By contrast, other single events were deemed of minor significance when they occurred, only later recognized as turning points. The assassination of a little-known European nobleman, Archduke Franz Ferdinand, on June 28, 1914, in the Bosnian town of Sarajevo was such an event; only after it touched off a chain reaction of political-military crises that escalated into the global conflict known as World War I did the murder's true significance become evident.

Other crucial turning points occurred not in terms of a few hours, days, months, or even years, but instead as evolutionary developments spanning decades or even centuries. One of the most pivotal turning points in human history, for instance—the development of agriculture, which replaced nomadic hunter-gatherer societies with more permanent settlements—occurred over the course of many generations. Still other great turning points were neither events nor developments, but rather revolutionary new inventions and innovations that significantly altered social customs and ideas, military tactics, home life, the spread of knowledge, and the human condition in general. The developments of writing, gunpowder, the printing press, antibiotics, the electric light, atomic energy, television, and the computer, the last two of which have recently ushered in the world-altering information age, represent only some of these innovative turning points.

Each anthology in the Greenhaven Turning Points in World History series presents a group of essays chosen for their accessibility. The anthology's structure also enhances this accessibility. First, an introductory essay provides a general overview of the principal events and figures involved, placing the topic in its historical context. The essays that follow explore various aspects in more detail, some targeting political trends and consequences, others social, literary, cultural, and/or technological ramifications, and still others pivotal leaders and other influential figures. To aid the reader in choosing the material of immediate interest or need, each essay is introduced by a concise summary of the contributing writer's main themes and insights.

In addition, each volume contains extensive research tools, including a collection of excerpts from primary source documents pertaining to the historical events and figures under discussion. In the anthology on the French Revolution, for example, readers can examine the works of Rousseau, Voltaire, and other writers and thinkers whose championing of human rights helped fuel the French people's growing desire for liberty; the French *Declaration of the Rights of Man and Citizen*, presented to King Louis XVI by the French National Assembly on October 2, 1789; and eyewitness accounts of the attack on the royal palace and the horrors of the Reign of Terror. To guide students interested in pursuing further research on the subject, each volume features an extensive bibliography, which for easy access has been divided into separate sections by topic. Finally, a comprehensive index allows readers to scan and locate content efficiently. Each of the anthologies in the Greenhaven Turning Points in World History series provides students with a complete, detailed, and enlightening examination of a crucial historical watershed.

Introduction

We are surrounded by the products of applied science. Science is the force behind the antibiotics that have conquered diseases, the technology that makes air travel possible, and the communication networks that allow us to see and hear events happening around the world. Science has allowed the average citizen of an advanced, industrial economy to enjoy products beyond the wildest dreams of the greatest rulers and richest people of just a century or two ago.

Perhaps more important, however, is that we have grown accustomed to thinking scientifically. Most educated Americans expect to be shown proof of claims. We expect logical arguments to be backed up by "hard evidence," that is, evidence one can see, hear, or touch. Many go even further. We have to some extent acquired the habit of weighing differing explanations for things against real-world evidence.

This way of thinking is not necessarily natural. For much of human history, people believed in superstition or let their religious beliefs shape their view of the natural world. However, around the middle of the sixteenth century things began to change. A young lawyer and astronomer named Nicolaus Copernicus wrote a treatise that, contrary to the accepted wisdom of the day, claimed to prove that Earth revolves around the sun.

A New Way of Thinking

Though Copernicus's theory was important in and of itself, it was more important as a turning point in the way people thought about the world. In the Middle Ages, knowledge had been pursued largely by looking back into the past. The primary example of a learned man was a monk, who sought knowledge in books; most did not engage in experimentation nor direct observation of nature.

Copernicus's theory was an impetus to change this system of learning. In order to prove (or disprove) his theory, astronomers throughout Europe initiated close observations of the skies. Their investigations became ever more thorough and systematic. Thus, a new way of thinking was born, one that emphasized testing theories against observed facts. To improve testing, scholars tried to increase the quality and quantity of observations.

This new attitude of testing beliefs by observation, of performing experiments to prove theories, was one of the greatest legacies of the scientific revolution. The "scientific method" of forming a theory, devising an experiment (whether in nature or in a laboratory) to test the theory, and then discarding the theory or revising it to fit the observed data has played a vital role in advancing both the theoretical knowledge of nature and the practical ability to control nature. Perhaps because of their awe at the scholars' very real achievements, many people tend to see the great scientists of the past as advancing from theory to critical experiment to improved theory in an unbroken chain of success.

Looking closer, however, the scientific revolution was not so straightforward. The discoveries were often preceded by years of work that was totally in error. Some of the greatest heroes of science held beliefs that today would be considered superstitious. They even dabbled in investigations that now look like utter foolishness. Robert Boyle, the "Father of Chemistry," for example, pursued the medieval pseudo-science of alchemy, the primary goal of which was the discovery of the "philosopher's stone," a substance that supposedly would change lead into gold and make humans immortal. Isaac Newton, whose discovery of the laws of motion and gravity were the greatest triumph of the scientific revolution, was also seduced by the mysteries of alchemy.

Discoveries that, looking back from a distance of hundreds of years, appear as sudden flashes of insight into nature turn out on closer inspection to be the result of slow trial and error, or completely wrong in the details. Author Arthur Koestler wrote about the sometimes unsure efforts of early scientists; he described the early scientists as "sleepwalkers" stumbling across discoveries whose importance they failed to recognize or pursuing ideas that seemed eminently scientific but turned out to be totally mistaken.

Yet in the years between the middle of the sixteenth century and the early 1700s, scientists changed their way of thinking and their way of approaching nature, which truly did have a revolutionary effect. And though perhaps not as rapid or as exciting to watch as a political revolution, the new science probably changed our world more than the events of the American or French revolutions. It is worthwhile, therefore, to investigate the Copernican revolution in more detail.

The Revolution Begins

The scientific revolution began in an unlikely place, the city of Torun. Torun, in what is now Poland, was a major settlement, but it was far from the new centers of learning that had developed during the Renaissance. However, it was where the young religious lawyer and astronomer Nicolaus Copernicus chose to settle after his legal studies in Italy. Copernicus had learned the habits of mind and techniques of inquiry that were characteristic of scholarly life in Renaissance Italy. Among these were a stress on observation and a healthy questioning of accepted dogma. On returning to his home country, Copernicus kept up with his study of astronomy. In 1543 he circulated a manuscript called the *Commentariolus*, which would lead to a full-scale revolution in the way people think about the universe.

Contrary to learned opinion at the time, Copernicus held that Earth revolved around the sun. In announcing this, Copernicus was overturning the whole belief system of the late Middle Ages. That belief system had two foundations: the literal truth of the Bible and the philosophy of the ancient Greek philosopher Aristotle.

Why was Copernicus's work such a challenge to the medieval system of thought? The answer is partly that the church, a powerful institution at the time, believed in the literal, word-for-word truth of the Bible. The Bible clearly stated that the sun moved (rather than Earth). Indeed, God had made the sun stand still in order to give the ancient Israelites an advantage in a battle. How could God make the sun stand still if it was not already moving? Perhaps more important was the symbolic nature of removing Earth from its position at the center of the solar system and therefore at the center of the universe. After all, Earth was humanity's home, and humaniy was God's finest creation. Would God put his finest creation anywhere but the center of the universe? Copernicus's theory took away the central nature of Earth.

A second problem was the dominance of the philosophy of Aristotle. Aristotle believed that Earth was the center of the universe. Moreover, his philosophy led him to believe that heavenly bodies are perfect; they behaved differently than objects on Earth. For example, their motion was said to form a per-

Nicolaus Copernicus

fect circle, because it was unthinkable to Aristotle that a heavenly body could travel in a path that he considered imperfect, such as an ellipse (oval).

Aristotle's philosophy, including his beliefs about the "perfect" nature of planets and their motions, influenced the greatest astronomer of the ancient era, Claudius Ptolemy. Ptolemy, a Greek who lived in Alexandria, Egypt, devised a solar system that conformed to Aristotle's beliefs. He put Earth at the center of the solar system and the universe. He had the planets travel in perfect circles. Ptolemy had a problem, however; the planets at times appeared to stop and even move backward in their path across the sky. Scientists today know that this is due to Earth overtaking planets, similar to how a car you are overtaking on the freeway, seems to move backward. But Ptolemy, believing Earth to be stationary at the center of the solar system, could not use the relative motion of Earth as a way of accounting for the apparent backward movement of planets. Instead, he devised a system of smaller circles called epicycles that the planets also moved along. The planets thus had a "great circle" orbit and smaller circles that were centered on the great circle. With this system of circles within circles, Ptolemy was able to account for many of the planets' apparent backward motions.

The Breakdown of the Ptolemaic System

Two things led to the breakdown of the Ptolemaic system. First, there was an ever increasing amount of data available for astronomers to analyze. The invention of the printing press made the reproduction of observations of astronomers much cheaper and easier than the laborious hand copying of this information. Now the observations of astronomers from all over Europe were available for calculation and recalculation of astronomical charts. With these new observations, the Ptolemaic system had to be readjusted constantly, with new epicycles added or old epicycles subtracted to make sense of the data.

Second, a general rediscovery of the culture of the ancient Greeks meant that the work of ancient philosophers and astronomers other than Aristotle and Ptolemy was being read for the first time in centuries. Some of these astronomers believed that the solar system was sun centered. Copernicus learned of these ancient thinkers during his time in Rome. He would continue to be influenced by them after his return to Poland.

Copernicus's Assumptions

With more data available to him, and inspired by other astronomers who thought the sun was the center of the universe, Copernicus set out to devise a system that would account for the apparent motions of the planets—especially their apparent changes of direction. He spent years on the project. His first writing on the subject, known today as the *Commentariolus*, was a brief outline of his ideas. In it, Copernicus, trying to account for the data that had been accumulating, starts out with a radical new set of assumptions.

His first assumption was that there was no one center around which all the heavenly bodies revolved. His second assumption was that Earth was not the center of the universe but only the center of gravity and the moon's orbit. His third assumption was that the sun was the center of the universe. These statements form the core of the Copernican system. By placing the sun at the center of the solar system and by having Earth revolve around the sun, Copernicus managed to simplify the motion of all the planets.

Copernicus almost achieved a completely accurate view of the solar system. Unfortunately, he still held to the belief that the heavenly bodies, because they were perfect, could travel only in a perfect motion. That is, they could travel only in spherical orbits. Today it is known that the planets, including Earth, travel in elliptical orbits around the sun. This small difference, small because the ellipses of the planets' orbits are very near to circles, was an error that would puzzle astronomers for a century after Copernicus's work. Paradoxically, this puzzlement led to scientific advance, as new theories were tested to try to account for the error in the Copernican system.

Controversy over the Copernican System

Copernicus's system was challenged and debated. At first the church did not seek to suppress it. Indeed, a high-ranking clergyman wrote a letter in support of Copernicus's work, which was published along with the *Commentariolus*. The system seemed to be just another system of so-called sky geometry, a way of conceiving the world to make accurate predictions of where the planets would be in the night sky. However, the Copernican system had more shattering implications than just another hypothetical system of looking at the universe. The quest to prove Copernicus correct led to more careful observation of the heavens, more compiling of data, and finally the breakdown of the medieval way of looking at the world.

Copernicus often couched his ideas so that they appeared as mere thought experiments or hypothetical situations, having nothing to do with the motion of real heavenly bodies. Meanwhile, Galileo Galilei, the genius Italian astronomer who was profoundly influenced by Copernicus, insisted on the reality of the motion of Earth and the planets. Galileo had an advantage over the Polish astronomer, the telescope. Galileo was the first to use the telescope for systematic investigation of the heavens.

The discoveries Galileo made were astounding. He discovered and mapped the craters of the moon, the rings of Saturn, and the moons of Jupiter. This last discovery was considered especially important, as it showed that Earth was not the center of every motion in the solar system; Jupiter was the center of motion for its moons. Perhaps more significant was Galileo's discovery of the phases of Venus. That is, he observed phases as the planet revolved around the sun. When it was on the opposite side of the sun from Earth, Venus appeared to be "full," just as the moon appears full when Earth is between it and the sun. (Both Venus and the moon are not hidden by the sun or Earth, respectively, because the orbits of revolution of Earth, Venus, and the moon lie on slightly different planes.) Conversely, when Venus and Earth were at right angles with respect to the sun, Venus appeared half in shadow. The phases, because they were exactly the same as those of the moon, proved that Venus revolved around the sun, just as the moon revolved around Earth.

Initially, Galileo's views were accepted by the educated public of his day. Even clergymen were open to his ideas. However, there was soon a backlash against Galileo. It was probably not helpful that he wrote a book in which the character who held to the old (non-Copernican) thinking about the solar system was called Simpleton. Galileo was duly brought before the religious authorities and ordered to recant his belief that Earth moved around the sun. Under threat of torture, Galileo recanted.

The Unstoppable Advance of Science

Although the religious authorities may have won the battle in Galileo's case, they were losing the war. The Protestant Reformation was under way in Europe. Astronomers and others with beliefs that would be condemned as heretical came under the protection of Protestant princes in northern Europe. As a result, they had the freedom to write the truth as they saw it. Thus the religious and political conditions in Europe were a great help in fostering the scientific revolution.

Perhaps because of the interest sparked by Copernicus and the Galileo trial, astronomers continued to compile data. In particular, the observations of the Danish astronomer Tycho Brahe set a new standard in accuracy and completeness. Tycho had a huge quadrant, a device for measuring the positions and angles of the planets at specified periods of time, built into his house. Again, the invention and spread of the printing press meant that the data from Tycho's observations was available to a wide audience of astronomers throughout Europe.

Astronomers continued to make advances in the analysis of the motion of the planets. Johannes Kepler refined Copernicus's system by reexamining Tycho Brahe's data. He had such confidence in Tycho's data that, when coming across what appeared to be an error, he repeatedly rechecked his calculations rather than question the accuracy of the data. Finally Kepler noticed a pattern in the data; if one assumed that orbits were elliptical (oval) rather than circular, the "error" disappeared. This insight led Kepler to formulate the laws of planetary motion.

Kepler's laws went beyond merely describing the shape of the orbits. He was able to work out a mathematical formula that related the speed of the planets' motions to their distance from the sun. Kepler thus showed that the planets accelerated and decelerated in their orbits. This was a major breakthrough. It pointed to a link between the force acting on the planets in motion around the sun and the forces that acted on objects on Earth. These could be the simple fall of an object from a tower or more complex motions like that of a cannonball in flight. Investigators such as Galileo had suspected such a link; Galileo had performed experiments that pointed in this direction and showed how such motions underwent acceleration with time. Kepler's insights, however, were more exactly formulated. They proved the key that Isaac Newton needed to fully understand the laws of motion and gravity. Newton explained those laws in his work *Philosophiae Naturalis Principia Mathematica* (*Mathematical Principles of Natural Philosophy*).

The Victory of the Scientific Revolution

In a way, Newton's *Principia* marks the end of the scientific revolution. This is not to say that discoveries ended; there have been thousands of significant discoveries in physics alone since Newton's time. But the revolutionary phase was over, and the scientific method had won. It was now accepted that laboratory experiments were central to science, as was the careful observation of phenomena in nature. It was accepted that mathematics was the language of science and that nature could best be described in concise mathematical formulas. The importance of testing theories against data from experiments or real-world observation was equally accepted. No longer would knowledge be limited to the study and restudy of ancient works. Discovery became the ideal of scholars, even of historians who dig in archives in the hope of discovering new documents.

The progression outlined above, from the first conception of a sun-centered solar system by Copernicus to Newton's discovery of the laws of motion, leaves out a host of other developments in science. The formation of scientific associations, like London's Royal Society, played a great role in expanding the new knowledge. Scientific journals spread the new ideas to a wider audience than the traditional exchange of personal correspondence between experimenters. In addition, something like modern research laboratories were founded, either by wealthy private individuals such as Robert Boyle or by monarchs seeking to increase the prestige of their kingdoms. All of these factors and more helped the scientific revolution achieve its ultimate victory. But in the end the triumph of science was primarily due to the diligent observations and calculations of Copernicus and those who followed him. Today we enjoy the fruits of the revolution that began almost five centuries ago when Copernicus first questioned accepted wisdom about the way the world worked.

Chapter 1

The Roots of the Scientific Revolution

Turning | Points
IN WORLD HISTORY

Ancient Scientists Anticipate Modern Discoveries

R.J. Harvey-Gibson

The ancient Greeks were the first people known to have developed the systematic investigation of nature using observation, experiment, and mathematics. As such, they are the first people to truly have practiced what is now called science. Although the Egyptians and the Babylonians observed and even predicted events such as flooding and eclipses, these peoples linked such observations with religious ritual. The Greeks freed science from ritual and thus gave thinkers more room to investigate and learn nature's secrets.

The modern image of science usually involves highly specialized scientists carrying out experiments in laboratories. The Greeks had a much broader view of scientific knowledge. For them, natural science, humanities, and the arts were all one. Those who pursued nature's secrets were called philosophers, lovers of wisdom. Thus a philosopher like Aristotle could investigate and write about physics, biology, drama, and politics. Some Greeks, however, like today's scientists, specialized in very specific areas.

In the following excerpts, botany professor R.J. Harvey-Gibson explains some of the achievements of those ancient Greek scientists who concentrated on a particular area of knowledge. Though most of their work was forgotten during the Middle Ages, its rediscovery during the Renaissance inspired the scientists of the early scientific revolution.

Solstices and Equinoxes.—We must go back very far indeed to find the name of the first enquirer into Nature's secrets; this was Thales of Asia Minor [now Turkey], who was in his

R.J. Harvey-Gibson, *Two Thousand Years of Science: The Wonders of Nature and Their Discoverers*. London: A&C Black, Ltd., 1929.

prime somewhere about 600 B.C. He was an astronomer of high rank, for he was the discoverer of the Solstices and the Equinoxes—terms we use to this day. The sun appears to rise in the east, to sweep across the sky and set in the west, but that journey is short in winter and much longer in summer. In mid-winter the sun reaches a certain height in the heavens, and keeps on reaching the same height for several days in succession—in other words, it appears to stand still; there is a solstice, or "sun-standing." As the sun's height above the horizon at noon is not very great, we have a short day and a long night; but, as the weeks pass by, the sun rises higher and higher and remains above the horizon longer and longer, until at length it is twelve hours above the horizon and twelve hours below it. This is the time of the spring equinox, when day and night are of equal length. Upwards still the sun mounts in the sky, the day lengthens and the night shortens, until, once more, the sun keeps on reaching the same height for several days. This is the period of the summer solstice. Another three months pass while the sun gradually fails to reach its previous height, and the day and night once more become of equal length. This is the autumn equinox. Finally the sun sinks to the level it reached at the winter solstice. Of course, with a little patience, anyone can follow this cycle of solstices and equinoxes for himself, but Thales has the credit of having been the first to note and record these phenomena.

Discoveries in Astronomy

Phases of the Moon.—About once a month we have a new moon, a slender crescent in the sky, which gradually thickens until the whole surface reflects the light of the sun, and then less and less of it shines on us until it disappears altogether. These different conditions are called the "phases of the moon," and are due to its position with regard to the sun in its journey round the earth. When the moon is between us and the sun its dark face is turned towards us; when it is a quarter of its way round its orbit we see half of its surface illuminated, and when it is opposite to the sun its full face is exposed—a full moon. In this last case it might be asked how do we come to see a full moon at all? Will not the earth block off the sun's rays from it? The explanation is that the plane of the moon's orbit does not quite coincide with that of the earth round the sun, so that the sun's rays may sometimes pass over, and at other times under it.

All this may seem a very simple matter to us nowadays, but to the ancients it meant a knowledge, not only of the fact that the moon shines only by reflected light, but also of the fact that it revolves round the earth in about a month. These facts were discovered by a friend of Thales, called Anaximander, who was also the first to teach the Greeks how to measure time by means of a sundial.

Mathematician, Astronomer and Geologist.—Pythagoras was also a native of the Ægean coast, and lived at about the same time. In philosophy, mathematics and natural science— in all alike he excelled, but it is in his discoveries in the last that we are most interested. He taught that the earth was a globe which revolved round a central fire; that the sea had once been land and the land had been sea; that islands had once formed parts of continents; that mountains were for ever being washed down by rivers into the ocean; that volcanoes were outlets for subterranean fires; that fossils were the buried remains of plants and animals turned into stone. These are commonplaces now in every school book on physical geography, but were very startling announcements to the Greeks, who saw in Etna the chimney of Vulcan's forge, and who believed that Olympus was the permanent abode of the immortal gods.

Physics and Medicine

The Atomic Theory.—In these early days most philosophers held that the earth was composed of four elements—earth, water, fire and air; but one thinker, called Democritus, a native of Thrace, explained the structure of the universe in another way. He said that it was made up of infinitely minute particles differing from each other in size, weight, shape, etc., and that these particles were indivisible, invisible, and indestructible—"atoms," he called them, i.e., particles that could not be cut in two, as the word means. At the beginning the atoms were in constant motion, but by and by they came together by chance and united in various ways to form solids, liquids and gases. Modern chemistry is founded on a somewhat similar idea, which we call the "atomic theory," although we interpret the facts differently.

The Father of Medicine.—These ancient thinkers had thus made a beginning in the study of four out of the five great sciences. There was left biology, the science of life, and it was only natural that they should commence their enquiries in that subject with the living organism that interested them most—the human body. This was done by a pupil of Democritus, Hippocrates, who has been called the "Father of Medicine." In those days ailments were thought to be inflicted by the gods, and thus the priests were obviously the appointed physicians, who made an excellent liveli-

Measuring the Earth

The ancient Greek mathematician Eratosthenes was able to estimate the size of the earth from the different lengths of shadows cast at different points of the earth. At Syene, an African city on the equator, no shadow was cast by a stone pillar (gnomon) at noon of the longest day of the year, while at Alexandria, a small shadow was cast. Eratosthenes used geometry to figure out the difference in the angles the pillars made with the vertical rays of the sun. From this he determined that Alexandria was about 1/50th of the circumference of the earth from Syene.

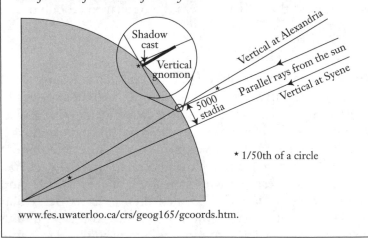

www.fes.uwaterloo.ca/crs/geog165/gcoords.htm.

hood out of the offerings of the patients who came to seek relief at the shrines of Æsculapius, the god of healing. Hippocrates introduced a new system of treatment; he began by making a careful study of the patient's body, and having diagnosed the complaint, set about curing it by giving directions to the sufferer as to his diet and the routine of his daily life, leaving Nature largely to heal herself. This was not, strictly speaking, biology as we understand it, but it was at least an attempt at the study of one living organism.

The First Research Centers

The Academy and the Lyceum.—In Ancient Athens there were two great schools, or rather universities, known as the Academy and the Lyceum. The head of the former was the renowned philosopher, Plato, and of the latter, the equally famous Aristotle. With Plato we have really nothing to do, for he was not a scientific man—indeed, he might almost be said to have despised natural science. On the other hand, Aristotle, although he also ranked as a philosopher, was a keen student of Nature, and it is fortunate that so many of his writings on scientific subjects have come down to us, although in a roundabout way. The goal he set before himself was the preparation of a treatise on the whole of natural science as it was then understood, a very ambitious scheme which he carried out very unequally. His writings on what might be called the physical sciences were of little value, but those on living things, and especially on animals, were considered of great importance almost down to our own times. He was a very competent anatomist, and excelled in his descriptions of the forms and habits of animals, but he knew little or nothing of the way in which the animal machine worked—physiology—as we term the subject.

The First Botanist.—Aristotle also wrote a book on plants, which has been lost, although that does not matter very much, since his pupil and successor as head of the Lyceum, Theophrastus, has left us two treatises on plants which, doubtless, contain all that Aristotle had to say on the subject. Theophrastus was a native of Lesbos, and, as a boy, studied first under Plato and later under Aristotle, whose heir he became. Attached to the Lyceum was a botanic garden in which he taught his pupils, and where he cultivated the plants whose characters and life stories he speaks about in his works. He died somewhere about 300 B.C., and with him died the science of botany, for we do not hear of a single new discovery in that subject for over eighteen hundred years.

The Great Library at Alexandria

The Alexandrine Museum.—A new university was meanwhile rising in Egypt to take the place of the Lyceum. This was the Museum, or Abode of the Muses, founded by Ptolemy Soter, one of the generals of Alexander the Great. To this centre of learning Ptolemy and his successors on the throne enticed as many of the great philosophers of Greece and Ionia as they could induce to settle in Alexandria, and begged, bought, and even stole every book they could lay their hands on to form the great library, which is said to have contained no less than 700,000 volumes.

One of the great scholars who migrated to the banks of the Nile [River] was Euclid, whom every schoolboy knows as the writer of a famous book on geometry called "Euclid's Elements," but a far greater than he was Archimedes, one of the most distinguished men in the history of science. He was born at Syracuse in Sicily, 287 B.C., and studied and afterwards taught in the Museum. He was a great mathematician, and wrote on the circle, the spiral, the parabola, the sphere and the cylinder. He was the first to make out the numerical relation between the circumference of a circle and its diameter, but his best work was done in the science of physics.

He is often credited with the discovery of the lever, but what he really did discover were the laws which governed its working. He found out also the principle of a system of pulleys, and towed a laden barge single-handed by their aid. He invented an endless screw for raising water, an apparatus still in use in some countries. It consists of a tube wound round an inclined axis, one end of the pipe dipping into the water to be raised, the other opening over a tank at a higher level. The water slowly mounts the tube as the handle is turned, as if up a spiral stairway.

Specific Gravity.—One of Archimedes's most important discoveries was the law of specific gravity. It is common knowledge how he exposed the fraudulent goldsmith who was commissioned to manufacture a golden crown for Hiero, ruler of Syracuse, by estimating the amount of water displaced by equal weights of gold, silver and an alloy of these two metals, and so determining the relative amounts of gold and silver in the crown. . . .

Charting the Heavens and the Earth

The last of the great men of the Alexandrine school was Ptolemy, or Claudius Ptolemæus, to distinguish him from the reigning house. He was an Egyptian, and lived in the middle of the second century of the Christian era. In spite of the fact that both Aristarchus and Hipparchus had taught in a quite convincing manner that the earth travelled round the sun, and that he was quite familiar with their views, seeing that he edited their works, it is extraordinary that Ptolemy put forward a theory of the universe of his own which was entirely erroneous, but which, nevertheless, was thoroughly believed in by the whole world, learned and unlearned, for well nigh fifteen hundred years. After weighing pros and cons, he decided that the earth was a stationary globe, and that the sun, moon and stars revolved round it. This is known as the Geocentric Theory, and it held its ground until Copernicus, in the middle of the sixteenth century, exposed the fallacies that underlay it. Ptolemy also attempted to describe the surface features of the earth itself—in other words, to write a textbook of geography. Here again he had the help of a Greek philosopher who had lived more than three and a half centuries before him—Eratosthenes.

The Measurement of the Earth.—Eratosthenes was the royal librarian at Alexandria, and was the first to draw parallels of latitude by the simple method of joining all the places known to him where, on a certain date, the length of the day was the same, for he rightly judged that all such places must be at the same distance from the equator. It was easy then to draw lines at right angles to these parallels and obtain those of longitude. From this he was led to make an attempt at measuring the circumference of the earth, which he did in the following manner. Almost on the line of longitude that passed through Alexandria there was another city, Syene, now called Assouan, and he noticed that, at the summer solstice, a pillar there cast no shadow at noon, while another pillar of the same height at Alexandria did cast a shadow. Now if a circle be described with a radius equal to the height of the pillar at Alexandria, the shadow will form a small arc on it, and the length of that arc will bear the same proportion to the circumference of the circle as the distance between Alexandria and Syene will bear to the circumference of the earth. Eratosthenes found the arc was 1/50 of the small circle, and that the distance between the two cities was 5,000 stadia, or, since a stadium is 607 feet, about 574 miles. Multiplying this figure by 50 gives the circumference of the earth as 28,700 miles, not a very accurate result, but not bad for a first attempt.

The Geographer.—Strabo, who lived about a century before Ptolemy, was a geographer of some note. He made a map of the then known world, and, more important still, travelled over much of it and described the things he saw. Although Vesuvius was not a "burning mountain" in his day, he compared its shape with that of Etna, and said it might spring into life again, as indeed it did, some sixty years after he died, when it destroyed Pompeii and Herculaneum. Strabo had no hesitation in saying that the presence of fossil shells in rocks many miles from the sea proved that these rocks must have been formed from silt brought down by great rivers, like the Nile, to form deltas in which these animals once lived.

The Decadence of Science

After Ptolemy's death, science in Alexandria, and indeed in the world generally, began to decay. The Romans, who succeeded the Greeks in the dominion of the world, had no taste for pure science, and those few scholars that were left contented themselves with reading and expounding the works of Aristotle and Ptolemy to their pupils, and made very few discoveries of their own.

The bud had passed into its long winter sleep.

Aristotle's Science Hinders Progress in the Middle Ages

A. George Molland

Today, Aristotle's scientific works are viewed as irrelevant curiosities. In most areas of science, Aristotle's theories were incorrect. In the following selection, Scottish historian of science and mathematics A. George Molland argues that, by influencing so many scientists, Aristotle's way of looking at the world hindered the development of modern science. Aristotle's teachings were so revered that scholars hesitated to believe their own investigations if they contradicted his. Therefore, Molland holds, it was necessary to escape from the "Aristotelian predicament" before science could advance.

Between the centre of the Aristotelian universe (where lay the earth) and its extremities a radical break occurred at the moon. From the moon outwards the world consisted of a number (perhaps 55) of spherical shells which moved continually with uniform circular motions and some of which carried planets or stars. The heavenly regions were composed of a special or fifth element, whose nature it was to be moved with such motion. The motion was not completely self-caused, for ultimately the spheres were moved by desire for Aristotle's First Cause or God, and sometimes Aristotle also posited the existence of intelligences as movers of the individual spheres.

Below the sphere of the moon we are in the realms of generation and corruption, and all bodies are composed of the four elements earth, water, air and fire. None of these are found in a pure state, and all bodies are a mixture of all four,

A. George Molland, "Aristotelian Science," *Companion to the History of Modern Science*, edited by R.C. Olby, G.N. Cantor, J.R.R. Christie, and M.J.S. Hodge. London: Routledge, 1996. Copyright © 1990 by Routledge. Reproduced by permission of the publisher and the author.

but naturally earth is the dominant element in solids and water in liquids. The elements are determined by two sets of defining properties. The first set comprises four qualities which are regarded as more fundamental than the elements—hot, cold, wet and dry. Earth is cold and dry, water cold and wet, air hot and wet and fire hot and dry. The elements are not immutable, but by changes in their qualitative structure may convert into one another. The other set of defining properties comprised heaviness and lightness. Earth is absolutely heavy and fire absolutely light, whereas water is relatively heavy and air relatively light. Associated with this is the doctrine of natural places and motions. The natural place of earthy bodies is at the centre of the world, whereas that of fiery bodies is at the periphery of the elementary regions. If a body is not in its natural place, then, if unimpeded, it will move towards it.

Aristotle's Biology

This idea of bodies fulfilling their own natures, and the general tendency to speak of things moving from potentiality to actuality, are characteristic of Aristotle's science, and can be associated with his predilection for biology. Aristotle may be said to be at his most 'scientific' in his biological works, which contain a wealth of meticulous observations (including evidence from dissections), along with some rather unreliable travellers' tales. By comparison with the physical works these treatises were not widely studied in medieval and early modern Europe, but it can still be plausibly argued that biological modes of thought permeate the physical treatises also. Unlike [the character] Timaeus in Plato's dialogue of that name, Aristotle does not explicitly say that the universe is a huge (and spherical) living creature, but it does have many of the appropriate characteristics. This is particularly evident in Aristotle's concern with teleology, as in the example above when a body fulfils its nature by moving to a natural place, just as an acorn fulfils its nature by growing into an oak tree.

Obviously not all motions were natural, for when a stone is being raised it is being moved violently, that is, against its own nature. There were also voluntary motions in which animate bodies moved themselves. This threefold (natural, violent and voluntary) labelling could produce problems. For instance, the voluntary motion of an animal, in itself natural, can also be unnatural, as when it jumps. Here Aristotle appealed somewhat unclearly to a distinction between whole and parts. 'The animal as a whole moves itself naturally: but the body of the animal may be in motion unnaturally as well as naturally.' 'It would seem that in animals, just as in ships and things not naturally organised, that which causes motion is separate from that which suffers motion, and that it is only in this sense that the animal as a whole causes its own motion.' Examples such as this show how much the Aristotelian texts (which for the most part come to us as notes rather than as polished treatises) were in need of explication and discussion. An even bigger difficulty concerned the unnatural motions of inanimate objects, notably projectiles. If a stone is thrown upwards, it continues to move upwards after it has left the hand. But what then can be moving it since, being an inanimate object, it certainly needs a mover? Aristotle grasped the nettle firmly: the only thing in contact with it is the air, and so the air must be the mover. While moving the stone upwards, the hand also transmitted to the air the power of continuing this motion and of transmitting this power from one part of the air to the next.

Reactions to Aristotle

This explanation did not find universal favour, and many commentators, Greek, Arabic and Latin, produced thought experiments to demonstrate its implausibility. The usual alternative was to posit that some force was communicated directly to the projectile, which then continued the motion. In the fourteenth century, [French priest and scholar] Jean Buridan spoke of an 'impetus', and in the late sixteenth century, the young Galileo [Galilei, the Italian astronomer,] suggested an impressed force (*virtus impressa*). It is instructive to compare their attitudes. Buridan is apologetic about diverging from Aristotle: 'In my judgement this question is very difficult, because, as it seems to me, Aristotle has not settled (*determinavit*) it.' Galileo on the other hand is delightedly anti-

Aristotelian: 'Aristotle, as in practically everything that he wrote about locomotion, wrote the opposite of the truth on this question too.' Discussions of this problem did not occupy a big place in the Aristotelian tradition, but later scholars have seen them as an important step towards the principle of inertia of classical mechanics. There is some truth in this, but it is important to note that even Galileo at this stage was asking Aristotelian questions, even though he gave non-Aristotelian answers. It was only when he tried to stop asking such questions, and when [French philosopher and mathematician René] Descartes and others conceived of motion as something that was naturally conserved, that we can really sense the transition to classical mechanics. We must, however, remember that even [English physicist Sir Isaac] Newton had an innate force (*vis insita*) to account for a body's continuance in a state of rest or uniform rectilinear motion, but this was clearly contrasted with the more active impressed forces, and was in fact a force of inactivity (*vis inertiae*). . . .

Aristotle and Mathematics

The holistic orientation of Aristotle's thought also caused him to have ambivalent attitudes towards the use of mathematics in science. Geometry was his paradigm for a demonstrative science, and geometrical examples abound in the corpus. Moreover, in a famous passage, he implied that in many cases in natural science, the mathematician has a distinctly superior role to the observationalist:

> The reason why differs from the fact in another fashion, when each is considered by means of a different science. And such are those which are related to each other in such a way that the one is under the other, e.g. optics to geometry, and mechanics to solid geometry, and harmonics to arithmetic, and star-gazing to astronomy. . . . For here it is for the empirical [scientists] to know the fact and for the mathematical [to know] the reason why; for the latter have the demonstrations of the explanations, and often they do not know the fact, just as those who consider the universal often do not know some of the particulars through lack of observation.

However, other passages reveal that Aristotle had considerable difficulty in incorporating what he called the 'more physical of the branches of mathematics', such as optics, harmonics and astronomy, into his scheme of knowledge, and, with the possible exception of a problematic discussion of the rainbow, he himself did little to extend the penetration of mathematics into physics.

The ambivalence towards mathematics continued in the Aristotelian tradition. Some thinkers, such as [the Islamic philosopher] Averroes and Albertus Magnus, saw mathematics very much as skimming over the surface of things and accordingly giving us only superficial knowledge, whereas others, such as [English monk and scholar] Roger Bacon and [French priest and mathematician] Nicole Oresme, strove to increase its domain in the natural world. In general, however, they cannot be held to have had a significant effect on the Scientific Revolution except by expressing a general desire to mathematise. A possible exception lies in considerations of motion, and this subject also provides useful case studies for the relationship of holism and mathematics.

Aristotle and Astronomy

For Aristotle astronomy gave a mathematical account of the heavenly motions, but there was no corresponding mathematical science to deal with sub-lunary [under the moon, i.e., on Earth] motions. Aristotle himself started with a very generalised idea of motion and proceeded to divide it into motions in the categories of quality (e.g. from hot to cold), quantity (change of size) and place. None of these is completely reducible to any of the others, but for simplicity we shall restrict our concern to local motion, which was the most fundamental. Aristotle gave no systematic quantification, but it is clear that our initial concentration should be on a motion as a whole, the motion of the whole body through the whole time from the beginning of the motion to its end. In the development of this notion by medieval thinkers, and particularly by Nicole Oresme, it became clear that we are in effect dealing with a five-dimensional object, with three spatial dimensions (the extension of the moved body), one temporal and one of intensity of speed, which could then, so to speak, be quantified in a number of different directions. The general procedure is to work from the outside inwards, whereas Galileo and other seventeenth-century thinkers tended to work from the inside out by concentrating initially on the motions of individual points of the body across the points of space. If there was a significant medieval influence on Galileo's science of motion (and the matter is still under dispute), it is probably confined to the habit of treating instantaneous speed as a continuous quantity that can be represented by a straight line.

Aristotelian holism also entered the very heartland of mathematics. To most seventeenth-century mathematicians it was quite natural to think of lines as being composed of an infinite number of points, and to this end later mathematicians would distinguish different orders of infinity. But all this would have been anathema to an orthodox Aristotelian. For Aristotle, a line like other continua was infinitely divisible, but only potentially so; the division could go on indefinitely, but at no stage did one meet a set of ultimate elements that composed the line. Once again wholes were prior to parts, and, while wholes had a well defined existence, parts were more shadowy, and sets of parts were rarely unique, for a line could be divided into other lines in an infinity of different ways. This apparently recondite [obscure] topic, to which Aristotle may seem to devote a disproportionate amount of attention, here emerges as a potent symbol of the difference between his biologically inclined world-view and the mechanical one of later thought.

Aristotelian Natural Philosophy

Aristotelian natural philsophy first became influential in the Latin west in the thirteenth century, but not unproblematically. Aristotle, even more obviously than Plato, had not been a Christian, and it was more difficult to assimilate him to the Christian tradition. It is therefore not surprising that there were repeated attempts to ban his natural philosophical works from the universities, or at least to censor them; nor, given the thirst for knowledge at the time, is it surprising that these attempts failed. There were several points of tension. Aristotle denied the Creation of the world from nothing, and claimed instead that it had always existed. He allowed at most only a shadowy form of individual survival after death. His God was not at all providential, but was engaged solely in contemplation of what was best in the universe, namely himself, and this left the way open for a thorough-going naturalism in philosophy. Aristotle often claimed that the world was a certain way because it had to be that way: to most Christians this put intolerable restrictions on God's freedom to have created the world in whatever way he chose. The tensions did not end in the thirteenth century, and it is instructive to remember that Galileo's friend and sparring partner, the rigid Aristotelian Cesare Cremonini, was continually having his own troubles with the Inquisition.

Nevertheless the intellectual Christian tradition became deeply imbued with Aristotelian concepts. In particular, these allowed an explication of the Eucharist in terms of transubstantiation: while the accidents of bread and wine remained, their substances were transformed into those of the body and blood of Jesus Christ. Mechanical philosophies, on the other hand, had notorious difficulties in coping with this. Moreover, Aristotelianism was the official philosophy of the Jesuits, an order that has often had a bad press from historians because of its members being on the 'wrong side' in certain famous disputes. But in fact the Jesuits were among the most scientifically advanced men of the age. Their colleges provided a rigorous education with greater than usual emphasis on mathematics, and figures such as Clavius, Scheiner, Cabeo, Kircher, Schott, Fabri and Pardies made no mean original contributions, even if their names are now over-shadowed by greater secular ones.[1] However, it can be argued that this was despite rather than because of their Aristotelianism, and that, if they had been liberated from this yoke, they would have soared even higher. And certainly some of the greater ones were very

1. Christopher Clavius, Christoph Scheiner, Nicolo Cabeo, Athanasius Kircher, Gaspar Schott, Honoré Fabri, and Ignace Pardies were Jesuit priests who made important contributions to science.

flexible in their Aristotelianism, and prepared to make significant modifications.

Aristotle and the Scientific Revolution

Positive Aristotelian influence has also been argued for in the cases of the undisputed leaders of the Scientific Revolution, notably Galileo and [English physiologist William] Harvey, both of whom significantly were associated with Padua, arguably the foremost Aristotelian centre of the time. It is now well established that many of Galileo's very early writings are drawn almost verbatim from works by Jesuits of the Colegio Romano, and it has been argued that a strong Aristotelian methodological influence remained in Galileo's mature writings. For my part I find it difficult to see much that was specifically Aristotelian in the later works, although we should remember that Galileo in his old age claimed that Aristotle would have regarded him as an Aristotelian. The case of Harvey is less problematic. He was steeped in Aristotelian thought, claimed to follow Aristotle as a leader, valued his methodology and appealed to Aristotelian analogies for the idea of circulation. In his case the dispute has been about how relevant was his Aristotelianism to his discovery of the circulation of blood.

For around 450 years Aristotelian science had been dominant in Europe. It had encouraged a rational approach to the natural world, and may in various particular ways have helped trigger off new developments in the seventeenth century. But Aristotelian science was more than a collection of theories about the world. It involved a whole attitude of mind and style of approaching natural philosophy. Like [philosopher of science Thomas] Kuhn's paradigms it determined the admissible questions about the world in a more fundamental way than that in which [it] provided the answers. To abandon it involved far more intellectual struggle than a simple rejection of error for truth, and I see no reason to revise the traditional view that sees as one of the most significant intellectual events of the seventeenth century what a recent scholar [C.B. Schmitt] has called the 'escape from the Aristotelian predicament'.

Islamic Scholars Build on Greek Scientific Tradition

David C. Lindberg

David C. Lindberg is a distinguished scholar at the University of Wisconsin. He is the author of numerous books on the history and philosophy of science and has been recognized for his work by the National Science Foundation, among other organizations.

In the following excerpt from his history of the early stages of Western science, Lindberg traces the spread of science to the Middle East. This area, which came under Islamic rule during the seventh and eighth centuries, had long been subject to Greek influence. Greek scientific ideas were part of that influence, and both Muslims and non-Muslims participated in scientific research under Islamic rule. Astronomy was of particular interest; astronomers under Islam made progress that extended the solid foundation of Greek knowledge regarding the movements of the heavenly bodies. Although there were few major breakthroughs in Islamic science, these scholars corrected Greek observations and added their own in astronomy, medicine, mathematics, and other fields. When the West began to regain the scientific spirit, its scholars learned not only from Greek knowledge passed on via the Arabs but also from the original scientific contributions that Middle Eastern scholars made.

Early in the twentieth century, the distinguished physicist-philosopher-historian Pierre Duhem threw out a challenge for historians of Islamic science when he wrote: "There is no Arabian [read "Islamic"] science. The wise men of Mohammedanism were always the more or less faithful disciples of

the Greeks, but were themselves destitute of all originality."
Duhem was clearly wrong, but his statement is useful nonetheless as a means of focusing our attention on the critical
issue: by seeing precisely what is wrong with Duhem's claim,
we stand to learn something important about the character
of the Islamic scientific achievement.

Muslims Are Heirs to Greek Scientific Tradition

It is simply not true that Muslim practitioners of Greek
science were "destitute of all originality"; and one possible
response to Duhem, therefore, is to demonstrate this by
enumerating the many original contributions of Islamic
physicians, mathematicians, and natural philosophers. To
offer but a single example, the eleventh-century Muslim Ibn
al-Haytham turned his critical powers on nearly the whole
of the Greek scientific achievement and made contributions
of the utmost importance and originality to astronomy,
mathematics, and optics. Unfortunately, to carry out this
program of recounting Muslim contributions to the various
sciences would require volumes, and we must be content
with more modest goals—though we will deal with Islamic
contributions to certain specific areas of scientific discourse.

But Duhem's statement offers us another point of entry
into the problem, which may lead us to the central issue.
Duhem maintains that Muslim scholars interested in the
foreign sciences "were always the more or less faithful disciples of the Greeks." He says this with derogatory intent, as
proof that the Muslims were not genuine scientists; that is,
he associates discipleship with an unscientific attitude
(which tells us something about his definition of science).
However, we can turn Duhem's point around and argue that
it was precisely by becoming the disciples of the Greeks that
Muslims entered the Western scientific tradition and became scientists or natural philosophers. Discipleship, on this
view, is essential, rather than antipathetic, to the scientific
enterprise; and Muslims became scientists not by repudiating the existing scientific tradition, but by joining it—by becoming disciples of the most advanced scientific tradition
that had ever existed.

What does it mean to be a disciple? For would-be Muslim scientists, it meant adopting both the methodology and the content of Greek science. By and large, Islamic science was built on a Greek foundation and carried out according to Greek architectural principles; Muslims did not attempt to pull down the Greek edifice and begin from the ground up, but applied themselves to completing the Greek project. This does not mean that originality and innovation were absent; it means that Muslim scientists expressed originality and innovation in the correction, extension, articulation, and application of the existing framework, rather than in the creation of a new one. If this seems to be a damning admission, let it be understood that the great bulk of modern science consists in the correction, extension, and application of inherited scientific principles; a fundamental break with the past is approximately as exceptional today as it was in medieval Islam.

Muslim scientists were aware of this relationship to the past. An early Muslim scientist, al-Kindī (d. ca. 866), who pursued the mathematical sciences under several early 'Abbasid[1] caliphs in Baghdad, acknowledged his debt to ancient predecessors and his membership in an ongoing tradition. Had it not been for the ancients, al-Kindī wrote,

> it would have been impossible for us, despite all our zeal, during the whole of our lifetime, to assemble these principles of truth which form the basis of the final inferences of our research. The assembling of all these elements has been effected century by century, in past ages down to our own time.

Al-Kindī conceived his obligation to be the completion, correction, and communication of this body of ancient learning. He continued:

> It is fitting then [for us] to remain faithful to the principle that we have followed in all our works, which is first to record in complete quotations all that the Ancients have said on the subject, secondly to complete what the Ancients have not

---

1. The 'Abbasids (750–1258) were the second Islamic dynasty.

fully expressed, and this according to the usage of our Arabic language, the customs of our age, and our own ability.

Two hundred years later al-Bīrūnī (d. after 1050) could still judge that the task facing Muslim scientists was "to confine ourselves to what the ancients have dealt with and endeavor to perfect what can be perfected."

Islamic astronomy is a good illustration of the relationship between Islamic and Greek science. Muslim astronomers produced a great deal of very sophisticated astronomical work. This work was carried out largely within the Ptolemaic framework (though we must acknowledge early Hindu influences on Islamic astronomy, largely displaced by subsequent access to [Greek astronomer] Ptolemy's *Almagest* and other Greek astronomical works). Muslim astronomers sought to articulate and correct the Ptolemaic system, improve the measurement of Ptolemaic constants, compile planetary tables based on Ptolemaic models, and devise instruments that could be used for the extension and improvement of Ptolemaic astronomy in general.

Islamic Astronomy

To give but a few examples, al-Farghānī (d. after 861), an astronomer employed at the court of al-Ma'mūn, wrote an elementary, nonmathematical textbook of Ptolemaic astronomy, which had wide circulation in Islam and (after translation into Latin) in medieval Christendom. Thābit ibn Qurra (d. 901), another court astronomer in Baghdad, studied the apparent motions of the sun and moon on Ptolemaic principles; he concluded that the precession of the equinoxes is nonuniform and devised a theory of variable precession (called "trepidation") to account for it. Al-Battānī (d. 929) introduced mathematical improvements into Ptolemaic astronomy, studied the motion of the sun and moon, calculated new values for solar and lunar motions and the inclination of the ecliptic, discovered the movement of the line of apsides of the sun (the shifting of the sun's perigee, or closest approach to the earth, in the heavens), drew up a corrected star catalogue, and gave directions for the construction of astronomical instruments, including a sundial and a mural quadrant. The fact that al-Battānī was still being cited in the sixteenth and seventeenth centuries (by [astronomers Nicolaus] Copernicus and [Johannes] Kepler, among others) testifies to the quality of his astronomical work. Finally, Islam saw a debate between defenders of the physically oriented concentric spheres of Aristotle and the mathematically oriented Ptolemaic system; this debate, conducted mainly in twelfth-century Spain, ended indecisively.

Optics is another example of distinguished scientific achievement in Islam. Here we find innovations at least as fundamental as those in astronomy—innovations, nonetheless, that grew out of the reconciliation and consolidation of a variety of ancient traditions. To be specific, Ibn al-Haytham (d. ca. 1040), who served at the court in Cairo (where a separatist Muslim dynasty had established its own caliphate), followed Ptolemy's lead in combining what had originally been separate Greek approaches to optical phenomena—mathematical, physical, and medical. In the case of Ibn al-Haytham, this synthesis produced a new theory of vision, built on the idea that light is transmitted from the visual object to the eye, which was to prevail first in Islam and then in the West until Kepler devised the theory of the retinal image in the seventeenth century.

The Decline of Islamic Science

The scientific movement in Islam was both distinguished and durable. Translation of Greek works into Arabic began in the second half of the eighth century; by end of the ninth century translation activity had crested, and serious scholarship was under way. From the middle of the ninth century until well into the thirteenth, we find impressive scientific work in all the main branches of Greek science being carried forward throughout the Islamic world. The period of Muslim preeminence in science lasted for five hundred years—a longer period of time than has intervened between Copernicus and ourselves.

The scientific movement had its origins, for practical purposes, in Baghdad under the 'Abbasids, though there came to be many other Near Eastern centers of scientific patronage. Early in the eleventh century, Cairo, under the Fatimids,[2] came to rival Baghdad. In the meantime, the foreign sciences had made their way to Spain, where the Umayyads [ruling dynasty from 756–1031], displaced in the Near East by the 'Abbasids, built a magnificent court at Cordoba [Spain]. Under Umayyad patronage, the sciences flourished in the eleventh and twelfth centuries. Instrumental in this development was al-Hakam (d. 976), who built and stocked an impressive library in Cordoba. Another large collection of scientific books was to be found in Toledo [Spain].

But during the thirteenth and fourteenth centuries, Islamic science went into decline; by the fifteenth century, little was left. How did this come about? Not enough research has been done to permit us to trace these developments with confidence, or to offer a satisfactory explanation, but several causal factors can be identified. First, conservative religious forces made themselves increasingly felt. Sometimes this took the form of outright opposition, as in the notorious burning of books on the foreign sciences in Cordoba late in the tenth century. More often, however, the effect was subtler—not the extinction of scientific activity, but alteration of its character, by the imposition of a very narrow definition of utility. Or to reformulate the point, science became naturalized in Islam—losing its alien quality and finally becoming Islamic science, instead of Greek science practiced on Islamic soil—by accepting a greatly restricted handmaiden role. This meant a loss of attention to many problems that had once seemed important.

Internal Warfare Hurts Islamic Science

Second, a flourishing scientific enterprise requires peace, prosperity, and patronage. All three began to disappear in late medieval Islam as a result of continuous, disastrous warfare among factions and petty states within Islam and attack from without. In the West, the Christian reconquest of Spain began to make serious, if sporadic, headway after about 1065

2. The Fatimids were a North Africa–based Islamic dynasty.

and continued until the entire peninsula was in Christian hands two centuries later. Toledo fell to Christian arms in 1085, Cordoba in 1236, and Seville in 1248. In the east, the Mongols began to apply pressure on the borders of Islam early in the thirteenth century; in 1258 they took Baghdad, thus bringing the 'Abbasid caliphate to an end. In the face of debilitating warfare, economic failure, and the resulting loss of patronage, the sciences were unable to sustain themselves. In assessing this collapse, we must remember that at an advanced level the foreign sciences had never found a stable institutional home in Islam, that they continued to be viewed with suspicion in conservative religious quarters, and that their utility (especially as advanced disciplines) may not have seemed overpowering. Fortunately, before the products of Islamic science could be lost, contact was made with Christendom, and the process of cultural transmission began anew.

Roger Bacon Uses Scientific Methods in the Middle Ages

M.M. Pattison Muir

Roger Bacon (1214–1294) was a monk who lived most of his life at Oxford University in England. In his era, learning meant the study and mastery of things such as logic, mathematics, and rhetoric. These subjects were self-contained; ideas in these subjects required no external confirmation by experiment or observation. Unlike Aristotle himself, the adherents of Aristotle's philosophy in the Middle Ages paid little attention to the natural world around them.

The alchemists were the exception to this rule. These men sought the philosopher's stone, a secret substance that was thought to be able to change common metals like lead or iron into gold. Other alchemists sought the "elixir," which also could transmute metals. Many of the alchemists' ideas were wrapped up in mysticism about the properties of substances. They used impenetrable vocabulary to shield their so-called secret knowledge from outsiders.

Although the alchemists were not scientists, their work with various metals, minerals, and acids resulted in some knowledge of chemical processes. In the following essay, Oxford scholar M.M. Pattison Muir shows how Bacon took what was best about the alchemists' techniques and united it with a genuine scientific attitude toward observing and measuring the results of experiments. Bacon was virtually alone in his time in pursuing experimental knowledge. Moreover, methods of travel, communication, and the production of written works (the printing press was not in use in Europe at the time) were not advanced enough to allow Bacon to communicate his ideas to oth-

M.M. Pattison Muir, "Roger Bacon: His Relations to Alchemy and Chemistry," *Roger Bacon: Essays*, edited by A.G. Little. Oxford: Clarendon Press, 1914.

ers. In short, Muir concludes that Bacon was a scientific genius trapped in a prescientific age.

Alchemists, both before and after Roger Bacon, formed, from their intellectual and emotional longings, a scheme of nature's method of working, and then observed natural changes through the distorted glass of their imaginings. Bacon at least tried to look first at external realities, and to base his intellectual explanation of material changes on observed facts. In his *Opus Tertium* [*Third Work*] he says of experimental science: 'This science works by perfect experiments, not by arguments as purely speculative science does, not by weak and imperfect experiments as operative science does. Therefore, this is the lord of all sciences, and the end of all speculation.' Again, in the same place, he says: 'The man who rejects anything ought to know the nature and circumstances of that thing, and so reject what is false, that what is true may remain unimpaired.' In the preceding chapter of the *Opus Tertium*, he asserts that many labour to make metals, and colours, and other things, without a real practical acquaintance with the methods of the laboratory. 'There are few who know how to distil properly, how to sublime and to calcinate, how to separate things.' There are not three men among the Latins [Western Europeans] who have given themselves to this that they may know speculative alchemy, which cannot be known without the operations of practical alchemy. 'There is only one man', Bacon says, 'who is instructed in all these questions; as so few people know these things, he does not deign to communicate with others, nor to associate with them, because he regards them all as asses and fools (*asinos et insanos*) delivered over to quibbles, and as charlatans who dishonour philosophy, medicine, and theology.'

Bacon often insists on the necessity of beginning with the study of the simpler inanimate things, of examining how 'simple and compound liquids, gems, marbles, gold, and other metals' are generated from their elements. It is impossible, he asserts, to gain any knowledge of the 'generation of animate things' without having first acquired a knowledge of the generation of the simpler inanimate things. Of this preliminary knowledge, he says, 'we find nothing in the books of Aristotle.'

In discoursing of the many errors of medical men, Bacon lays stress on their ignorance of alchemy. A knowledge of alchemy, he says, enables men to recognize the differences between medicines, and the virtues of different medicines; this knowledge also is necessary for the proper preparation of medicines. Here, as elsewhere, Bacon lays much importance on alchemy as a practical art which deals with real things.

Bacon Concerned with Practical Knowledge

Bacon's leaning to the practical and useful side of knowledge should be noticed, as it is characteristic of him, and marks him off both from his contemporaries and his predecessors. In *Opus Tertium* he says that practical alchemy is more important than all the other sciences, because 'it is productive of more advantages' than they. 'The utility of everything must be considered; for this utility is the end for which the thing exists.'

How different this is from the gibe of the modern absolutist philosophers against the 'irrelevant appeals to practical results which are allowed to make themselves heard'! Of the many experiences which philosophers of the absolutist school say create 'a passing show of arbitrary variation', these same philosophers assert that 'they themselves, and the manner of their connexion, are excluded from the theory of knowledge'. Not only was Roger Bacon in advance of his predecessors and his contemporaries in his method of seeking knowledge, he was also far in advance of those who today reject the experience of the seven centuries which separate them from him.

The following quotation from *Communia Naturalium* [*General Principles of Natural Philosophy*] gives a vivid picture of the genuinely scientific character of Roger Bacon. It shows clearly the great importance he placed on the careful examination of external facts, and makes us realize his skill in determining the kind of facts which ought to be studied for this or that particular purpose. Bacon divides natural philosophy into separate sciences. The fifth of these separate sciences is *agriculture*. Of this department of knowledge he writes as follows:

> Next [after alchemy] comes the special science of the nature of plants and all animals, with the exception of man; who, by reason of his nobleness, falls under a special science called medicine. But first in the order of teaching is the science of animals which precede man and are necessary for his use. This science descends first to the consideration of every kind of soil and the productions of the earth, distinguishing four kinds of soil, according to their crops; one soil is that wherein corn and legumina are sown; another is covered with woods; another with pastures and meadows; another is garden ground wherein are cultivated trees and vegetables, herbs and roots, as well for nutriment as for medicine. Now this science extends to the perfect study of all vegetables, the knowledge of which is very imperfectly delivered in Aristotle's treatise on that subject; and therefore a special and sufficient science of plants is required, which should be taught in books on agriculture. But as agriculture cannot go on without an abundance of tame animals; nor the utility of different soils, as woods, pastures and deserts, be understood, except wild animals be nurtured; nor the pleasure of man be sufficiently enhanced without such animals; therefore this science extends itself to the study of all animals.

In these words, Bacon draws the outlines of a true science of agriculture, based on observation and experiment, fitted to yield results useful to mankind.

Experiments and Mathematics

By using the method of observation and experiment, and reasoning on the results obtained, Roger Bacon arrived at just and fruitful conceptions regarding plant life, the growth and nutrition of animals, tides, rainbows, the density of air, and other natural events. This method also led him to the invention of instruments of much usefulness in optics, astronomy, and other branches of physical science. Bacon often insists on the need of mathematics in the investigation of physical occurrences. He tried to form a general science which should bring the actions of bodies, and of natural agents, under the principles of mathematics. Nevertheless, he taught that the experimental sciences are more useful to men than mathematics, for they stir curiosity and make possible the understanding of many things. Without experience, he said, no satisfactory investigation is possible. Experience shields us from erroneous judgements. His own discoveries, made by experimenting and observing, had shown him, he says, that there is nothing too hard to believe either in human or divine things.

Most of the alchemists appealed to the authority of men of renown who had gone before them for justification of their outlook on nature. Roger Bacon opposed the custom of constantly discussing ideas, generalities, principles, stated by Aristotle and other ancient writers. He insisted on the need of observing and discussing facts. He said that scholastic science was too greatly concerned with intellectual definitions, and the supposed causes of natural events, and neglected the accurate observation of these events (*Non oportet causas investigare* [one should not investigate causes]). He altogether rejected occult [hidden] causes. He taught that undue respect to worthless authority is one of the causes of ignorance, and that the conceit of learned men, which makes them hide their ignorance under a display of apparent knowledge, is another potent cause of error and mental darkness.

Bacon Was a Prisoner of His Times

It was impossible that Bacon should shake himself quite free from the trammels of authority. He taught the need of obedience to the Church, although he was imprisoned for a supposed lack of proper humility to authority. He despised the ignorance and stupidity of the multitude. 'Men are so ready to go astray', he said, 'that they must have some trustworthy guide.' He placed theology at the head of his hierarchy of sciences, and though he appealed again and again to observation and experiment, he carried over theological methods into scientific inquiries.

Bacon was obliged to paint his mental picture of the mutations of material things with the pigments he found in his colour-box. He could not do otherwise. We all do that. He could not but use the conception of the four elements—hotness, dryness, coldness, wetness—as guides in his attempt to make an intellectual arrangement of the facts he had to set in order. Roger Bacon was necessarily influenced by the intellectual conceptions of his time. Nevertheless, [French historian Émile] Charles can justly say of him: 'His greatest discovery is that of the feebleness and faults of scholasticism; his originality is to belong as little as possible to his own time.' In the thirteenth century there were no methods, no instruments, for making minutely accurate investigations of material changes. Bacon was born into a mental atmosphere of vague principles, and grew up in that environment. Desirous of finding *how* the changes of things happen, he thought of these changes in terms of fire, air, earth, and water; for these were at once the simplest and the most ingathering conceptions which came to his hand. The instruments which he found in use, and used for investigating natural changes were not sufficiently incisive, not sufficiently plastic, not penetrative nor scarifying enough, to be completely effectual for sweeping away the images, the prejudices, the mental atmosphere, in which his intellectual life was steeped. He had to do his best with the mental apparatus which he inherited. He accomplished much.

Early Scientists' Investigations Were Not Scientific

Lynn Thorndike

Lynn Thorndike was a longtime Columbia University professor. His major interest was medieval history and science. Thorndike had a lifelong interest in the connection between magic and science. His research led him to conclude that early science grew out of, or was at least associated with, the dubious practices of late medieval alchemists and conjurers.

The early scientists left the professor much material on which to build his case. Here, he investigates articles published in the earliest British science journal, the *Transactions of the Royal Society*. The material published in these early issues seems very unscientific today. There are accounts of "monsters," tales of deformities much like a seventeenth-century freak show, and strange recipes for "cures" of various illnesses. Thorndike concludes that the conventional story of science—the tale of the intrepid skeptic overcoming medieval superstition—must itself be met with skepticism.

It has been said that the Proceedings of the Royal Society[1] in [British chemist Robert] Boyle's time abounded in "papers on the medicinal power of gems and the astrological influences of the planets as physical problems worthy of the new experimental methods of inquiry," [according to P.P. Weiner]. Similarly it has been recognized that many of the members of the Royal Society in the seventeenth century "were merely

---

1. The Royal Society London was founded in 1660 to promote collaboration among scholars interested in experimental science.

Lynn Thorndike, "Academies and Scientific Societies," *A History of Magic and Experimental Science*. New York: Columbia University Press, 1958.

dilettantes seeking amusement," and that the early records of the Society are "a weird agglomeration of trivialities and discoveries which the attrition of subsequent investigation has shown to be of basic importance," [write authors Henry W. Robinson and Walter Adams].

Monsters, Snakes, and Salamanders

In the first volume of the *Philosophical Transactions* of the Royal Society in 1665, are communications from Boyle concerning a "very odd monstrous calf" and the monstrous head of a colt. Also some "observations and Experiments upon May-Dew [the morning dew from the first day of May]," which would putrefy in the shade but not in the sun, and the killing of a rattlesnake in Virginia in July, 1657, in less than half an hour by holding bruised pennyroyal or dittany to its nose, and the additional observation that no rattlesnakes are seen where this herb grows. Secrets are mentioned every now and then, such as an admirable secret, not yet revealed, to keep ships from being worm-eaten. The Portuguese build their ships of hard wood and scorch them, while a Londoner suggests the use of pitch. A letter from [early geologist Nicholas] Steno reports that a knight named Corvini assured him of the following experiment with a salamander which he had imported from the Indies. When Corvini threw it into the fire, it soon swelled up and vomited a quantity of thick slimy matter which quenched the neighboring coals. As soon as they rekindled, the salamander put them out again in the same way, and by this means saved itself for two hours, when Corvini removed it for fear it could not survive much longer. It lived for nine months afterwards, although for eleven months it had no other sustenance than what it got by licking the earth on which it was brought from the Indies, and which it moistened with its urine, as the earth dried up. When Corvini substituted Italian soil, the salamander expired in three days time. New teeth crop out in a man of eighty-one and a woman of seventy-five.

Monstrosities continued to be recorded in subsequent volumes. A monstrous birth was in the form of an ape with a mass of flesh over its shoulders like a little cloak, because the mother had seen an ape thus clothed upon the stage, when she had gone five months with child. Passing over two monstrous sheep, we note a headless child which lived for four days, thus refuting the theory of [French philosopher and mathematician René] Descartes that the pineal gland is the connection between mind and body. Or we hear of hailstones eight, nine and twelve inches in circumference and of 96 stones in a boy. Somewhat fantastic experiments also continue, such as [British experimental scientist Robert] Hooke's preserving animals alive by blowing air with a bellows through their lungs, or [British physiologist] Dr. Richard Lower's making a dog draw its breath "exactly like a wind-broken horse." Yet along with such trivialities are announced [French experimental scientist Edme] Mariotte's discovery of the blind spot by experiment, and [French experimental scientist Jean] Pecquet's showing, also by experiment, that it is in the retina, not in the optic nerve. . . .

Royal Society Considers Practical Topics

As for topics considered by the members of the English Royal Society, its contemporary historian, [Thomas] Sprat, lists along with such practical or would-be practical matters as growing potatoes, planting verjuice grapes in England, brewing beer with ginger instead of hops, and making wine from sugar canes, and along with scientific subjects such as the manner of the circulation of the blood in fish, strata seen in a well at Amsterdam and in diverse cliffs, a report of two new stars observed in 1666, one in [the constellation] Andromeda, the other in [the constellation] Cygnus, and both in the same place where they appeared sixty years before and had not been seen since, the following more curious and marvelous topics. A way of turning water into earth, a reported rain of fish and frogs, that silk worms in Virginia are not hurt by thunder, of swallows living after they had been frozen under water, of barnacles and solon geese, of several monsters, and of sympathetic cures and trials. For, as Sprat remarks later, "there are many qualities and figures and powers of things that break the common laws and transgress the standing rules of nature." Even in the early eighteenth century [English geologist John] Woodward was expelled from the Council of the Royal Society for refusing to apologize for remarks he had made reflecting upon [British physician] Dr. Hans Sloane who had stated that gallstones caused colic, which Woodward denied.

On March 27, 1686, [English astronomer Edmond] Halley as secretary of the Royal Society wrote to [St. George] Ashe of the Philosophical Society at Dublin:

> Your new method of demonstrating the knottiest Propositions of Euclid, your new-invented Dial, your Experiments of Injections of Liquors into Animals, and the account of your mathematical Girl, are things that will be very acceptable to us: as likewise whatsoever, whether Natural, Artificial or Mathematical Curiosity comes before you.

On May 27 of the same year he acknowledges the receipt from [William] Molyneux of the same Irish society of

> the figure of the Horny Girle, which is certainly a most extraordinary curiosity, and which I belive very much puzles the Physicians to account for; wee are made to belive we shall see her here at Bartholomew faire.

On July 9 he writes to yet another correspondent:

> I have this day seen a great curiosity viz a Calicoe shirt brought from India, which is wove without a seam all of one piece, which I should have thought impossible had I not seen it. It explains the Scripture relation of our Saviours coat which was without seam.

On November 13 he writes to the noted mathematician [John] Wallis:

> The child you mention to have seen with 6 fingers on a hand & as many toes on each foot, is a great curiosity, especially if they be so contrived that the hand be not therby made less fit to do its office. Nor is the quantity of Water found in the Dropsicall[2] maid less prodigious, it being hardly conceaveable how the Muscles of the Abdomen should be distended to so great a Capacity.

2. having a swelling due to accumulation of fluid in bodily tissue or cavity

A little later in the same letter he mentions a dwarf only 16 inches high "said to have been presented lately to the French King." The next year in another letter to Wallis he tells somewhat sceptically of "a very odd relation of an Hermaphrodite"[3] at Toulouse. In 1696 Halley writes to Hans Sloane concerning a monstrous birth from a greyhound of which Wallis had informed the Society.

Stubborn Survival of Superstition

Some further idea of the stubborn survival of such notions and traditions, and of the half credulous, half sceptical attitude which was maintained towards them may be had from the questionnaires sent out to different parts of the world by the Royal Society. Among 38 questions addressed to correspondents in Surat [a British outpost in India] and other parts of the East Indies the following may be noted. 1) Whether diamonds and other gems grow again after a few years in the mines whence they have been dug? 5) Whether in [the East Indies island of] Sumatra there is a fountain of medicinal oil? . . .

The Inquiries for Egypt, by [member of the Royal Society] Thomas Henshaw Esq., published in *Philosophical Transactions*, are largely concerned with what truth there is in a number of old statements and beliefs. 3) "Whether the earth of Egypt, adjoyning to the river Nile, preserv'd and weigh'd daily, keeps the same weight till the 17th of June and then grows daily heavier with the increase of the river?" 4) Whether deaths from the plague cease after that day? 9) Whether the ichneumon [wasp] can kill a crocodile by "skipping into his mouth and gnawing his way out?" 10) Whether there are on the banks of the Nile talismans or astrological images which the crocodiles cannot pass? 13) Whether legs and arms still continue to stand out of the ground on Good Friday? "And how that imposture is performed?" 14) "Whether children born there in the eighth month do usually live, contrary to what is believed to happen in other countries?". . .

Of twenty-two queries addressed to [German astronomer Johannes] Hevelius at Danzig,[4] one asked what amber was,

3. A person possessing physical elements of both a male and a female.   4. Now Gdansk, Poland.

another whether swallows lived in the winter under the ice on the surface of bodies of water, and whether there were sub-terranean passages between the maelstroms in the Sea of Norway and Bodnick Bay. Hevelius replied that amber was a kind of fossil pitch or bitumen; that fishermen affirmed that swallows hibernated under ice, but that he had never seen it himself; and that [Johannes] Scheffer asserted the existence of such passages, but on hearsay evidence.

Dr. Stubbes [a contributor to the Royal Society's journal] confirmed the observation of Oviedo [Spain] that lice "leave the Spaniards as they go to the Indies . . . and meet them again in the same latitude in their return." The explanation was given that they began to sweat excessively as they ap-proached the tropics and thus drowned the old lice, while the perspiration did not lodge in the pores long enough to produce any new vermin by spontaneous generation. But

> In their return, the sweat lodgeth longer in the pores and habit of the body, and the particular forms or ferments, being exalted and unloosen'd and put into activity, shape out those creatures, and so they breed them.

A French Natural History of the Antilles affirmed that *l'herbe aux flesches*,[5] "being stamped," would cure wounds made with poisoned arrows. The fruit of the mancenille tree would kill anyone who ate it except crabs; the touch of a juice from its bark made the skin swell and blinded the eye for several days; even its shadow made the bodies of those resting under it swollen; and meat boiled over a fire of its wood burned the mouth and throat. Dr. Stubbes, in a later communication, remarked:

> About the Manchinel-Tree I shall only say, it is a wood of an excellent grain, equalling the Jamaica-wood, but large to four foot diameter. The Spaniards turn it into beds, and the En-glish usually floor their rooms with it in Jamaica; yet it is as malignant, I am told, as 'tis described.

---

5. the "arrow-plant"

The skin of the animal called Tatou (armadillo) was bullet-proof and cured deafness and earache.

Obsession with Mad Dogs

Mad dogs received repeated attention in the sixteenth volume of *Philosophical Transactions*. By royal command, Sir Robert Gourdon contributed to the Royal Society "A Receipt [recipe] to cure mad dogs or men or beasts bitten by mad dogs." For beasts one was to take a handful each of agrimony roots, primrose roots, dragon roots, single peony roots and leaves of box; two handfuls of the Starr of the Earth; one ounce each of black of crabs' claws and Venice treacle. These were to be beaten and bruised together, boiled in a gallon of milk until the half of it evaporated, put unstrained in a bottle, and administered three or four spoonfuls at a time for three mornings before new and full moon. The animal was to be bled a little the day before the medicine was given. For human use the decoction was to be infused in two quarts of strong white wine for at least twelve hours, strained, and taken a gill [five fluid oz.] at a time evening and morning for three days preceding the new and the full moon.

Another communication was made by Sir Theodore de Vaux, Knight, from the papers of Theodore Turquet de Mayerne (1573–1655). First seven diseases of dogs were distinguished: hot madness in which they attack every thing and can hold out but four days; running madness, when they attack only other dogs and may live for nine months; *la rage mue*, which is in the blood; falling madness, a sort of epilepsy having its seat in the head; blasting or withering in the bowels which shrivel up; a sleepy sickness from little worms in the mouth of the stomach; and rheumatic disease with swelling of the head and yellowing of the eyes. Only the first two of these were properly madness and incurable. In the other five the dog won't eat and, unless remedies are applied, dies of hunger after eight or nine days without hurting anybody. "The first two are catched by the breath of dogs being together, as is the plague among men; the latter are likewise contagious but curable."

Four recipes follow. "A never-failing remedy for the bite of a mad dog by Sir Theodore Mayern" consists of equal portions of Virginia snake-root and flowers of St. John's wort gathered in their prime and finely powdered. Another prescription is of rue, London (or better, Venice) treacle, garlic, fine tin filings, taken in white wine or ale after fasting three hours, with the dregs bound on the wound and renewed every twenty-four hours. "This remedy I have given many times by Sir Theodore Mayern's direction, and I have never found it to fail." A simpler cure is to pluck the feathers from the breech of an old cock and apply them severally to the bite or bites. If the dog was mad, the cock will die and the patient recover. If the cock doesn't die, the dog wasn't mad. The last recipe is the most complex. First the victim is to be plunged fasting as soon as may be nine times into the sea. Then the bite is to be washed in lye of ashes of oak wood and urine, and a cataplasm applied of London treacle, hedge garlic, rue and salt. Next one takes of dried rue and *scordium* two drams each, one and a half of Virginia snake-root, three of flowers of St. John's wort, four drams each of tin filings and garlic, and an ounce of London treacle. These are beaten and mixed all together and enough syrup of lemon added to make an electuary of four and one half ounces, which is to be divided into nine equal parts of a half ounce each and taken one daily, followed by a small draught of good strong ale, a walk, and not dine for four hours.

Despite all these remedies and sure cures, a subsequent issue of the *Transactions* could only record the death of a child of three who was bitten by a mad dog. He grew delirious and soon "the malignity had made so virulent an impression upon the animal spirits," that he made signs as if to bite, his voice became like the bark of a dog, he foamed at the mouth, and died.

We turn for a moment to a bit of wholesome scepticism. [Early biologist Antoni von] Leeuwenhoek, in a letter of April 5, 1697, to the Royal Society, wrote very sceptically concerning a German at Amsterdam who claimed to work great cures by applying a sympathetic powder to the patient's urine, but could give no satisfactory physiological or anatomical explanation how it could operate at a distance. A married couple known to Leeuwenhoek died of consumption despite the promise of a cure by this powder made to them by this empiric.

[Historian of science] George Sarton has recently written:

> The revolution completed by the middle of the seventeenth century implied at least three things: the experimental method, the sceptical or critical spirit, rationalism. The academies were extremely helpful in the development of these, chiefly the first two.

We may agree that the academies helped to foster the experimental method, but the specific cases which we have noted show that their spirit was curious and credulous rather than sceptical and critical.

Chapter 2

Pioneers of the Scientific Revolution

Turning Points

IN WORLD HISTORY

Copernicus's New Astronomy Marks the Beginning of the Scientific Revolution

Owen Gingerich

Nicolaus Copernicus's development of the sun-centered (heliocentric) view of the solar system is traditionally held to be the start of the scientific revolution. His book *De revolutionibus orbium coelestium* (*On the Revolutions of the Heavenly Spheres*), published in 1543, relied on his own observations and data from other astronomers to build the case that Earth moves around the sun. Copernicus's motivations, however, may sound somewhat strange today. He was trying to determine when the Christian celebration of Easter should take place. Moreover, Copernicus's reasons for adopting the heliocentric view do not seem to be based on science but on beauty. He believed that the natural and most pleasing place for the sun was at the center of the universe, as the sun was the "lamp" that lit all of God's creation. Thus, the reasons for Copernicus developing his system are hardly what would be considered scientific motivation today.

In the following excerpt, Harvard professor of astronomy and history of science Owen Gingerich explains that Copernicus's system sparked the scientific revolution because changes in society allowed Copernican ideas to flourish. The development of printing meant that his book could be reproduced and his work read by scholars throughout Europe. The discovery of the Americas showed the insufficiency of medieval knowledge. And the Protestant Reformation brought with it a spirit of free inquiry into fundamental questions. Copernicus, the diligent and creative

Owen Gingerich, "A Copernican Perspective," *UNESCO Courier*, April 1973. Copyright © 1973 by United Nations Education, Scientific and Cultural Organization. Reproduced by permission.

thinker, was certainly a good candidate to initiate the scientific revolution. Despite the Catholic Church's attempt to suppress his idea of a sun-centered universe, he was fortunate to live during an era when his ideas could be accepted by Protestants and other free thinkers.

To a modern scientist, science of the 15th century has a strange and unfamiliar quality. When Copernicus was born, men believed that a weightless, crystalline sun whirled daily around the earth. Celestial motions were explained in terms of strivings inherent in matter itself. Professors of physics said that a stone thrown from the hand flew straight until it ran out of "impetus" and then fell directly down to the ground.

Start of a Revolution

In 1543 Copernicus' masterpiece, *De revolutionibus* ("Concerning the Revolutions"), was published, and in the century that followed, the curious, time-honored scientific explanations of antiquity and the Middle Ages gave way to the ideas that form the foundations of today's science. A great change—indeed a revolution—took place in that age, with Copernicus at its forefront. Far more than political struggles, with their attendant fleeting changes, the work of Copernicus and his intellectual successors has shaped our contemporary world.

If indeed Copernicus' contributions triggered the entire sequence of ideas that have become modern science, we may well ask why this is a phenomenon only 500 years old. What prevented the appearance of a Copernicus a century or two before? Was an earlier great unfolding of science prevented by bonds of dogma and ignorance?

Or, in a contrary view, should we consider creative science a delicate and fragile plant that blossoms forth only in particularly germinal conditions? Perhaps it was not mere coincidence that the great astronomer lived as a contemporary of [Christopher] Columbus, [German artist Albrecht] Dürer, Leonardo [da Vinci], [Dutch philosopher Desidarius] Erasmus, and [German Protestant theologian Martin] Luther. In that case we can make a fascinating inquiry: What factors contribute to the remarkable flowering of science, such as that typified by Copernicus? . . .

A Crisis in Astronomy

The geocentric astronomy of Copernicus' day had served well for over a thousand years; it meshed perfectly with man's view of himself and with the primitive physics of Aristotle. To be sure, learned prelates recognized that Easter was coming too early in the calendar year, and a few astrologers knew that the planets were sometimes found several degrees from positions predicted by tables based on the venerable Ptolemaic theory. But if there were a crisis in astronomy, Astronomia had just as much of a problem on her hands after Copernicus as before, for the calendar remained the same and planetary predictions were improved only a little.

No one knows precisely how or when the Polish astronomer first seized upon the idea of a sun-centered system; in any event, by 1515 he had circulated a précis of his innovation, and within a few years was hard at work on his manuscript of *De revolutionibus*—a book that encompassed both his new cosmology and a careful reexamination of old and new planetary observations. Nor do scholars know *why* he adopted a heliocentric view of the cosmos, for the observations of his day could neither prove nor disprove his idea. Nevertheless, there is a clue in his own writings. A euphoric sense of beauty pervades the entire composition of the book: "For in this most beautiful temple, who would place this lamp in another or better position than that from which it can light up the whole thing at the same time? . . . We thus discover a marvelous commensurability of the universe and a fixed harmonious linkage as can be found in no other way. . . . So vast is this divine handiwork of the most excellent Almighty." Surely an aesthetic vision gripped Copernicus and guided his analysis of the heavens.

Yet it is a curious and nearly forgotten fact that the Copernican Revolution was nearly stillborn. Two decades after he had begun his book, Copernicus was running out of steam. By then in his sixties, he had written the most profound astronomical treatise in a millennium, but the small technical details lacked a final polish and inner consistency. His manuscript was a work of beauty, with exquisitely drafted figures and two-color tables, but these paper folios had apparently been designed as the end product itself.

Publishing the Manuscript

His post as canon of the Frombork cathedral in Prussian Poland had given him financial security and time for contemplation, but it deprived him of stimulating intellectual companionship. In short, there was no one to talk to about his remarkable book, which had been so long in the making.

Although Copernicus had found printed works essential in his own studies, printing was still a comparatively new invention, one that had begun to flourish only during his own lifetime. There was as yet no printer in Frombork, and the aging astronomer apparently had no intention to publish his work elsewhere. *De revolutionibus* seemed destined to gather dust in the cathedral library, to be forgotten and ignored. Such a fate seems incredible to us today—yet it must have overtaken scores of astronomical achievements of the Middle Ages.

In 1539, during Copernicus' last years, a young mathematician from Germany appeared in Frombork, eager to learn the details of the astronomer's ideas. Georg Joachim Rheticus, already a professor at Wittenberg [University in Germany], though just in his mid-twenties, had heard rumors of the innovative Copernican astronomy. Although the young Rheticus came from the hotbed of Lutheranism, the Catholic Copernicus received him with courage and cordiality. Caught up by the enthusiasm of his young disciple, Copernicus made last-minute revisions to his opus and then entrusted a manuscript copy to Rheticus for publication. Rheticus took the manuscript to a printer in Nuremberg, who finished the production of several hundred copies in 1543. These were sold to scholars and libraries throughout Europe. Thus it came about that the new technology of printing was able to play an absolutely essential role in preserving and disseminating the new astronomy.

The readers of Copernicus' treatise gladly accepted his new planetary observations and his careful attention to the details of planetary orbits, but the heliocentric world view itself found little support. In our own age of space exploration, when men have looked back upon the spinning earth suspended in the skies, the Copernican system seems natural, almost obvious; but to most astronomers of the late 1500s, imbued with the physics of Aristotle, a moving earth had little appeal. Instead, they chose a primitive form of relativity. Keeping the earth as their fixed reference framework, they viewed the Copernican system as a clever mathematical model, somewhat more complicated than the old Ptolemaic system, but not a true description of the physical world. There was certainly nothing obvious about a moving earth and a fixed, central sun; [Italian astronomer] Galileo later remarked that he could not admire enough those who had accepted the Copernican system *in spite of* the evidence of their senses. Nevertheless, Copernicus' *De revolutionibus* acted like a delayed time bomb. Around 1600 two great scientists, each in his own individual way, grasped a truth in the heliocentric system that

Johannes Kepler

went beyond geometrical model building. Johannes Kepler saw in the sun-centered spacing of the planets a harmonious, aesthetic relation that could be expressed mathematically. He envisioned a force emanating from the sun and built a "new astronomy or celestial physics based on causes."

In Italy, Galileo Galilei turned the newly invented telescope to the heavens, where he found one astonishing surprise after another. The moon, filled with mountains and plains, traversed the skies as another earthlike planet. Jupiter, with its own retinue of moons, became a miniature Copernican system. To Galileo the universe was comprehensible as a unity only if the earth was a planet revolving about the distant fixed sun.

Mathematical Model or True Picture?

Both Kepler and Galileo differed strongly from an anonymous introduction that had been added to *De revolutionibus* when it was printed. In that introduction the Lutheran theologian Andreas Osiander stated a widely held philosophical opinion: Astronomical theories were mathematical models intended for predictions of astronomical phenomena, and whether they were ultimately true or false was irrelevant. Such a view is logical and self-consistent, but Kepler and Galileo were convinced that their astronomy gave a true picture of the universe. This claim, plus their opinion that in matters of science the Bible simply spoke in terms of the common man so as to be understood, brought them into conflict with the Catholic Church, and consequently several of their works were placed on the *Index of Prohibited Books*.

To a 20th-century scientist familiar with the concept of relativity, it may seem ultimately irrelevant whether the earth or the sun is the chosen fixed reference point. But the 17th-century collision between religious dogma and an innovative world view has had a profound impact on mankind's views concerning the source and nature of truth about our physical world. And in the 17th century, it *did* make a difference whether the universe was conceived in geocentric or in heliocentric terms, because only a heliocentric solar system leads onward to Newtonian physics. In turn, Newton's laws of motion and his law of universal gravitation describe the orbits of satellites and space probes. Thus, there is a direct line from Copernicus through Kepler, Galileo, and Newton to the marvels of our own space age.

No doubt Copernicus would have been astonished to learn that the world would link his birthday to a celebration of modern science. An unwitting revolutionary, his goal was to return science to a purer state, conceived in terms of the perfect circles of the ancient Greeks. He sought a view "pleasing to the mind," and he gave to the mind's eye a fruitful new way of looking at the cosmos.

Still, our earlier question comes back to haunt us. Why did this new view wait until the early 1500s? The answer lies not so much in the science as in the society and in new-found patterns of communication. The invention of printing and the rise of universities encouraged the flow of information and new ideas. The discovery of America, while Copernicus was a student at Cracow, helped demonstrate the inadequacy of traditional knowledge. A seething intellectual milieu, absent a century or two earlier, characterized the age. Furthermore, Copernicus had a patrol—the Frombork cathedral chapter—that enabled him to travel to Italy for graduate study and that freed him from financial worries. More importantly, he had the time and freedom to contemplate and choose innovative views. In that age of change, a new mobility of ideas brought Copernicus fresh knowledge that he required for building his system, and at the end of his life this same combination of travel, freedom, and printing saved his work from oblivion.

The new-found freedom of inquiry, combined with the requisite intellectual resources and the discipline to work out the consequences and to test the data—this is without doubt more important for the rise of modern science than the specific idea of a sun-centered cosmos. We learn more for our own age from Copernicus' persistence, his eagerness to seek learning beyond his own provincial boundaries, and his willingness to share with those outside his own religion and nation than we learn from his formidable astronomical tome or from his paeans to the heliocentric cosmology.

From his "remote corner of the world," Nicolaus Copernicus set into motion not only the earth, but the entire spirit of inquiry that has so richly increased our understanding of the universe. But the ultimate reason for the anniversary celebration—and indeed its challenge—is a rededication to preserve the fragile freedom of inquiry and the resources that make inquiry possible.

Galileo Makes Remarkable Discoveries with His Telescope

Laura Fermi and Gilberto Bernardini

Galileo Galilei (1564–1642) was both a craftsman and a scientist. Originally planning to be a physician, Galileo attended the University of Pisa in Italy. He was halfhearted about his medical studies, however, and gravitated toward mathematics. He began teaching mathematics privately at Siena (Italy) in 1585 and also began writing and experimenting.

Galileo was interested in both experimental science and artisanship. He would often go to arsenals and shipyards to speak with and observe master craftsmen. He became something of a craftsman himself, and his masterpieces were his telescopes. Galileo realized that the telescope was more than a piece of fine artisanship for amusement; it had real potential as a scientific instrument. Accordingly, he began using his invention to explore the sky. With his telescope, he was able to gather evidence supporting the heliocentric (sun-centered) view of the solar system proposed by Copernicus. More importantly, he shattered the conventional belief that the heavens consisted of "perfect" forms. The reality was much more complex and interesting.

Laura Fermi was a writer and the wife of the famous physicist Enrico Fermi. Gilberto Bernardini was a physicist who specialized in the study of cosmic rays.

The first telescope [Galileo] built had a magnification of three diameters, the second of eight diameters, and finally he built one magnifying 33 diameters. He increased the size of his lenses but stopped at the point where further increase

Laura Fermi and Gilberto Bernardini, "The Universe Through the Telescope," *Galileo and the Scientific Revolution*. New York: BasicBooks, 1961.

would cause distortion of images. Later he built many more telescopes, some of which are preserved and are still objects of admiration.

Telescopes Extend Human Perception

Yet, more than a clever craftsman, he was a true scientist. No one before him so clearly realized that instruments serve two essential purposes: First, they make observations both objective and quantitative, transforming them into "measures." Second, they extend the power of human senses beyond their normal physiological limits. No instrument but the telescope could give Galileo the feeling of how much, above all expectations, the power of the senses could be enlarged. For the first time eyes could see very distant things as well as if they were close by and discover the existence of objects that up to then had been too far away to be visible.

To make full use of the telescope as a scientific instrument Galileo did something that no one had done before. He turned it to the sky.

We are so used to the "extension of our senses"—to loudspeakers and other amplifiers increasing the power of our hearing; to powerful telescopes and microscopes enlarging our vision—that we cannot easily recapture the intensity of Galileo's experience. He, first of all men, could realize how much larger God's creation is than that which is revealed to the unaided senses, and for this privilege he devoutly offered frequent thanks to God in his writings.

For tens of centuries men had seen the same objects in the sky, and they had come to believe that they had learned all there was to be learned in it. But Galileo saw new depths and a new population in the heavens. Everywhere he turned his telescope he saw stars never seen before, in the most crowded constellations and in the thinly scattered regions. He recognized that the Milky Way is not a long luminous cloud but is made of numberless stars so dim and close together that the naked eye cannot distinguish them.

The moon appeared very different to him, and among its new strange features were prominences and cavities in its surface. ". . . Many of the prominences there are in all respects similar to our most rugged and steepest mountains, and among them one can see uninterrupted stretches hundreds of miles long. Others are in more compact groups, and there are also many isolated and solitary peaks, precipitous and craggy. But most frequent there are certain ridges . . . very much raised, which surround and enclose plains of different sizes and shapes, but mostly circular. In the middle of many of these there is a very high mountain, and a few are filled with rather dark matter. . . ."

Galileo calculated the height of lunar mountains and concluded correctly that some are as high as four miles. He thought that this was higher than *any* mountain on the earth. (Mount Everest, we know, is about five and a half miles high.)

Jupiter's Satellites

The telescope held still more marvels in store. Galileo soon discovered four small planets (or satellites) revolving around the planet Jupiter, as the moon revolves around the earth. (More satellites of Jupiter were discovered later, with more powerful telescopes than his and with photographic methods. There are twelve in all.) Galileo attached a great importance to this astronomical discovery, and even in later years it remained his favorite. Accordingly he named Jupiter's satellites *Medicean Planets*, in honor of his beloved former pupil Cosimo [de Medici] who had become Grand Duke, and in honor of Cosimo's family.

"Behold, then, four stars reserved to bear your famous name," Galileo wrote in the dedication of his book *The Starry Messenger*, "bodies which belong not to the inconspicuous multitude of fixed stars, but the bright ranks of the planets. Variously moving about most noble Jupiter as children of his own, they complete their orbits with marvelous velocity—at the same time executing with one harmonious accord mighty revolutions every dozen years about the center of the universe; that is, the sun."

We see from this paragraph that Galileo not only had observed Jupiter's planets but also was studying their motion. Indeed, he hoped to arrive at a complete understanding of this motion and to predict the satellites' positions so accurately that navigators would then be able to rely on them to direct the course of their ships. Jupiter's satellites are more suitable than planets for this purpose because their periods of revolution are shorter. (The satellite 10, 262,000 miles from Jupiter, completes an orbit around Jupiter in 42½ hours.) He spent evening after evening, year after year, studying the motion of the Medicean Planets with his telescope, indifferent to the chill of night that increased his arthritic pains or to the strain that prolonged observation put on his eyes. He came close to his goal but did not quite reach it.

When he turned his telescope on the planet Saturn, he found that this did not always look like a round body but seemed of strange variable shape. He thought Saturn to be "three-bodied; that is, it . . . was an aggregate of three stars arranged in a straight line parallel to the ecliptic, the central star being much larger than the others." His telescope was not sufficiently powerful to let him distinguish the three, possibly four, rings we now know are around Saturn. It was the Dutch astronomer and inventor Christian Huygens (1629–95) who discovered Saturn's rings. . . .

The Phases of Venus

Less than a month later Galileo announced "another detail newly observed by me, which drags along the decision of very great controversies in astronomy, and in particular contains a vigorous argument for the Pythagorean and Copernican constitution."[1]

Although Galileo called it "a detail," this was a true discovery, the discovery of the phases of Venus. On this occasion, as after his observation of Saturn's shape, Galileo wrote an anagram.[2] *Haec immatura a me frustra leguntur o y*, which he later explained as meaning: *Cynthiae figuras aemulatur mater amorum* [the mother of love (Venus) emulates the shapes of Cynthia (the moon)]. He described the phases of Venus toward the end of 1610:

---

1. The Copernican constitution is the theory, invented by astronomer Nicolaus Copernicus, that Earth revolves around the Sun.   2. That is, he jumbled the letters of his announcement to make a new phrase.

". . . about three months ago I began to observe Venus with my instrument, and I saw it of rounded shape and very small: It went on growing daily in size, still keeping its roundness, until eventually, arriving at a very great distance from the Sun, it started to lose its roundness on its eastern side, and in a few days diminished to a half circle. In this shape it stayed several days, growing however in size: now it starts to become of horned shape, and so long as it will appear as evening star, its small horns will diminish [it will become thinner] until it will vanish; but when it will appear again as morning star, it will be seen with very thin horns, and also turned against the Sun, and it will grow to become semicircular at its maximum departure [from the sun]. It will then remain semicircular for several days, decreasing however in size; and then from semicircular it will get to full roundness in a few days, and after that for several months it will be seen completely round, both when [it appears] as morning star and evening star, but rather small in size."

Copernicus had been disappointed not to see phases of Venus and variations in the apparent size of the planet. The fact is that the unaided eye cannot detect them. Their discovery through the telescope came as a strong argument against the hypothesis of an earth-centered universe—a much stronger argument than the Medicean Planets provided. (Indeed, to the foes of Copernicus it did not matter that satellites went around Jupiter; so long as Jupiter was moving around the earth, the satellites partook of Jupiter's motion and did not disturb Ptolemy's geocentric universe.) . . .

Sunspots

All Galileo's astronomical discoveries mentioned so far were made in 1610. Shortly afterward he made another important observation, that of sunspots. We do not call it a discovery because sunspots had been observed before, probably even in ancient times, and a booklet mentioning them, by [Lutheran pastor and astronomer] Johann Fabricius of Wittenberg, had appeared in 1611, before Galileo published their description. But Galileo seems not to have known of this booklet and said that he was the first discoverer of sunspots. So did another astronomer, the German Jesuit father Christopher Scheiner (1575–1650), and the two entered into a bitter dispute which played an important role in Galileo's controversy with the Church. We are concerned here only with Galileo's observations. In his own words:

". . . the dark spots seen in the solar disk by means of the telescope are not at all distant from its surface, but are either contiguous to it or separated by an interval so small as to be quite imperceptible. . . . Some are always being produced and others dissolved. They vary in duration from one or two days to thirty or forty. For the most part they are of most irregular shape, and their shapes continually change, some quickly and violently, others more slowly and moderately. They also vary in darkness, appearing sometimes to condense and sometimes to spread out and rarefy. In addition to changing shape, some of them divide into three or four, and often several unite into one. . . . Besides all these disordered movements they have in common a general uniform motion across the face of the sun in parallel lines. From special characteristics of this motion *one may learn that the sun is absolutely spherical, that it rotates from west to east and around its own center, carries the spots along with it in parallel circles, and completes an entire revolution in about a lunar month.*" Thus the sun itself, the most resplendent of celestial bodies, has blemishes on its surface, and it rotates around its axis as the earth and moon do.

The Aristotelian Universe Is Shaken

News of the telescope and its marvels spread with a rapidity unprecedented in the history of scientific discovery. Even 67 years after Copernicus died, he was known only in restricted circles of mathematicians and astronomers; Kepler's outstanding contribution to astronomy was not appreciated in his lifetime. But Galileo's discoveries were the subject of discussion throughout Europe within a few weeks of the time he made them.

Galileo himself greatly helped to spread the news by talking and writing. It seems he could not keep his discoveries to himself for even a short while. He sent out many scientific letters, and by March 1610 had finished a book, *The Starry Messenger*, in which he described the observations he had made so far. He wrote this book in Latin because he wanted astronomers in foreign countries to read it, and he certainly achieved his purpose. As soon as Kepler read it, he had it reprinted in Germany; five years after its publication it appeared in China, translated into Chinese—an astounding feat, if we consider the slow means of transportation available at that time.

The great publicity that Galileo received was favorable in most circles. Friends hailed him, poets wrote poems in praise of his telescope, painters reproduced it with their brushes, and innumerable people asked for a telescope or at least a chance to look through one. Among scientists, however, there were many unbelievers. For one thing, only Galileo could build telescopes powerful enough to reveal all his discoveries, and he never gave away the secret of how he ground his lenses. Though he built a large number of telescopes, not all were equally successful; only ten were suffi-

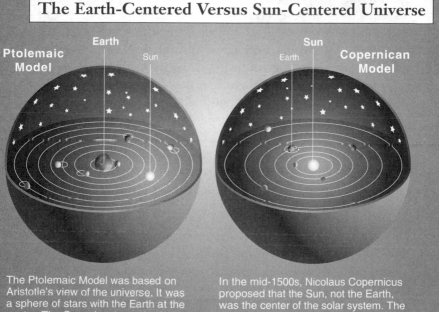

The Earth-Centered Versus Sun-Centered Universe

Ptolemaic Model — Earth — Sun

Copernican Model — Sun — Earth

The Ptolemaic Model was based on Aristotle's view of the universe. It was a sphere of stars with the Earth at the center. The Sun, planets, and sphere of stars all revolved around the Earth.

In the mid-1500s, Nicolaus Copernicus proposed that the Sun, not the Earth, was the center of the solar system. The Copernican Model was accepted science until modern times.

ciently good to show all the new phenomena. Thus even Kepler doubted the existence of the Medicean Planets at first, and only when he obtained a telescope made by Galileo did he admit that Jupiter's satellites were real and not a misinterpretation stemming from a flaw in the lenses or some other accident. He then wrote Galileo a letter ending: "*Galileae vicisti* [You have won, Galileo]."

More stubborn unbelievers were the Aristotelian philosophers[3] one of whom refused even to look through the telescope. Those who did look said either that they could see nothing new or that what they saw was mere optical illusion, tricks created by the telescope. Their mental bias is not hard to understand. They wanted to save at all costs the Aristotelian universe, which the telescope was shaking to its foundations.

In the universe of the telescope the sky contained many more stars than Aristotle had believed; his distinction between "terrestrial" and "celestial" bodies made no sense. The Medicean Planets circling around Jupiter formed a miniature Copernican system and disproved an argument of the Peripatetics: namely, that the earth could not be a planet, because it had a moon whereas the planets in the sky did not. Jupiter's satellites put the earth and Jupiter on the same level. The sunspots proved that perfection did not belong even to the sun, and, most important of all, the phases of Venus demonstrated that a planet *could* circle around the sun.

The tremendous blow that Galileo delivered to a well-rooted way of thinking, this opening of new vistas in a universe that had been thought unchangeable, is a greater contribution to astronomy than his discoveries. He could have gone far beyond and advanced the theory of astronomy had he not committed a serious mistake—he never really read Kepler's books.

---

3. Scholars who rigidly followed the ancient doctrines of the Greek philosopher Aristotle, also known as Peripatetics.

Galileo's Fight to Reconcile Science and Faith

William Bixby

Galileo Galilei is a candidate for the scientist who suffered most for the cause of science. Galileo was convinced of the truth of the Copernican (sun-centered) solar system, and he was determined to publish his ideas to spread this doctrine. However, he met with resistance from die-hard Aristotelians. These scholars, many of them clergymen, believed that Aristotle's writings expressed the truth of the physical world just as the Bible expressed the truth of the spiritual world. Any challenge to Aristotle's physics (and the Copernican system was such a challenge) would cause a crisis in faith.

Galileo did not make matters easier for himself. While he was careful to present Copernican ideas as merely plausible, not absolutely true, he also wrote condescendingly of his enemies. For example, he named the Aristotelian character he is arguing against in his *Dialogue Concerning Two World Systems* "Simpleton." Galileo's enemies eventually prevailed. He was brought before the Inquisition, the church council that judged whether individuals and beliefs were heretical. Despite having a friend as pope, Galileo was forced to publicly withdraw his belief that Earth moves around the sun.

William Bixby is an author who has written about explorer Robert Scott and other figures from history.

Galileo's early experiments on the motion of falling bodies had disproved [ancient Greek philosopher] Aristotle; his later astronomical discoveries were interpreted as casting doubt on the Bible. Angry churchmen pointed to the contradiction be-

William Bixby, *The Universe of Galileo and Newton*. New York: American Heritage Publishing, 1964. Copyright © 1964 by American Heritage, A Division of Forbes, Inc. Reproduced by permission.

tween Galileo's belief that the earth moved about the sun and the biblical assertion that Joshua had commanded the sun to stand still. Stubbornly, these dogmatists argued that if the sun was fixed at the center of the universe—as Copernicus and Galileo insisted—then how could Joshua have observed the sun to be moving? Their interpretation of the Bible was literal and unyielding.

Galileo the Heretic

In Pisa and in Florence, the rumor spread that Galileo was a heretic who questioned biblical truth. The sarcasm with which he replied to his critics did nothing to win new allies, and the ranks of his enemies grew. Soon university officials at Pisa ordered that no theory or discovery of Galileo's was ever to be mentioned or taught—to which Galileo responded once again contemptuously. He declared that the ignorance of his enemies had been the best master he had ever had, since their blindness had forced him to make many experiments to demonstrate the validity of his discoveries.

Galileo was waging a fight over the right of a scientist to teach and defend his beliefs. Thus, even though he recognized the undercurrent rising against him, he refused to suppress his discoveries or temper his statements. He had proof, he insisted, that Aristotle's concept of a changeless heaven was false. Further, he said he felt no compunctions about modifying or revising outmoded theories: Nature, he said, "in order to aid our understanding of her great works, has given us two thousand more years of observations, and sight twenty times as acute as that which she gave Aristotle." This explanation, despite its logic, would not satisfy his enemies, and Galileo knew it. He was always aware that his work would provoke criticism, even condemnation. In a letter to a friend, following an important discovery, Galileo expressed certainty that the Aristotelians would immediately "put forth some grand effort to maintain the immutability of the heavens.". . .

The First Attacks Against Galileo

The first overt clerical attack took place in December, 1614. Standing in the pulpit of the Dominican Church of Santa

Maria Novella in Florence, Father Thomas Caccini delivered a sermon that denounced mathematics as inconsistent with the Bible and detrimental to the State. And then, to drive home his venomed attack, the angry monk declaimed this biblical passage:

> Then spake Joshua to the Lord in the day when the Lord delivered up the Amorites before the children of Israel, and he said in the sight of Israel, Sun, stand thou still upon Gibeon. . . . So the sun stood still in the midst of heaven . . .

Word of Caccini's sermon, which was an indirect censure of Galileo, spread quickly through Florence. Many people were shocked, and Galileo's friends grew fearful and uneasy. It had begun to seem that Galileo's beliefs really did contradict the Bible. Not so, said the scientist, and then explained his reasoning:

> . . . I do not think it necessary to believe that the same God who gave us our senses, our speech, our intellect, would have us put aside the use of these, to teach us instead such things as with their help we could find out for ourselves, particularly in the case of these sciences, of which there is not the smallest mention in the Scriptures . . .

Many intelligent churchmen sided with Galileo, and a high dignitary in the Dominican order, Father Maraffi, even apologized to Galileo for Caccini's outburst. But the damage had been done, and Florence was in an uproar. In Rome, however, many of the strictest clerics seemed unconcerned—and were still reading Galileo's works with interest. A number believed, in fact, that his writings were destined to be recognized as established truths. . . .

A Roman prelate, Robert Cardinal Bellarmine, who served as a member of the Holy Office (the Inquisition), summed up the view of the Church in the matter of how the heavens went in this extract from a letter written to a Carmelite monk, Paolo Antonio Foscarini:

> . . . the words 'The sun also ariseth, and the sun goeth down, and hasteth to his place where he arose' were written by Solomon, who not only spoke by divine inspiration, but was

a man wise above all others and learned in the human sciences and in the knowledge of all created things, which wisdom he had from God . . .

Implied strongly in the text of this statement was Bellarmine's assertion that anyone who believed the theories of Copernicus was questioning the wisdom of Solomon and hence the Bible. Galileo was obviously in this category.

Although Bellarmine had been present when Galileo had been denounced by Caccini, the Cardinal's evaluation of Galileo's argument was not reported to the Inquisition. Bellarmine knew that the scientist was being investigated, but at this point he did not press for a ruling against him. Nor was he particularly eager to have Galileo come to Rome to answer his critics. Probably Bellarmine knew that the Inquisition did not yet have a solid case against Galileo. He must also have realized that despite frequent illnesses, Galileo was a persuasive and dynamic man whose presence in Rome might score heavily against Church opposition.

Galileo Galilei

But in December, 1615, Galileo did go to Rome, and soon his efforts to win clerical approval seemed to be meeting success. Even Caccini, the man who had maligned him, was told to apologize. Galileo's eloquence won him many admirers. As one witness to his forceful debating wrote to a certain Cardinal d'Este in Florence:

> Your Reverence would be delighted with Galileo if you heard him holding forth, as he often does, in the midst of fifteen or twenty, all violently attacking him, sometimes in one house and sometimes in another. But he is armed after such fashion that he laughs all of them to scorn . . .

Certainly Galileo was well armed against verbal attack, but against the forces that were already conniving against him, there was no defense. At last he was summoned to appear before Cardinal Bellarmine. To Galileo's surprise the Cardinal told him that the Copernican theory had been determined to be "in error." Therefore, Bellarmine advised, Galileo should abandon the idea that the sun was the center around which the earth and the other planets revolved.

The meeting apparently took place in February, 1616, although the only official record of it is a note in the Inquisition files. The note, which was unsigned and lacked a notary's seal, states that after the Cardinal had spoken, the Commissary General of the Inquisition stepped forward, and Galileo was "commanded and enjoined, in the name of His Holiness the Pope and the whole Congregation of the Holy Office, to relinquish altogether the said opinion . . . nor further to hold, teach, or defend it in any way whatsoever, verbally or in writing; otherwise proceedings would be taken against him by the Holy Office; which injunction the said Galileo acquiesced in and promised to obey.". . .

He knew he was forbidden to "hold, teach, or defend" what he felt certain was true. Some historians suggest that key phrases of the injunction may have been added later, which would explain why the document did not appear to have been authenticated.

Galileo's subsequent actions raise doubt that he ever realized the seriousness of his situation. He never imagined that he was liable to immediate arrest if he ever showed "in any way whatsoever" his Copernican leanings. Even so, he left Bellarmine's palace shaken and somewhat depressed. He had lost the battle to convince his Church that truth—even scientific truth   need not be considered contrary to belief in God.

By this time his problems were no longer theoretical, but actual. Rome was blackened by rumors that Galileo had at last been brought down, that he had been forced to recant. Hearing this whispered gossip, Galileo requested a statement from Cardinal Bellarmine describing what had occurred at their meeting. The Cardinal responded willingly. He certified that Galileo had not been forced to recant or to do penance for his erroneous beliefs but had been advised that the Copernican theory was contrary to the Bible and therefore was not to be held or defended. Apparently Bellarmine was unaware of the intervention of the Commissary General—or perhaps pretended to be.

Armed with the Cardinal's certificate, Galileo hoped once more to suppress his enemies, and for a time it appeared that he had done so. He lingered four more months in Rome, and before his departure he was received by Pope Paul V. The Pope, and many high churchmen, bore Galileo no ill will. How could they? for many had not read his books thoroughly nor thought out his logical and upsetting conclusions. Despite the pardon from the Church, Galileo still feared persecution. He expressed this concern in an audience with Paul V and was assured that neither the Pope nor the Holy Office would give heed to rumors spread against him. . . .

A Friend Becomes Pope

In 1621 Pope Paul V died. The next pope, Gregory XV, lived only two years. Then to Galileo's delight, Maffeo Cardinal Barberini, a friend and admirer, was elected to the papacy, choosing the name Urban VIII. Galileo was determined now to go back to Rome. He would press for the withdrawal of the 1616 prohibition against his publicly championing the Copernican theory. . . .

Galileo, no less of a wrangler than before, felt compelled to fight. In 1624, he traveled to Rome to talk with the Pope. To his dismay he found that as a cardinal Barberini had been able to hold private views favorable to Galileo and his scientific endeavors, but as pope he must steer a different course. Urban VIII welcomed his old friend from Florence, feted him, assured him of his warmest regard, and even conferred a pension on the learned scientist. But he would not withdraw the admonition. Instead he suggested that Galileo put his literary skills at the service of the authorities and enumerate all the pros and cons relative to new scientific theories. One stipulation was that Galileo should conclude his dissertation by stressing that the problem had not been solved, that God might have solved it by means beyond human consideration, and that Galileo must not constrain divine omnipotence within the limits of his theories. The Pope even dictated this conclusion for the proposed work, but Galileo would not agree to undertake the project.

For years Galileo had dreamed of giving the Copernican theory to the world, of explaining it so persuasively that no one could fail to see its truth. He had been admonished by the Church to which he remained loyal and, in spiritual matters, subservient. But he could not stop searching for a way to satisfy both his love of scientific truth and his love for his Church.

Galileo's Skill in Writing Creates Enemies

Finally, a way had become apparent. During the years of his semiretirement in Florence, he had worked on a book called *The Assayer.* It dealt with the nature of comets but was in reality a reply to attacks made on his physical discoveries. His views in it were erroneous, for he believed that comets, like rainbows, were atmospheric peculiarities that reflected sunlight. However, the significance of *The Assayer*, as far as Galileo's immediate future was concerned, was in its skillful writing rather than in its science. For the book managed to discomfit his enemies without violating Church doctrine; and though it stung the opposition, the book received the applause of the Pope himself, who had been cool to Galileo's pursuit of scientific discovery.

Galileo's method, which proved a most successful tactic, was to present his own theories simply as plausible ideas without stressing his firm belief that they were true. And as he deftly skirted the question of Copernicanism, he could not be accused of lending support to theories that were in conflict with the dogma of the Church.

The Assayer was printed in Rome in October, 1623, and its success had been one of the reasons Galileo had ventured to Rome to plead before the new pope. Its success also encouraged Galileo to turn to a long-cherished project, *Dialogue Concerning the Great World Systems*, after his return from Rome. He was sixty when he began it, and for five years thereafter, despite recurrent illness, he poured his best reasoning and most skillful writing into the volume. It is the book that introduces the three characters Salviati (champion of Galilean physics), Simplicio (an Aristotelian dogmatist), and Sagredo, the object of their persuasive speeches. . . .

With great expectations Galileo set out once more for
Rome. [His friends Benedetto] Castelli [mathematician to
the pope], [Niccolo] Riccardi [chief censor to the Vatican],
and Pope Urban each received him warmly. His manuscript
was read, and after minor alterations had been made, it was
returned to him with the censor's general approval. Galileo
had also written a preface and an epilogue designed to fore-
stall all possible criticism and even incorporating conclusions dictated by the Pope. But at this point Riccardi began
to realize that the text might not be so harmless as he had
imagined and that by allowing it to be published he was becoming a kind of accomplice.

Galileo was allowed to return to Florence with the text,
but the chief censor withheld the preface and the conclusion,
thus preventing the book's publication. With the exercise of
some pressure by Galileo, and with the help of the Tuscan
ambassador to Rome, Galileo was given permission to submit the text to ecclesiastical censors in Florence and to have
it approved there. With further prodding from the Tuscan
ambassador, Galileo managed to retrieve the preface and the
conclusion from Rome. So at last, after more than a year's
delay, the book was published in February, 1632. . . .

Book Banning

Shortly after its publication, orders came from Rome to stop
printing the book. And in another order, the printer was
commanded to remit to the Vatican all copies of the book remaining in stock. The printer wrote that he could not com-
ply with the order as his stock was completely sold out.

Friends of Galileo pleaded with Pope Urban to intercede,
but they were quickly informed that the Pope had grown fu-
rious with the scientist. Urban had come to believe that the
Simplicio of the *Dialogue*, the Aristotelian, was a caricature
of himself. Angrily he described Galileo as a man "who did
not fear to make game of me." The scientist's friends did not
doubt that the papal wrath would find an outlet.

On September 23, 1632, a message from Rome arrived at
the residence of the Florentine Inquisitor. It directed him to

"inform Galileo in the name of the Holy Office that he is to appear as soon as possible in the course of the month of October, at Rome, before the Commissary General of the Holy Office.". . .

His *Dialogue* had received the censor's approval; all the requested corrections had been made; the book had been granted the seal of approval required for the publication of any book in a Catholic country. Thus there seemed to be no basis upon which to substantiate charges against him. But one day someone riffling through the Inquisition files discovered the unsigned note setting forth the injustice of 1616. In it was the statement that Galileo had agreed no longer to "hold, teach, or defend it [the Copernican theory] in any way whatsoever, verbally or in writing . . ."

Galileo was sure that the words "in any way whatsoever, verbally or in writing" had not appeared in the original admonition of Cardinal Bellarmine or in the prelate's later explanatory note. He was certain too that though he had agreed not to hold or defend the controversial theory— which the *Dialogue* gracefully avoided—he had not been asked to refrain from teaching it.

Galileo Forced to Recant

Had his memory failed him? Was this an error, a forgery? Galileo would never know, for with these words as evidence, the Inquisition now had the means to deliver the final blow against him. On June 21, 1635, Galileo was convicted of disregarding the prohibition of 1616. The following day he knelt before his inquisitors and read slowly in a halting voice from a prepared apology:

> I, Galileo . . . kneeling before you, most Eminent and Reverend Lord Cardinals Inquisitors-General against heretical depravity throughout the whole Christian Republic, having before my eyes and touching with my hands the Holy Gospels, swear that I have always believed, do believe, and by God's help will in the future believe, all that is held, preached, and taught by the Holy Catholic and Apostolic Church. But whereas—after an injunction had been judi-

cially intimated to me by the Holy Office to the effect that I must altogether abandon the false opinion that the sun is the center of the world and immovable, and that the earth is not the center of the world, and moves, and that I must not hold, defend, or teach in any way whatsoever, verbally or in writing, the said false doctrine . . .

His voice droned on and on as he enumerated the sins he had committed and of which the tribunal had found him guilty. Upon completing his recantation—the true purpose of the trial—Galileo was not imprisoned, as many people believe. He was allowed to return to Florence and remained there under house arrest. His movements were restricted, and he was continually watched. The father of modern science had been humbled at last by his enemies—but not wholly subdued.

Kepler Makes a Key Discovery in Astronomy

René Taton

Johannes Kepler's laws of planetary motion are some of the most important discoveries in early science. As well as describing accurately the true, elliptical nature of planetary orbits, the laws relate motion to time. The relation of motion to time, especially motion along a curved path, paved the way for Isaac Newton to develop his theory of force and gravity, which unified motion in the heavens and on Earth. Moreover, the laws were derived in classic scientific style.

In this article, the French academic René Taton, one of the pioneers of the history of science, shows how persistent differences between Kepler's calculations and Danish astronomer Tycho Brahe's extremely accurate (for the era) observations led to the discovery of the true shape of the planets' orbits. Proceeding from the idea that Earth's orbit was circular, Kepler noticed his calculations were incorrect, but by a fixed amount. He did not believe Tycho's observations could be in error, but he did notice that all the observations fell within the calculated circular orbit. Kepler recalculated the orbit, but assumed an ellipse (oval) with a focus at the sun. The fit was perfect; Kepler had overthrown the theory of "perfect" circular motion and made a key discovery of how the solar system works.

It is certain that in the very large majority of cases errors of observation, of calculation or of interpretation are harmful to scientific research. Mistaken conclusions can often be put right only after long and unproductive verifications. Fur-

René Taton, *Reason and Chance in Scientific Discovery*, translated by A.J. Pomerans. London: Hutchinson Scientific and Technical, 1957. Copyright © 1957 by Random House Group, Ltd. Reproduced by permission.

thermore, there are some errors which, having been misunderstood for a long time, impair or retard the development of very large fields of science. Nevertheless there are other errors which, by the incentives or simplifications that they contain, have played an essential role in the discovery of facts or of fundamental principles. This fact may well appear paradoxical on first examination, but if we realize that the apparent simplicity of numerous physical phenomena is nothing but a first approximation of a very much more complex reality, we shall understand that many laws could only have been discovered by means of over-simplified hypotheses and of observations, in which grossly approximate measurements minimized certain difficulties that otherwise might have prevented progress in thought. A . . . particularly characteristic example is Kepler's statement of the three laws governing the motion of the planets of the solar system. This will give us a very good idea of the many ways in which erroneous theories or even material errors of many kinds can play a favourable role in the discovery of fundamental laws, and the example will also lead to some general considerations. Thus we shall devote quite some space to it, particularly since it is an example that deals with the foundations of celestial mechanics. . . .

Born in Weil, in Würtemberg [modern-day Germany], on the 27th December, 1571, Johann Kepler studied at the University of Tübingen, where the astronomer Michael Mästlin determined Kepler's vocation by introducing him to the heliocentric system of [Polish astronomer Nicolaus] Copernicus. In 1596, at the age of twenty-six years, he published his first work, the *Mysterium Cosmographicum* [*Cosmographic Mystery*], in which he produced new arguments in favour of the Copernican theory, and where he showed that the planes of the planetary orbits are close to one another but distinct. Copernicus was wrong in thinking that these different planes pass through the centre of the terrestrial orbit—an error which had disturbed and partially impaired his research work —and Kepler established that in reality their common point is the Sun.

But this work shows, in the case of its author also, conceptions which might strike us as very strange. In fact Kepler thought that the planetary system was organized according to the five regular polyhedra[1] known from the time of the ancient geometers. This mystical conception, to which Kepler always remained faithful, was taken from the Platonic theories on the affinity between geometrical figures and the perceptible properties of the elements which they are supposed to represent. For Kepler this was more than a mere intellectual diversion. Kepler, like many scientists of his time, was filled with mystical ideas, and in order to relate the motion of the stars in the solar system to regular polyhedra and to musical harmonics, he attempted an accurate determination of the geometry and kinematics [science dealing with motion and time] of the trajectories of the stars. True, such a mystic approach in itself could not suffice for creating so important a work as his, and very fortunately Kepler had, along with his mysticism, all the apparently incompatible qualities and resources of the authentic scientist. In fact it was observation and concrete fact which he considered as the basis to which he must adjust all his hypotheses, abandoning those that would not fit and modifying those he thought capable of improvement. It was thus that he directed his patient and exemplarily painstaking calculations towards trying to verify the validity of the ideas that sprang from his creative imagination. This was to lead him to his main discovery and gave him the courage to persevere in the face of the many difficulties that he was to meet during a life often marked by painful and dramatic incidents.

An Age of War and Witchcraft

It is understandable that such a man might look somewhat irrational to the eyes of the modern scientist. To appreciate him we must enter into the spirit of the beginning of the seventeenth century when wars and pillage, witch-hunts and religious strife were the background to a scientific life. Here a love for tradition and for the hard work that preceded the

1. Three-dimensional shapes whose surfaces (sides) are all the same. For example, a cube has a square for all six sides.

creation of new scientific concepts was tempered by an infatuation with ancient myths, scholastic discussions, and the speculations of astrologers, alchemists and the disciples of [Swiss alchemist] Paracelsus.

We are, in fact, in a period in which the first mutterings of the experimental method and the progress of observational science revealed, in the concrete structure of the universe and of nature, a variety and an order that had previously been beyond even the imagination. Thus it was natural that attempts were made to explain these marvels by new and audacious theories. If today we can easily distinguish between rational and mystical conceptions in these theories, such a distinction was very much more difficult for scientists at the beginning of the seventeenth century, whose entire education had conditioned them to seeing a constant intervention of the supernatural in the development of physical phenomena.

That fundamental errors were the basis of a great deal of progress during this time is a fact which can be seen in all branches of science, ranging from astronomy to chemistry, physics, anatomy and medicine. The realms to be tackled were so vast that, however erroneous the starting-point, the working hypotheses and the interpretations, any systematic research work had to lead to an increase in knowledge.

Within this framework, however, Kepler's situation is a very particular one. His emphasis on mysticism was a little unusual even in his period, but nevertheless the laws which he discovered are typical examples of strict modern scientific laws.

In a rapid sketch of the genesis of his famous laws on the motion of the planets of the Solar system we shall try to show how some misconceptions were able to play a favourable role, while others stood in the way of the progressive development of ideas. We shall also find that, for Kepler, it was observation alone that decided the validity of the scientific laws, and that it is to this conception, which is the basis of modern science, that the success of his research work is due.

In his *Mysterium Cosmographicum* of 1597, Kepler had already directed his attention to the study of the structure of the Solar system. However, in order to continue his research work he had to start from more precise astronomical observations than those which were then at his disposal. Circumstances were soon to provide these indispensable data in bringing to his knowledge the considerable number of observations of the best observer of the times, the Danish astronomer Tycho Brahe (1546–1601). In fact when, in the course of the year 1600, the publication of an edict against Protestants obliged Kepler to quit the Chair which he had occupied in Gratz since 1594, Tycho Brahe, who was then mathematician to the Emperor Rudolph II at Prague, invited him to come to work with him. The Danish astronomer was then trying to perfect a new theory of the planet Mars, and Kepler assisted him actively in his research work. Tycho Brahe died in the following year and Kepler succeeded him as court mathematician. Tycho's heirs left him the manuscripts and the observational notes of the

Kepler's Analysis of Error Leads to Key Discovery

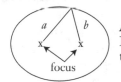

An Ellipse Showing the Foci. Kepler showed that planets' orbits take this shape.

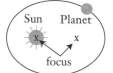

Kepler's First Law of Planetary Motion. The planet orbits in an ellipse with one focus at the Sun's location.

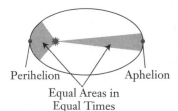

Kepler's Second Law of Planetary Motion. The area "swept out" by the radius drawn from the Sun to the planet are proportional to time. Thus for equal times, the areas will be equal.

www.physics.uc.edu/~hanson/ASTRO/LECTURENOTES/F01/Lec5/Page 2.html.

great observer. Kepler profited from these, and began a new and highly individual study of the theory of Mars, and after long efforts his research work led to his three famous laws which are one of the pillars of modern astronomy.

Kepler's First Two Laws of Planetary Motion

In 1604 and 1605 he had discovered the two first laws of the planetary system, viz. the law of areas which gives an accurate kinematic determination of the motion of every planet by stating that the area traversed by the radius vector joining it to the Sun is proportional to the time; and the geometric law stating that the orbits of the planets are ellipses with one focus at the Sun. These laws put an end to the thousand-year-old belief, which had still been held by Copernicus, in the absolute pre-eminence of circular motion.

This double discovery, which Kepler announced in 1609 in his *Astronomia Nova* [*New Astronomy*], published under the auspices of Emperor Rudolph, was the result of a long series of hypotheses, arguments and calculations.

To determine the displacement of a planet such as Mars, the astronomer had to overcome considerable obstacles resulting from the simultaneous displacement of his point of observation. In the first stage of his work Kepler had tried to gain a better knowledge of the orbit of the earth. To do so he needed a fixed reference system, for which purpose he chose intervals of 687 days, which Tycho Brahe had shown to be the duration of a full revolution of Mars. Thus having a fixed line of reference, viz. the line joining the Sun to that point of the orbit of Mars to which the planet returns after each revolution, Kepler could fix different points of the earth's orbit. His first calculations showed him that these points could be represented by a circle whose centre is at a distance from the Sun equal to $\frac{18}{1000}$ of its radius. During the first phases of his researches this seemed to confirm, at least as a working hypothesis, Ptolemy's theory of eccentricities, and enabled him to improve the corresponding data for the earth's orbit. The small eccentricity of this orbit favoured Kepler's calculations and justified, at least as a first approximation, this false but simplifying hypothesis. . . .

Error Leads to the Truth

Having now an accurate enough terrestrial orbit and a correct kinematic law, Kepler tried to determine the orbit of Mars. Based on two observations made at an interval of 687 days (the duration of one revolution of Mars), one particular position of Mars and the two corresponding positions of the earth could be determined by the law of areas, and a simple process of triangulation would then give the distance of Mars. In repeating this operation a sufficient number of times, different points are obtained which should have given an adequate idea of the trajectory of this planet.

When, after long calculations, Kepler had obtained this result, he tried to interpret it. Starting first of all from the theory of epicycles, he determined the assumed circles by means of points in the neighbourhood of the apsides.[2] But when he compared the other positions observed by Tycho Brahe with those obtained by this theory, Kepler discovered an error of eight minutes [that is ⁸⁄₆₀ of a degree] in some of these.

With great acumen he saw that the cause of this error was not to be sought in the imperfections of Tycho's observations but in the erroneous character of his starting hypothesis.

'Divine Mercy,' he wrote later on, with the calm assurance which comes once success is assured, 'has given us in Tycho an observer so faithful that he could not possibly have made this error of eight minutes. We must thank God and take advantage of this situation; we must discover where our assumptions have gone wrong. . . . These eight minutes, which we dare not neglect, will give us a means of reforming the whole of astronomy.'

A Key Observation

In trying to create a new theory that would agree better with the observational data, Kepler noticed that all the discrepant points lay inside the circle that he had constructed. He then tried to replace the circle by an oval whose point was at the perihelium, the point of the orbit nearest to the Sun; but the application of the law of areas to such a trajectory proved to be

2. The extremities of major axes of the planetary orbit.

particularly difficult, and also led to imperfect agreement with the observations. Finally, after new fruitless attempts, complicated at one time by an error of calculation, he discovered that the hypothesis of an ellipse, of which the sun is one of the foci, agreed perfectly with the observational data and led to an easy application of the law of areas. Then his enthusiasm knew no bounds. 'I awoke,' he wrote, 'from a deep sleep and a new light fell upon me.' And, in the dedication to the Emperor Rudolph II in his *Astronomia Nova*, he speaks of this achievement in allegorical terms, unfamiliar to the modern reader:

'I am presenting your Majesty with a noble prisoner, the fruit of a laborious and difficult war waged under your auspices. . . . No other human invention has ever triumphed more completely; in vain had all astronomers prepared for the struggle, in vain had they put their resources to work, their troops into the fields. Mars, laughing at their endeavours, had destroyed their machines and ruined their hopes; quietly, he had entrenched himself in the impenetrable secret of his empire and had camouflaged his cunning path from the enemy's search. . . . As for me, I must above all praise the work and the devotion of the valiant captain Tycho Brahe. . . . His observations, which have guided me, have helped me to banish this vague and undefined fear which one experiences when first confronted with an unknown foe. . . . During the uncertainties of the struggle, what disasters, what scourges have not devastated our camp. The loss of an illustrious captain, mutiny of the troops, contagious diseases, all added to our distress. Domestic fortunes and misfortunes robbed me of precious time. Soldiers, deprived of everything, deserted *en masse*; the new recruits were ignorant of the manœuvres, and to add to our misery, provisions were lacking.

'Finally, the enemy resigned himself to peace, and by the intervention of his mother, Nature, he sent me note of his defeat, became a prisoner on parole, and Arithmetic and Geometry escorted him unresisting into our camp.'

After having declared his intention of tackling the study of the trajectories of other planets, Kepler finished with a pressing demand for money.

The Printing Press Was Key to Disseminating Scientific Knowledge

Anthony Corones

The development of the printing press in Europe, around 1450, had a profound effect on all aspects of European life. Science was no exception. The printing press made knowledge much less expensive and much more widely available than it had been when books were copied by hand. The astronomer Nicolaus Copernicus, for example, had access to data from astronomers throughout Europe when devising his theory of the solar system. Alternative theories to explain the data were put forward, also by means of the printed word, and these too were disseminated throughout Europe. Printing had a real impact on the way scientific research was carried out.

Printing was not viewed as a blessing by all scientists, however, including Copernicus. As the Australian historian of science Anthony Corones, the director of the History of Science and Technology Program at the University of New South Wales, shows in the following excerpt, Copernicus was wary of putting his ideas before the public. He was worried that he would be ridiculed by readers who would not understand his thoughts on the solar system. In this fear he followed a long tradition of philosophers going back to the ancient Greeks; the philosopher Pythagoras thought that knowledge should be communicated just to an elite group of thinkers. The printing press was too valuable a technology, however, and Copernicus's friends soon pressured him into publishing his work.

Anthony Corones, "Copernicus, Printing, and the Politics of Knowledge," *1543 and All That*, edited by Guy Freeland and Anthony Corones. Dordrecht, Netherlands: Kluwer Academic Publishers, 2000. Copyright © 2000 by Kluwer Academic Publishers. Reproduced by permission of Springer Science and Business Media and the author.

Despite some notable exceptions, printing does not generally feature in histories of science. There is a good reason for this. In so far as historians of science have tended to focus on the content of science, printing is presumed to be a mere tool—convenient for the communication of ideas, but not in itself a factor in the conceptual development of science. On this view it is not obvious that printing even counts as a positive adjunct to that development, since it could just as easily serve the spread of 'non-progressive' ideas and theories as 'progressive' ones. Why, then, take it into account?

Technology Affects Scientific Ideas

The most direct response to such a position is to question the assumption of the neutrality of printing. Why restrict printing to being a mere carrier of ideas? Could it not also affect the content of science? The most strident versions of this view are, of course, forms of technological determinism; but while technological determinism has a certain reductive charm, it is not enjoying much favour among historians at the moment. In particular, the noted historian of printing, Elizabeth Eisenstein, makes a point of distancing herself from such a thesis: 'The very idea of exploring the effects produced by any particular innovation arouses suspicion that one favours a monocausal interpretation or that one is prone to reductionism and technological determinism'.

Eisenstein's monumental book, *The Printing Press as an Agent of Change*, is unquestionably the most important exploration of the impact of printing on the development of science. It is, nonetheless, a very guarded and well-hedged exploration. Commenting on the title of her book, Eisenstein stresses that 'it refers to *an* agent of change not to *the* agent, let alone *the only* agent of change'. For all that, however, she does think that printing constituted a profound shift in communications, and that this shift has been largely neglected by historians. Her revisionist thesis is stated as follows:

> As *an* agent of change, printing altered methods of data collection, storage and retrieval systems and communications networks used by learned communities throughout Europe.

It warrants special attention because it had special effects. In this book I am trying to describe these effects and to suggest how they may be related to other concurrent developments. The notion that these other developments could ever be *reduced* to *nothing but* a communications shift strikes me as absurd. The way they were reoriented by such a shift, however, seems worth bringing out.

Despite the criticism which Eisenstein has received for claiming that the shift from script to print precipitates a 'revolutionary' rupture in European history, I think she is right to emphasise the discontinuities. In any case she does not ignore the continuities, though she is critical of the deep-rooted historical conventions of 'gradualism and continuity'. As opposing historiographical strategies, continuist and discontinuist metanarratives should not blind us to the fact that both are concerned with change, and with how best to characterise the changes being studied. So long as both strategies are in use, historians will be kept on their toes.

Printing as an Agent of Change

To talk of printing as an 'agent' of change invites causal analysis (one speaks, for example, of 'chemical agents' which cause particular reactions to occur; or of human agents, typically responsible for doing things). Indeed, what is significant about printing for Eisenstein is that it had *special* effects—causal language again. It might seem, then, that the task at hand is to determine in what sense printing caused certain things to happen, and to weave this in with other causes and their effects in order to arrive at the full story. In her conclusion to *The Printing Press as an Agent of Change*, however, Eisenstein makes a rather striking claim which indicates that there is more to it than that; that printing is not just one cause among others:

> One cannot treat printing as just one among many elements in a complex causal nexus for the communications shift transformed the nature of the causal nexus itself. It is of special historical significance because it produced fundamental alterations in prevailing patterns of continuity and change.

It's not that there weren't books before the invention of printing, but the way in which the production, marketing and distribution of books was affected by printing (at least, in the European context—the story was not the same in China) made a difference. A more subtle position on the question of whether printing affected the content of science is required, then, than that suggested by the opposition presented earlier between the claim that printing is neutral with respect to content, and the technologically determinist position which assumes that the medium is the message. The 'middle way' would be to establish that there is an indirect, but important, sense in which printing affected the content of science—namely, by showing how printing affected the deliberative and problem-solving activities of scientists.

Printing Increases the Information Available to Copernicus

One strategy is to show that printing increased the cognitive resources available to scientists. Another is to show how those increased resources affected the problem-solving activities of scientists. Yet a third strategy, one which is geared especially to discontinuity in scientific thought, is to claim that students 'who took full advantage of technical texts which served as silent instructors were less likely to defer to traditional authorities and more receptive to innovating trends'. These are the basic strategies adopted by Eisenstein, and she employs them across a wide range of sciences. So far as Copernicus is concerned, however, these strategies are realised in the following way. Firstly, as 'a post-print astronomer, Copernicus had an opportunity to survey a wider range of records and to use more reference guides than had any astronomer before him'; and being freed from the need to slavishly copy texts, Copernicus was in a position to do more with more. Secondly, not only did access to many records enable him 'to tackle certain technical problems relating to long-term cycles that had remained out of the reach of astronomers who were served by scribes', but the availability of different texts exposed him to a diversity of views (and possible problem solutions, though Eisenstein does not make this point) about celestial motions. Thirdly, the multiplicity of conflicting models, inconsistently used, was a goad to innovation.

Interesting as these points are, however, they do not go very far. Certainly, printing gave Copernicus access to a great deal, and supplied him with cognitive resources; but this tends to limit the consideration of printing to largely 'internal' matters—that is, to the data available to Copernicus, the problem-solutions and mathematical models to hand, and the 'state' of the field of astronomy. This analysis is exemplified by Eisenstein's telling remark that 'Perhaps the most significant contribution made by Copernicus was not so much in hitting on the 'right' theory as in producing a fully worked out *alternative* theory and thus confronting the next generation with a problem to be solved rather than a solution to be learned'. The language of 'alternatives', problems to be solved and 'contributions' suggests an evolutionary or developmental model of scientific progress focussed on the problematic of the field. This is well and good as far as it goes, but it does not necessarily owe anything to printing—access to the great library of Alexandria in antiquity could have served similar ends just as well. Further, despite Eisenstein's leaning towards 'internalist' historiography, she has little to say about the specifics of Copernicus' theory, and how printing bears on those specifics. Finally, and most especially, she has nothing to say about Copernicus' cautious attitude to printing. . . .

The Danger of Printing

Copernicus himself provides us with a significant clue to the role of such considerations in his appeal to the Pythagorean tradition of philosophical secrecy. What he seems to approve of in this tradition is a certain kind of epistemic elitism whereby what can be said publicly is constrained by an assessment of the audience; that is, certain things (philosophical mysteries) should only be passed on to certain people; and then 'not in writing but by personal contact'. The reason why writing (and by extension printing) was mistrusted was because there was no control over possible readers. By restricting the communication of ideas to personally 'screened' listeners, one could better control the distribution and reception of those ideas. According to Copernicus, the Pythagoreans resorted to this strategy:

> . . . not as some think from a certain jealousy of communicating their doctrines, but so that their greatest splendours, discovered by the devoted research of great men, should not be exposed to the contempt of those who either find it irksome to waste effort on anything learned, unless it is profitable, or if they are stirred by exhortations and examples of others to a high-minded enthusiasm for philosophy, are nevertheless so dull-witted that among philosophers they are like drones among bees. Accordingly as I thought it over, the contempt which I had to fear because of the novelty and absurdity of my opinion had almost driven me to suspend completely the work which I had begun.

Theories Shared Among Friends and 'Great Men'

The rhetorical nature of this Pythagorean reflection by Copernicus should not be allowed to mask the seriousness of his concerns about printing De revolutionibus [On Revolutions]. It was one thing personally to inform friends and 'devoted great men' about this theory concerning the motion of the earth but it was quite another to print a book and put it out into the public domain where just anybody could read it. No wonder Copernicus feared a contemptuous response. That same fear had crippled him some three decades earlier—Copernicus was not even prepared to put his name or give a title to the first brief sketch of his heliocentric theory. The Commentariolus [Little Commentary], as it came to be called much later, was not printed by Copernicus; and he only dared to distribute a few handwritten copies to friends.

Of course, given the fact that De revolutionibus was printed, how was it that his reservations had been overcome? Copernicus lays the responsibility on his friends, claiming that despite *his* resistance, they insisted on publication. Copernicus tells us that Tiedemann Giese, Bishop of Kulm, 'often urged me, and demanded of me, sometimes with reproaches as well, to issue this book . . . after I have kept it suppressed and hidden not just for nine years but almost four times nine years already'. The astronomer (and teacher of Kepler) Michael Maestlin (1550–1631), being steeped in the classics, noted the allusion to [Roman poet] Horace's *Ars poetica* in Copernicus' claim to have suppressed the book. In recommending that a poet not publish work until nine years had passed, Horace shrewdly observed that 'What you have not published you can destroy; for the word once set forth can never come back'. The manuscript of *De revolutionibus* was not, however, lying in a locked closet for thirty-six years. The book was in fact not completed until just before its publication. Why feign Horatian prudence? Although Copernicus' humanist contemporaries may have appreciated the literary conceit for its own sake, Copernicus uses it as a rhetorical device to heighten the responsibility of his friends for the publication of the book. Indeed, by the end of this passage in his preface to *De revolutionibus*, Copernicus says that 'I was induced by their persuasion . . . eventually *to allow my friends to publish this work* [my emphasis], as they had long been asking me'.

Women Contribute to Italian Science

Paula Findlen

Science, like most other areas of eighteenth-century society, was dominated by men. However, science was different in that it offered some opportunity for women to make a career. Unlike traditional areas of scholarship such as law and medicine, women were not formally barred from studying the new subject. This allowed several women, such as the mathematician Emilie du Châtelet, to make important contributions early in the development of scientific knowledge.

Only in Italy, however, were women invited to participate fully in academic life. In France, women typically discussed their ideas in the confines of salons, discussion groups that met in private homes. Several Italian academies, on the other hand, included women as full members. Laura Bassi, an early physicist, exemplified this trend. She was able to take advantage of the Italian openness to women in science, joining the *Istituto delle Scienze* (the Italian Academy of Sciences) and eventually being appointed lecturer at the University of Bologna.

The author of this selection, Paula Findlen, is a historian of science. Among her accomplishments is the establishment of an academic program on science and society. Findlen is currently a cochair of the Science, Technology, and Society Program at Stanford University.

In 1732 Laura Bassi (1711–1778) became the second woman to receive a university degree and the first to be offered an official teaching position at any university in Europe. While

Paula Findlen, "Science as a Career in Enlightenment Italy: The Strategies of Laura Bassi," *History of Women in the Sciences*, ISIS, vol. 84, 1993, pp. 441–69. Copyright many other women were known for their erudition, none received the institutional legitimation accorded Bassi, a graduate of and lecturer at the University of Bologna and a member of the Academy of the Institute for Sciences (Istituto delle Scienze), where she held the chair in experimental physics from 1776 until her death in 1778. In Germany she was held up as a model to encourage other learned women to receive formal recognition for their studies. In France she earned the praise of contributors to the article on "Woman" that appeared in the *Encyclopédie* [the French encyclopedia]; the *Journal des Dames* [*Women's Journal*] devoted an article to her accomplishments in March 1775. Bassi left behind little of her scientific work, but her correspondence amply testifies to her accomplishments in and centrality to the learned world. . . . As [French writer] Voltaire wrote to her in 1744, "There is no Bassi in London, and I would be much happier to be added to your Academy of Bologna than to that of the English, even though it has produced a [physicist Isaac] Newton."

Bassi Plays a Central Role in Italian Science

Bassi is one of the most interesting women natural philosophers of the early modern period. During her long tenure as a professor at the University of Bologna and the most prominent female member of Italy's leading scientific society, she played a central role in the introduction of new forms of learning into the university science curriculum and in the constitution of a network of experimenters that connected Italy to the scientific culture of France and England. Other women natural philosophers published more than she did— for example, [English science critic] Margaret Cavendish, [natural historian] Maria Sybilla Merian, and Voltaire's celebrated companion, [French mathematician] Émilie du Châtelet—but Bassi was best at inserting herself within the academic world of science. This essay explores the conditions that made her success possible. . . .

Bassi's activities began in the period that ushered in early discussions about Newton, in the form of poems about the *Opticks* and cautious explorations of the *Principia* [*Mathematica*, Newton's work on physics]; by the time she died the general principles of Newtonianism had become a basis for explorations of all facets of the natural world. When Bassi first became associated with the University of Bologna, Newtonianism had only just begun to enter Italian academic discourse. Bassi studied primarily Aristotelian and Cartesian philosophy prior to receiving her degree, and she did not explore Newton's thought until the mid 1730s, under the tutelage of the mathematician Gabriele Manfredi. She became one of the first scholars in Italy to teach Newtonian natural philosophy, beginning with her lectures on the less controversial *Opticks* in the late 1730s and continuing with the course in experimental physics that she conducted in her home and ultimately at the Institute. In 1749 she presented a dissertation on the problem of gravity and in 1763 one on refrangibility [the capability of being refracted, or bent, e.g., light waves], before her colleagues at the Institute: in 1757 she published a paper on hydraulics in the *Commentaries of the Bolognese Institute and Academy for Sciences and Arts* that worked out certain theorems posed by Newton. From the 1760s onward, in collaboration with her husband Giuseppe Veratti, she made Bologna a center for experimental research in electricity, attracting the interest of well-known scholars of this subject such as [French scientist-monk] Abbé [Jean] Nollet. Right until the end of her career, she made the dissemination of Newtonian ideas one of her principal goals. As late as 1774 she lectured on the work of [botanist] Stephen Hales, well known for his applications of Newtonian ideas to explorations of fluids in works such as his *Vegetable Staticks* (1727).

Teaching, Publishing, and Raising a Family

Despite Bassi's importance to the scientific culture of Enlightenment Italy, we know very little about her intellectual activities because so few of her dissertations and lectures have survived. In addition to the forty-nine theses printed for her doctoral defense and various poems, Bassi published only four works in her lifetime. . . . Another was published posthumously. . . . These represent only a fraction of the dissertations that she prepared and defended annually at the Institute academy. And, as [Italian historian of science] Alberto Elena observes, they tell us very little about Bassi's experimental and pedagogical activities. Unlike Émilie du Châtelet, Bassi did not derive her fame from her publications. In addition to the normal obstacles that faced women writers, she had to divide her time between teaching, experimenting, and raising a family of eight children (five of whom survived to adulthood). Equally important, Bassi did not need to publish to stake her claim within the community of natural philosophers. Instead, the unique opportunities that early modern Italian academic culture afforded Bassi made it possible for her to achieve recognition for her work in physics and mathematics through her actions rather than her pen. Her correspondence and contemporary reports of her activities allow us to follow her career as a natural philosopher in Enlightenment Italy.

By the early eighteenth century science increasingly was a legitimate pursuit for exceptional women of unquestionable virtue. Women had become an audience for philosophical speculations, and their role as patrons and consumers of natural philosophy was increasingly acknowledged by contemporaries. The popularity of scientific activities in the Baroque Italian courts gave noblewomen the opportunity to observe and moderate the culture of experimentation and debate. In this context, women such as the grand duchess of Tuscany [a region in Italy], Christina of Lorraine [a region in France], and Queen Christina of Sweden emerged as patrons of science. The visibility of female patrons at court and the expansion of roles for women in the literary, artistic, and scientific academies of Italy set the background for the increased participation of socially prominent and intellectually gifted women in natural philosophy. Equally important were the possibilities that Cartesian philosophy offered. [French philosopher René] Descartes's famous dedication of his *Principles of Philosophy* (1644) to Elizabeth of Bohemia was seen by a number of scholars, male and female, as clear evidence that women were capable of philosophizing. Taking Descartes's praise of Elizabeth of Bohemia literally, Giuseppa-Eleonora Barbapiccola translated the work into Italian in 1722 in order "to make it accessible to many others, particularly women, who, as the same René says in one of his letters, are more apt at philosophy than men." Bassi, in her studies of Cartesian philosophy in preparation for her thesis defense, may even have read Barbapiccola's translation. Certainly her family and mentors acted in accordance with these principles when they chose to make natural philosophy an important part of her education. Learned women had long been known for their skill in ancient languages and, in a city such as Bologna, law. Mastery of natural philosophy, particularly the tenets of the new scientific learning, added a novel dimension to this topos [theme].

Women Find a Place in Italian Academic Institutions

During the same period, Italian intellectuals explored the desirability of women's education. Most famously, the Accademia de' Ricovrati, known for its admission of women, conducted a series of debates in 1723 about whether "women should be allowed to study Sciences and the Fine Arts" that expressed well the range of opinions of this issue. While many natural philosophers continued to oppose the entry of women into academic discourse, others, such as the president of the Accademia de' Ricovrati, the anatomist Antonio Vallisneri, encouraged their participation. Thus the Academy of the Institute for Sciences had important precedents to draw upon when it chose to add several women to its ranks, first among them Bassi. While claiming to imitate the new scientific societies such as the Royal Society, the Paris Academy of Sciences, and the Accademia del Cimento, none of which included women as members, the Institute academy nonetheless acknowledged its debt to the flourishing tradition of Italian academies that made the presence of women in their assemblies a necessary part of their composition.

The presence of women within academic institutions in Italy stood in marked contrast to the situation elsewhere. In countries like France women's participation occurred primarily in the salons. Excluded from the universities, women were allowed no role in organizations such as the Paris Academy of

Sciences. As François Poulain de la Barre wrote in 1673, "They [men] founded Academies to which women were not invited; and in this way [women] were excluded from learning as they were from everything else." In contrast, the Italian academies welcomed French women of learning, capitalizing on the dearth of possibilities within French academic culture. Upon hearing of Émilie du Châtelet's admission to the Institute academy in 1746, one philosophe [French philosopher] lamented:

> When Bologna proudly displays, in Italy,
> Its register adorned with the fair name of Émilie
> Why is the fair sex, so greatly loved by us,
> Excluded, in France, from the Academy?

While other regions discarded the Renaissance model of the academy as a place in which learned men and women of high social standing could interact, Italian practice enhanced this image. Rather than creating a salon culture that served to formalize the separation of the world of the academies from the society of learned women, scholars in numerous Italian cities formed academies that linked the university, the salon, and the leisure activities of the urban patriciate. In Bologna, Bassi soon became the centerpiece of such a network. Her presence strengthened preexisting ties between different sectors of the political and cultural elite and contributed to the enhancement of the city's position within the Republic of Letters.

Francis Bacon Charts the Course of Science

Edward O. Wilson

Edward O. Wilson is one of the foremost scientists today. He is an entomologist whose study of ants led him to the study of other social animals, including humans. Wilson founded the controversial field of sociobiology, which argues that human behavior and institutions have biological roots.

Wilson's wide-ranging interests naturally led him to study the history of science. In the following excerpt, he paints a picture of one of the great figures of the scientific revolution, Francis Bacon (1561–1626). Bacon was critical to the scientific revolution, but not for his brilliance in the laboratory or his mathematical ability. Rather, he thought about how science should be done, by what methods the scientist could advance knowledge about nature, and how these methods should be nurtured.

Bacon sought the best means for communicating scientific discoveries, both among scientists and to the educated public. He encouraged the creation of scientific institutions by which investigators could share their knowledge. He also used his writing talents to spread his gospel of science, for example, by outlining a fictitious "science governed" society in his work *New Atlantis*.

Science was the engine of the Enlightenment. The more scientifically disposed of the Enlightenment authors agreed that the cosmos is an orderly material existence governed by exact laws. It can be broken down into entities that can be measured and arranged in hierarchies, such as societies, which are made

Edward O. Wilson, *Consilience: The Unity of Knowledge*. New York: Alfred A. Knopf, Inc., 1998. Copyright © 1998 by Edward O. Wilson. Reproduced by permission of Alfred A. Knopf, Inc., a division of Random House, Inc.

up of persons, whose brains consist of nerves, which in turn are composed of atoms. In principle at least, the atoms can be reassembled into nerves, the nerves into brains, and the persons into societies, with the whole understood as a system of mechanisms and forces. If you still insist on a divine intervention, continued the Enlightenment philosophers, think of the world as God's machine. The conceptual constraints that cloud our vision of the physical world can be eased for the betterment of humanity in every sphere. Thus [French philosopher the Marquis de] Condorcet, in an era still unburdened by complicating fact, called for the illumination of the moral and political sciences by the "torch of analysis."

Bacon as Architect of Enlightenment

The grand architect of this dream was not Condorcet, or any of the other *philosophes* [French Enlightenment philosophers] who expressed it so well, but Francis Bacon. Among the Enlightenment founders, his spirit is the one that most endures. It informs us across four centuries that we must understand nature, both around us and within ourselves, in order to set humanity on the course of self-improvement. We must do it knowing that destiny is in our hands and that denial of the dream leads back to barbarism. In his scholarship Bacon questioned the solidity of classical "delicate" learning, those medieval forms based on ancient texts and logical expatiation. He spurned reliance on ordinary scholastic philosophy, calling for a study of nature and the human condition on their own terms, without artifice. Drawing on his extraordinary insights into mental processes, he observed that because "the mind, hastily and without choice, imbibes and treasures up the first notices of things, from whence all the rest proceed, errors must forever prevail, and remain uncorrected." Thus knowledge is not well constructed but "resembles a magnificent structure that has no foundation."

> And whilst men agree to admire and magnify the false powers of the mind, and neglect or destroy those that might be rendered true, there is no other course left but with better assistance to begin the work anew, and raise or rebuild the sciences, arts, and all human knowledge from a firm and solid basis.

By reflecting on all possible methods of investigation available to his imagination, he concluded that the best among them is induction, which is the gathering of large numbers of facts and the detection of patterns. In order to obtain maximum objectivity, we must entertain only a minimum of preconceptions. Bacon proclaimed a pyramid of disciplines, with natural history forming the base, physics above and subsuming it, and metaphysics at the peak, explaining everything below—though perhaps in powers and forms beyond the grasp of man.

He was not a gifted scientist ("I can not thridd needles so well") or trained in mathematics, but a brilliant thinker who founded the philosophy of science. A Renaissance man, he took, in his own famous phrase, all knowledge to be his province. Then he stepped forward into the Enlightenment as the first taxonomist and master purveyor of the scientific method. He was *buccinator novi temporis*, the trumpeter of new times who summoned men "to make peace between themselves, and turning with united forces against the Nature of things, to storm and occupy her castles and strongholds, and extend the bounds of human empire."

Proud and reckless phrasing that, but appropriate to the age. Bacon, born in 1561, was the younger son of Sir Nicholas and Lady Ann Bacon, both of whom were well educated and extravagantly devoted to the arts. During his lifetime England, ruled successively by Elizabeth I and James I, passed tumultuously from a feudal society to a nation-state and fledgling colonial power, with its own newly acquired religion and an increasingly powerful middle class. By the year of Bacon's death, 1626, Jamestown was an established colony with the first representative government in North America, and the Pilgrims were settled at Plymouth. Bacon saw the English language come to first full flower. He ranks as one of its grand masters, even though he regarded it as a crude parochial language and preferred to write in Latin. He lived in a golden age of industry and culture, surrounded by other global overachievers, including, most famously, [explorer Francis] Drake, [colonist Walter] Raleigh, and Shakespeare.

Bacon enjoyed the privileges of rank through every step of

his life. He was educated at Trinity College at Cambridge, which had been enriched some decades earlier by land grants from Henry VIII (and a century later was to serve as home to [Isaac] Newton). He was called to the bar in 1582 and two years afterward appointed to membership in Parliament. Virtually from infancy he was close to the throne. His father was Lord Keeper of the Seal, the highest judicial officer of the land. Elizabeth took early notice of the boy, talking with him often. Pleased by his precocious knowledge and gravity of manner, she fondly dubbed him The Young Lord Keeper.

He became a confirmed courtier for life, tying his political beliefs and fortunes to the crown. Under James I he rose, through flattery and wise counsel, to the heights commensurate to his ambition: Knighted in 1603, the year of James' accession, he was then named successively Attorney General, Lord Keeper, and, in 1618, Lord Chancellor [highest adviser to the monarch]. With the last office he was created first Baron of Verulam and soon afterward Viscount St. Alban.

Impeached and Imprisoned

Then, having flown too close too long to the royal flame, Bacon at last sustained near-fatal burns. He was targeted by a circle of determined personal enemies who found the wedge to his destruction in his tangled finances, and in 1621 successfully engineered his impeachment as Lord Chancellor. The charge, to which he pleaded guilty, was acceptance of bribes—"gifts," he said—while in high public office. He was heavily fined, escorted through the Traitor's Gate and imprisoned in the Tower of London. Unbowed, he at once wrote the Marquis of Buckingham: "Good my Lord: Procure the warrant for my discharge this day. . . . Howsoever I acknowledge the sentence just, and for reformation sake fit, [I was] the justest Chancellor that hath been in the five changes since Sir Nicholas Bacon's time."

He had been all that, and more. He was released in three days. Shorn at last of the burden of public ambition, he spent his last days totally immersed in contented scholarship. His death in the early spring of 1626 was symbolically condign, the result of an impromptu experiment to test one of his favorite ideas. "As he was taking the air in a coach with Dr. Witherborne towards High-gate," John Aubrey reported at the time, "snow lay on the ground, and it came into my Lord's thoughts, why flesh might not be preserved in snow, as in salt. They were resolved they would try the experiment presently. They alighted out of the coach and went into a poor woman's house at the bottom of High-gate hill, and bought a hen, and made the woman exenterate it, and then stuffed the body with snow, and my Lord did help to do it himself. The snow so chilled him that he immediately fell so extremely ill, that he could not return to his lodgings. . . ." He was taken instead to the Earl of Arundel's house close by. His condition remained grave, and he died on April 9, most likely of pneumonia.

The ache of disgrace had been subdued by the return to his true calling of visionary scholar. As he wrote in one of his oft-quoted adages, "He that dies in an earnest pursuit is like one that is wounded in hot blood, who for the time scarce feels the hurt." He saw his life as a contest between two great ambitions, and toward the end he regretted having invested so much effort in public service with an equivalent loss of scholarship. "My soul," he mused, "hath been a stranger in life's pilgrimage."

His genius, while of a different kind, matched that of Shakespeare. Some have believed, erroneously, that he *was* Shakespeare. He melded great literary gifts, so evident in *The Advancement of Learning*, with a passion for synthesis, two qualities most needed at the dawn of the Enlightenment. His great contribution to knowledge was that of learned futurist. He proposed a shift in scholarship away from rote learning and deductive reasoning from classical texts and toward engagement with the world. In science, he proclaimed, is civilization's future.

Bacon defined science broadly and differently from today's ordinary conception to include a foreshadowing of the social sciences and parts of the humanities. The repeated testing of knowledge by experiment, he insisted, is the cutting edge of learning. But to him experiment meant not just controlled manipulations in the manner of modern science.

It was all the ways humanity brings change into the world through information, agriculture, and industry. He thought the great branches of learning to be open-ended and constantly evolving ("I do not promise you anything"), but he nonetheless focused eloquently on his belief in the underlying unity of knowledge. He rejected the sharp divisions among the disciplines prevailing since Aristotle. And fortunately, he was reticent in this enterprise when needed: He refrained from forecasting how the great branches of learning would ultimately fall out.

Bacon elaborated on but did not invent the method of induction as a counterpoint to classical and medieval deduction. Still, he deserves the title Father of Induction, on which much of his fame rested in later centuries. The procedure he favored was much more than mere factual generalizations, such as—to use a modern example—"ninety percent of plant species have flowers that are yellow, red, or white, and are visited by insects." Rather, he said, start with such an unbiased description of phenomena. Collect their common traits into an intermediate level of generality. Then proceed to higher levels of generality, such as: "Flowers have evolved colors and anatomy designed to attract certain kinds of insects, and these are the creatures that exclusively pollinate them." Bacon's reasoning was an improvement over the traditional methods of description and classification prevailing in the Renaissance, but it anticipated little of the methods of concept formation, competing hypotheses, and theory that form the core of modern science.

The Psychology of Discovery

It was in psychology, and particularly the nature of creativity, that Bacon cast his vision farthest ahead. Although he did not use the word—it was not coined until 1653—he understood the critical importance of psychology in scientific research and all other forms of scholarship. He had a deep intuitive feel for the mental processes of discovery. He understood the means by which the processes are best systematized and most persuasively transmitted. "The human understanding," he wrote, "is no dry light, but receives an infusion from the will and affections [impulses or desires]: whence proceed sciences which may be called 'sciences as one would.'" He did not mean by this to distort perception of the real world by interposing a prism of emotion. Reality is still to be embraced directly and reported without flinching. But it is also best delivered the same way it was discovered, retaining a comparable vividness and play of the emotions. Nature and her secrets must be as stimulating to the imagination as are poetry and fables. To that end, Bacon advised us to use aphorisms, illustrations, stories, fables, analogies—anything that conveys truth from the discoverer to his readers as clearly as a picture. The mind, he argued, "is not like a wax tablet. On a tablet you cannot write the new till you rub out the old; on the mind you cannot rub out the old except by writing in the new."

Common Errors in Reasoning

Through light shed on the mental process, Bacon wished to reform reasoning across all the branches of learning. Beware, he said, of the *idols of the mind*, the fallacies into which undisciplined thinkers most easily fall. They are the real distorting prisms of human nature. Among them, idols of the *tribe* assume more order than exists in chaotic nature; those of the imprisoning *cave*, the idiosyncrasies of individual belief and passion; of the *marketplace*, the power of mere words to induce belief in nonexistent things; and of the *theater*, unquestioning acceptance of philosophical beliefs and misleading demonstrations. Stay clear of these idols, he urged, observe the world around you as it truly is, and reflect on the best means of transmitting reality as you have experienced it; put into it every fiber of your being.

I do not wish by ranking Francis Bacon so highly in this respect to portray him as a thoroughly modern man. He was far from that. His younger friend William Harvey, a physician and a real scientist who made a fundamental discovery, the circulation of the blood, noted drily that Bacon wrote philosophy like a Lord Chancellor. His phrases make splendid marble inscriptions and commencement flourishes. The unity of knowledge he conceived was remote from the present-day concept of consilience [the synthesis of knowledge across traditional scholarly boundaries], far from the deliberate, systematic linkage of cause and effect across the disciplines. His stress lay instead upon the common means of inductive inquiry that might optimally serve all the branches of learning. He searched for the techniques that best convey the knowledge gained, and to that end he argued for the full employment of the humanities, including art and fiction, as the best means for developing and expressing science. Science, as he broadly defined it, should be poetry, and poetry science. That, at least, has a pleasingly modern ring.

A New Beginning

Bacon envisioned a disciplined and unified learning as the key to improvement of the human condition. Much of the veritable library that accumulated beneath his pen still makes interesting reading, from his often quoted essays and maxims to *Advancement of Learning* (1605), *Novum Organum* (*The New Logic*, 1620), and *New Atlantis* (1627), the latter a utopian fable about a science-based society. Most of his philosophical and fictional writing was planned to implement the scheme of the unification of knowledge, which he called *Instauratio Magna*, literally the Great Instauration, or the New Beginning.

His philosophy raised the sights of a small but influential public. It helped to prime the scientific revolution that was to blossom spectacularly in the decades ahead. To this day his vision remains the heart of the scientific-technological ethic. He was a magnificent figure standing alone by necessity of circumstance, who achieved that affecting combination of humility and innocent arrogance present only in the greatest scholars. Beneath the title of *Novum Organum* he had the publisher print these lines:

FRANCIS OF VERULAM
REASONED THUS WITH HIMSELF
and judged it to be for the interest of the present and future
generations that they should be made acquainted
with his thoughts.

Chapter 3

Building the Scientific Revolution

Turning | Points

IN WORLD HISTORY

Robert Boyle and English Thought

Meyrick H. Carré

Robert Boyle is a key figure in the development of the scientific revolution. Generally considered to be the Father of Modern Chemistry, he implemented the ideas of Francis Bacon, the first philosopher of science. The laboratories he set up with his own personal wealth greatly advanced the cause of the new knowledge. As for method, he insisted on experimental proof for every scientific idea. Only the lack of mathematics in his work keeps him from ranking as high as Isaac Newton on the scale of greatness.

Philosopher and historian of science Meyrick H. Carré explains Boyle's role in the following selection. Carré shows Boyle's insistence on the correctness of the mechanico-corpuscular view of nature (the view that nature behaved like a mechanism made of small, basically identical particles that combined in various ways to make the multitude of forms evident in the universe). Boyle did not believe in dogma, however, and viewed grand hypotheses as essentially ephemeral, to be regarded as temporary learning tools that were valuable until improved ideas were developed. Carré also touches on Boyle's attempt to reconcile science to religion. The chemist viewed nature as being made by design. For Boyle, the scientist's job was to discover that design.

In the early years of the seventeenth century men who were interested in scientific questions gathered at Gresham House, in Bishopsgate, London, where mathematical lectures were given to all who cared to attend. At first many of those who formed the audiences at the lectures were makers

Meyrick H. Carré, "Robert Boyle and English Thought," *History Today*, vol. 7, May 1957, pp. 322–27. Copyright © 1957 by History Today Limited. Reproduced by permission.

of instruments, such as astrolabes, compasses, clocks and other useful inventions. An increasing number were attracted by the theories of William Gilbert and by the strange discoveries reported from Italy and France. Various groups began to meet at regular intervals to discuss the new theories, but it was not until after 1640 that these casual meetings assumed the shape of definite associations. The most organized of these bodies met weekly at the lodgings of the Professor of Astronomy or at the house of the eminent physician, Dr. Goddard, in Wood Street. The discussions were conducted with some formality; rules of procedure were drawn up and members paid a subscription. Political and religious questions were rigorously excluded; a necessary precaution among men divided between support of the King's party and loyalty to the Parliamentary cause.[1] The names of the Gresham circle included men who afterwards became leading figures of the Royal Society. There remains some record of the comprehensive subjects that were discussed, ranging over recent advances in astronomy, mechanics, mathematics, chemistry, physiology and medicine. At each meeting an experiment or some improved instrument was demonstrated.

Introduction to Scientific Society

One evening in the year 1644 a remarkable young man was introduced to the group. Robert Boyle was the seventh son of the formidable Earl of Cork, who had acquired by unscrupulous ability large estates in Ireland. Robert was born in 1627 and was educated at Eton, where he is described by a school-fellow as a pale and sickly boy. After leaving Eton he travelled extensively abroad in the company of a tutor, and during a visit to Italy he read carefully the works of Galileo. On his return to London he was introduced to the society of natural philosophers at Gresham House by his sister, Lady Ranelagh, who was a leader of intellectual culture in the capital. The group welcomed the eager and intelligent

---

1. These meetings were held in the period leading up to the English Civil War, a conflict between the king and Parliament.

young aristocrat to its discussions. But he soon left London for his manor house at Stalbridge in [the English county of] Dorset and applied himself, as he wrote to his old tutor, to the production of "divers little essays both in prose and verse" and to the study of works on "natural philosophy, the mechanics and husbandry, according to the principles of our new philosophical college that values no knowledge, but as it hath a tendency to use." There speaks the disciple of Francis Bacon. The young virtuoso[2] had already entered upon some inquiries into minerals and natural history before renewing his associations with the group in London. In 1648 several of its leading investigators left to take up appointments at Oxford where the house of Dr. John Wilkins, the Warden of Wadham College, became the centre of renewed discussions and experiments. A number of brilliant young men, interested in the new learning, debated the implications of recent advances in physics and the Cartesian philosophy in Dr. Wilkins' famous upper room.

Boyle Establishes Laboratories

The arrival of Boyle at Oxford in 1653 gave a powerful stimulus to the Philosophical Society which had been founded two years earlier. His wealth enabled him to establish laboratories, to hire assistants and to direct his extraordinary intellectual energies to a multitude of physical problems. He was now in his twenty-seventh year, tall, lean and emaciated, modest and unassuming in his demeanour, temperate and frugal in his habits. Indeed it was only by careful attention to his diet and by a strict regimen that he was able to accomplish the enormous quantity of work indicated in his published writings. He suffered from frequent spells of painful illness, and an increasing weakness of the eyes which often prevented him from working. Under these disablements his prolonged scientific exertions appear heroic.

Beyond these incessant scientific activities, he became immersed in a press of business. He was occupied with the management of his estates; he threw himself into the promotion

---

2. Virtuoso here means someone skilled in conducting experiments.

of the Gospel in foreign parts; he was an inspector of minerals for the government and a director of the East India Company. He was deeply concerned with questions of religion and wrote a number of theological works. He even composed a religious novel. The establishment of the *Royal Society of London for the Promotion of Natural Knowledge* owed much to his advice and support; the Society finally received its charter of incorporation in 1662. Its activities were greeted with suspicion and ridicule. Prominent members sprang to its defence; among them was the eloquent [English philosopher] Joseph Glanvil, whose case on behalf of the new philosophy, set forth in *Plus Ultra*, 1668, included an impressive eulogy of the work of Boyle. In his later years Boyle removed to London and lived at the house of his sister, Lady Ranelagh, where, writes a contemporary, "he has a noble laboratory and several servants to look to it." The writer adds, "he has not only a high renown in England, but abroad; and when foreigners come hither, 'tis one of their curiosities to make him a visit." He died on December 31st, 1691, in the sixty-fifth year of his age.

A Genius in the Laboratory

No man of his time was more generally revered and no thinker of the period did more to educate the men of his day in the new ways of truth. He was the genius of experimental inquiry in the seventeenth century. "In my laboratory," he wrote, "I find that water of Lethe[3] which causes me to forget everything but the joy of making experiments." The appearance of his first scientific book, *On the Spring and Weight of Air*, in 1661 excited lively interest and the public exhibitions in London of "the pneumatic engine" promoted discussion of the new methods and conceptions. Boyle soon described a number of further ingenious experiments on the properties of air, and in these publications he not only exploded cardinal principles of the traditional physics but also recommended to thoughtful persons the experimental procedure in natural enquiry. The book on the properties of air states in a

---

3. A river in Greek mythology whose water, when drunk, made the drinker forget everything.

clear and attractive style the problems to be investigated, describes the apparatus by which the factors under consideration can be controlled and measured, and presents a sequence of over forty experiments. Many notable contributions to physical and chemical knowledge followed, *The Sceptical Chemist, Physiological Essays, The History of Colours*, and other works. He wrote a long series of papers for the newly-formed Royal Society, the pages of which are crowded with records of experiments. One biographer writes of him during the wonderful years from 1660–1673, "His range was so catholic [universal], the mass of observations and experiments so astonishing, and his discussions of the new outlook so numerous, that he appears more as an institution than as an individual." His classical contributions to the development of physics and chemistry cannot here be described. This is no place for more than a bare mention of the work on the composition and pressure of air, the advance towards the theory of chemical elements and the investigation of the properties of respiration, fluidity and combustion. What may be concisely acknowledged here are the broader tendencies of his thought. Such trends include the mechanical philosophy of nature, the experimental and empirical view of knowledge and the religious frame of belief in which both these conceptions are set. The association of these principles in the mind of Robert Boyle gave rise to long reverberations in the thought of the seventeenth and eighteenth centuries. The cycle of ideas repeatedly expounded by him shaped the characteristic design of speculative ideas in England. Let us briefly review these articles of the new intellectual faith.

The Mechanical Philosophy of Science

Boyle's persistent application of the mechanical explanation of natural phenomena is displayed in the titles of many of his works, *The Mechanical Origin of Heat and Cold, The Mechanical Production of Magnetism, The Mechanical Production of Tastes and Odours*, and, for a general consideration, *The Excellence and Grounds of the Mechanical Philosophy*. The treatise that contains his most explicit account of the principles of mechanism is *The Origin of Forms and Qualities, Serving as an Introduction to that Mechanical Philosophy.* The treatise appeard in 1666; a further and enlarged edition was published in 1670. The paper is a deliberate challenge to the traditional notions of Aristotelian doctrines that were still maintained at the Universities. In place of the endless perspective of internal forms and essences, the new outlook reduces all natural things and processes to two embracing principles. First, there is one universal matter, common to all bodies in the universe. This substance is extended, that is to say, occupies space, and is impenetrable. The infinite diversity of things and qualities in nature is due to the operation on primary matter of a second principle, motion. The opinion of the ancient physicists that motion is inherent in matter must be rejected, for matter is essentially inert. The origin of motion must be sought beyond the world of matter; and Boyle does not hesitate to ascribe it to the divine activity of the Creator when the world was framed by Him. The rules of motion that were then established are the mechanical laws by which the parts of matter operate upon one another. The parts of matter are themselves due to the work of motion, for motion breaks matter into fragments. The ultimate elements of matter are certain primitive indivisible particles that constitute the *minima naturalia* [smallest natural parts, what we now call atoms] of the material world. Each of these infinitely minute particles may be conceived to have a determinate motion, shape and size; and since there are numerous modes and rates of motion, and many shapes and sizes of particles, "what a vast number of variations may we suppose capable of being produced by the compositions and re-compositions of myriads of single invisible corpuscles that may be contained and concreted in one small body?" Corpuscles, in Boyle's terms, are clusters of particles, that form the basic textures of bodies. Chemical experiments on iron, salt, amber, copper and many other substances confirm the corpuscularian hypothesis. On the basis of the calculable effects of the impact on one another of particles and corpuscles of varying bulk, figure and speed, it would be possible to show how the special natures of bodies arise and why changes in them occur, without recourse to the metaphysical powers of the old physics. If a substance, such as saltpetre, can be dissolved by chemical agents into a solution and then be re-united into its original nature, we may infer that the "form" of a body, which, according to the accepted teaching, gives the body its special nature from which its qualities are believed to flow, is actually a modification of common matter, the minute parts of which are disposed in a particular manner. If the same parts were arranged in different ways, they would constitute other kinds of bodies. All compounds are made of the same fundamental elements; the differences between them spring from the mode in which the elementary factors and forces are related to each other. A species of body is generated by the accession or withdrawal of corpuscles and by their transposition and arrangement. Boyle illustrates the plan of the mechanical philosophy by means of the favourite simile of seventeenth-century scientific theory. In seeking to understand the complex elements that make a substance, the philosopher must suppose that they combine in the manner of the weight, spring, wheels and hands of a clock. A substance and its qualities can, in principle, be explained by means of the determined inter-action of parts; by employing no other factors beside calculable forces between fixed items of matter. The laws of motion govern not only the action of engines but also the movements of the minute particles of bodies; and those who deny this speak as though "the laws of the mechanism may take place in a town-clock and not in a pocket-watch." With the comprehensive enthusiasm of a virtuoso of the Royal Society, Boyle extends the theory to many ranges of natural history, medicine and physiology. And he dwells upon the services which the mechanical philosophy may bring to the arts of health, trade and the daily comforts of men.

Boyle's Work Lacks Mathematics

It must be admitted that Boyle's speculative physics lack definition. The account of the nature and activities of the corpuscles is vague, and the process by which they form bodies is obscure. The chief failure is the absence of all attempt to express the mechanism, which he everywhere proclaims, on mathematical lines. In these respects Newton made signal advances upon Boyle's mechanical philosophy. But the classical view of nature, the unity of all kinds of material things in a comprehensive mechanical, atomic physics, was first and most elaborately proclaimed in England by Boyle.

Yet the temper of his mind was constitutionally averse to dogmatism. Here we turn to the second quality of his thought, its empiricism. He displays a profound distaste for rigid schemes and for speculation that outruns evidence. "When an author," he writes, "after having cultivated a particular branch of physics, sets himself down to give a complete body of them, he finds himself, by the nature of his undertaking and the laws of method, engaged to write of many things wherewith he is unacquainted; whence he is reduced, either idly to repeat what, perhaps, has already been impertently delivered on the subject; or to say anything of it, to avoid saying nothing." What he demands is that the makers of systems should offer evidence in proportion to the extensiveness of the theory to be built on it, and in the meantime he requests that such superstructures should be looked upon as temporary. It is in this spirit that he embraces the corpuscular or mechanical philosophy. The scheme is no more than an hypothesis, a useful key with which to read the cipher of the natural world. We cannot find whether it is the right key save by trial, nor can we prove *a priori* that ours is the right key and that those of others are ill-fitting.

Tireless accumulation of evidence, systematic experiment, cautious theorising, these methods proved to be vastly more valuable in science than the rational procedure of [philosopher René] Descartes. They became equally important in philosophy. The first great exponent of modern empiricism in philosophy, [political philosopher] John Locke, was intimate with Boyle, and described himself as "an underlabourer" to such "master-builders" as Boyle and [physician Thomas] Sydenham. "Those who are diligent and judicious enough, thoroughly to study any part of philosophy," writes Boyle, "will, from the difficulties and uncertainties they find therein, be the most backward of all men to write systems." Everywhere in his voluminous works he sets an example of openness of mind, humility before facts, and experimental ardour which influenced English thought for generations. The "corpuscularian hypothesis" of universal mechanism walks with the conviction that the details of the mechanism could be decided only by experimental inquiry. The mechanistic philosophy in his hands remains throughout a pragmatic ideal.

Religious Faith and Science

Finally, this scheme of thought is blended with religious faith. In early youth, amid the mountains of Switzerland, Boyle experienced a profound spiritual crisis and thereafter all his activities were coloured with religion. He wrote extensively upon the relations between natural philosophy and Christian belief, and warmly contested the opinions of those divines who feared that the new science would encourage irreligion. In *The Christian Virtuoso* and other writings he showed at length how experimental philosophy conduces to a firm persuasion of the existence and attributes of God. The more carefully the intricate contrivances of nature are examined, the more impressively are discerned the marks of supreme power, wisdom and goodness. Tiny creatures display traces of omniscience too delicate to be ascribed to any other cause. "The silk-worm raises my wonder more than those outlandish monsters, which multitudes flock to pay to see." And again, "The contrivance of every animal, and especially of a human body, is so curious and exquisite, that 'tis almost impossible for any one, who has not seen a dissection well made and anatomically considered, to conceive how much excellent workmanship is displayed in that admirable engine." Such passages, which abound in Boyle, associate mechanism with theology and gave birth to the elaborate developments of the argument from design in the following centuries. . . . In other passages Boyle argues on lines that bring him into touch with more recent views. He points out that the natural philosopher who trusts the evidence of attested experience will not lightly dismiss the records of "theological experience" obtained from spiritual men. In Boyle there is attained a synthesis of the mechanical ideal in science, of the empirical and exploratory view of knowledge, and of belief in the providential order of the world, the influence of which is prominent in the thought of the succeeding centuries.

Descartes Devises a Method of Mapping Space

John Gribbin

The Italian astronomer and pioneer of science Galileo Galilei is supposed to have said, "Mathematics is the language of science." If that is true, then the most fluent speaker of science at the beginning of the scientific revolution must be the French mathematician and philosopher René Descartes. Descartes had a varied career as a military man, adventurer, philosopher, and scientist. But he is most remembered for his gift to every student of algebra, the Cartesian coordinates.

In the following excerpt, the popular English science writer John Gribbin relates how Descartes came up with the idea of mapping space with a coordinate system. While sick in bed, watching a fly buzzing around the room, Descartes realized that the position of the fly could be described by three numbers: the distance of the fly from each of the walls, and the height of the fly above the floor. True to the spirit of the scientific revolution, Descartes had managed to split space into each of its dimensions. This concept is commonplace today, especially in the two-dimensional case; almost everyone has used Cartesian coordinates to read a map. However, the coordinate system was a momentous advance, as it allowed the separation of motion into vertical and horizontal components, thereby greatly simplifying the mathematical models used to describe motion.

René Descartes was born at La Haye, in Brittany, on 31 March 1596. He came from a prominent and moderately

John Gribbin, *The Scientists*. New York: Random House, 2002. Copyright © 2002 by John and Mary Gribbin. Reproduced by permission.

wealthy local family—his father, Joachim, was a lawyer and a Counsellor in the Brittany parliament and although René's mother died not long after he was born, she left him an inheritance which was sufficient to ensure that, although by no means rich, he would never starve, and could choose whatever career (or lack of career) he liked without worrying unduly about money. There was a real prospect, though, that he would never live long enough to have a career of any kind—René was a sickly child, who might not have lived to adulthood and often suffered ill health in later life. When he was about 10 years old (possibly a little younger), Descartes was sent by his father (who hoped that the boy might follow in his footsteps as a lawyer, or perhaps become a doctor) to the newly established Jesuit College at La Flèche, in [the French region of] Anjou. This was one of several new schools that Henry IV, the first Bourbon King of France (also known as Henry of Navarre), allowed the Jesuits to open around this time. . . .

Descartes Studies in Paris

Two years after the death of Henry IV (or possibly in 1613; the records are not clear), Descartes left the Jesuit college and lived for a short time in Paris, before studying at the University of Poitiers, where he graduated with qualifications in law in 1616 (he may have studied medicine as well, but never qualified as a doctor). At the age of 20, Descartes now took stock of his life and decided that he was not interested in a career in the professions. His childhood illness had helped to make him both self-reliant and something of a dreamer, who loved his creature comforts. Even the Jesuits had allowed him considerable indulgence, such as permission to get up late in the morning, which became not so much a habit as a way of life for Descartes. His years of education convinced him primarily of his own ignorance and the ignorance of his teachers, and he resolved to ignore the textbooks and work out his own philosophy and science by studying himself and the world about him.

To this end, he took what seems at first sight a rather bizarre decision, upping sticks and moving to Holland, where he signed up for military service with the Prince of Orange [the ruler of Holland]. But the comfort-loving Descartes wasn't a fighting soldier; he found his military niche as an engineer, using his mathematical skills rather than his less-developed physical abilities. It was while he was at the Military School at Breda that Descartes met the mathematician Isaac Beeckman, of Dordrecht, who introduced him to higher aspects of mathematics and became a long-term friend. Not much is known about Descartes's military life over the next few years, during which he served in various European armies, including that of the Duke of Bavaria [a region in southern Germany] although we do know that he was present at the coronation of Emperor Ferdinand II in Frankfurt in 1619. Towards the end of that year, however, the most important event of Descartes's life occurred, and we know exactly when and where it happened because he tells us in his book *The Method*—in full, *Discours de la Méthode pour bien conduire la raison et chercher la Vérité dans les sciences* (*A Discourse on the Method of Rightly Conducting Reason and Seeking Truth in the Sciences*)— published in 1637. It was 10 November 1619, and the army of the Duke of Bavaria (gathered to fight the Protestants) was in winter quarters on the banks of the river Danube. Descartes spent the whole day snugly tucked up in bed, dreaming (or daydreaming) about the nature of the world, the meaning of life and so on. The room he was in is sometimes referred to as an 'oven', which is a literal translation of the expression used by Descartes, but this does not necessarily mean that he had literally crawled into some hot chamber usually used for, say, baking bread, since the expression could have been metaphorical. Either way, it was on this day that Descartes first saw the road to his own philosophy and also had one of the greatest mathematical insights of all time.

Mapping Space

Idly watching a fly buzzing around in the corner of the room, Descartes suddenly realized that the position of the fly at any moment in time could be represented by three numbers, giving its distance from each of the three walls that met in the corner. Although he instantly saw this in three-dimensional terms, the nature of his insight is now known to every schoolchild who has ever drawn a graph. Any point on the graph is represented by two numbers, corresponding to the distances along the x axis and up the y axis. In three dimensions, you just have a z axis as well. The numbers used in the system of representing points in space (or on a piece of paper) in this way are now known as Cartesian co-ordinates, after Descartes. If you have ever given someone instructions on how to find a location in a city by telling them something along the lines of 'go three blocks east and two blocks north, you have been using Cartesian co-ordinates—and if you go on to specify a certain floor in the building, you are doing so in three dimensions. Descartes's discovery meant that any geometric shape could be represented simply by a set of numbers—in the simple case of a triangle drawn on graph paper, there are just three pairs of numbers, each specifying one of the corners of the triangle. And any curved line drawn on paper (or, for example, the orbit of a planet around the Sun) could also be represented, in principle, by a series of numbers related to one another by a mathematical equation. When this discovery was fully worked out and eventually published, it transformed mathematics by making geometry susceptible to analysis using algebra, with repercussions that echo right down to the development of the theory of relativity and quantum theory in the twentieth century. Along the way, it was Descartes who introduced the convention of using letters at the beginning of the alphabet (a, b, c . . .) to represent known (or specified) quantities, and letters at the end of the alphabet (especially x, y, z) to represent unknown quantities. And it was he who introduced the now familiar exponential notation, with x^2 meaning $x \times x$, x^3 meaning $x \times x \times x$ and so on. If he had done nothing else, laying all these foundations of analytical mathematics would have made Descartes a key figure in seventeenth-century science. But that wasn't all he did.

Descartes Settles Down in Holland

After his insights in the 'oven', Descartes renounced the military life in 1620, at the end of his service with the Duke of

Bavaria, and travelled through Germany and Holland to France, where he arrived in 1622 and sold off the estate in Poitiers that he had inherited from his mother, investing the proceeds to allow him to continue his independent studies. With his security established, he spent several years wandering around Europe and doing a bit of thinking, including a lengthy spell in Italy (where, curiously, he seems to have made no attempt to meet [Italian astronomer] Galileo), before deciding at the age of 32 that the time had come to settle down and put his thoughts into a coherent form for posterity. He visited Holland again in the autumn of 1628, spent the winter of 1628/9 in Paris, then returned to settle in Holland, where he stayed for the next twenty years. The choice of base was a good one. The Thirty Years War still kept central Europe in turmoil, rumblings from the Wars of Religion still surfaced from time to time in France, but Holland was now securely independent; although it was officially a Protestant country Catholics formed a large part of the population, and there was religious tolerance.

Descartes had a wide circle of friends and correspondents in Holland, including: Isaac Beeckman and other academics; Constantijn Huygens, a Dutch poet and statesman (father of [mathematician] Christiaan Huygens), who was secretary to the Prince of Orange; and the family of the Elector Palatine of the Rhine, Frederick V. The latter connection provides a link, of sorts, between Descartes and Tycho [Brahe, the Danish astronomer] since Princess Elizabeth, the wife of Frederick V, was the daughter of James I of England. Like Galileo, Descartes never married, but, as [English writer] John Aubrey puts it, 'as he was a man, he had the desires and appetites of a man; he therefore kept a good conditioned hansome woman that he liked'. Her name was Hélène Jans, and they had a daughter, Francine (born in 1635), who he doted on, but who died in 1640.

Descartes's Greatest Work

While reinforcing his already good reputation as a thinker and man of learning in conversations and correspondence with these friends, Descartes spent four years, from 1629 to 1633, preparing a huge treatise in which he intended to put forward all of his ideas about physics. The work was titled *Le Monde, ou Traité de la Lumière* [*The World, or Treatise on Light*], and it was on the verge of being published when news of Galileo's trial and conviction for heresy reached Holland. Although the full story of the trial did not become clear until later, what seemed to be clear at the time was that Galileo had been convicted for Copernican beliefs [i.e., supporting Copernicus's belief in a sun-centered universe] and Descartes's manuscript very much supported Copernican ideas. He stopped the publication immediately, and the book never was published, although large parts of it were used as the basis for some of Descartes's later works. Even granted that Descartes was a Catholic, this does seem to have been a rather hasty overreaction, since there was nothing the Jesuits in Rome could do to harm him in far-away Holland, and it didn't take much urging from his friends and acquaintances, many of whom had seen parts of the work or had it described in letters, to persuade Descartes to publish something sooner rather than later. The first result was *The Method*, which appeared in 1637, accompanied by three essays, on meteorology, optics and geometry. Although not all of the ideas he presented were correct, the important thing about the essay on meteorology is that it attempted to explain all the working of the weather in terms of rational science, not by recourse to the occult or the whim of the gods. The essay on optics described the workings of the eye and suggested ways to improve the telescope. And the essay on geometry considered the revolutionary insights stemming from that day in bed on the banks of the Danube.

Return to France

Descartes's second great work, *Meditationnes de Prima Philosophia* [*Meditations on the First Philosophy*], appeared in 1641, and elaborated the philosophy built around Descartes's most famous (if not always correctly interpreted) line, 'I think, therefore I am.' And in 1644 he produced his third major contribution to learning, *Principia Philosophiae* [*Principles of Philosophy*], which was essentially a book about physics, in which Descartes investigated the nature of the material world and made the correct interpretation of inertia, that moving objects tend to keep moving in a straight line, not (as Galileo had thought) in a circle. With the publication of that book out of the way, Descartes made what seems to have been his first trip to France since 1629, and he went there again in 1647—a significant visit, since on that occasion he met the physicist and mathematician Blaise Pascal (1623–1662) and suggested to the younger man that it would be interesting to take a barometer up a mountain and see how the pressure varied with altitude. When the experiments were carried out (by Pascal's brother-in-law in 1648) they showed that the atmospheric pressure drops with increasing altitude, suggesting that there is only a thin layer of air around the Earth and the atmosphere does not extend for ever. Another visit to France, in 1648, was curtailed by the threat of civil war, but it now looks clear that in the late 1640s Descartes, who was 52 in 1648, was, for whatever reason, becoming restless and no longer seemed committed to spending the rest of his life in Holland. So in 1649, when Queen Christina of Sweden invited him to join the circle of intellectuals that she was gathering in Stockholm, Descartes leaped at the chance. He arrived in Stockholm in October that year, but was horrified to discover that in return for the favours he would receive and the freedom to spend most of his time working at what he pleased, he was expected to visit the Queen each day at 5 am, to give her personal tuition before she got on with the affairs of state. The combination of the northern winter and early rising proved too much for Descartes's comfort-loving body. He caught a chill, which developed into pneumonia, which finished him off on 11 February 1650, just short of his fifty-fourth birthday.

Descarte's influence was profound, most importantly because of the way in which (although he believed in God and the soul) he swept away from his thinking any vestige of mystic forces and insisted that both the world we live in and the material creatures that inhabit the world (including ourselves) can be understood in terms of basic physical entities obeying laws which we can determine by experiment and observation.

Newton Discovers Universal Laws of Motion

I. Bernard Cohen and George E. Smith

Isaac Newton (1643–1727) was without a doubt the premier scientist of the scientific revolution. His work represents the triumph of the revolution that Copernicus (who first proposed the sun-centered view of the solar system) began almost two centuries before. Although Copernicus, Galileo, and others had made important observations and some progress in developing theories to account for their observations, Newton's theories of motion and gravity tied the whole universe together with a few simple, elegant rules.

Newton did pioneering work in optics and other areas, but his most famous work is his theory of gravity. The law of universal gravitation developed by Newton showed that falling bodies near Earth and the motion of planets around the sun obeyed the same principle. This was contrary to the ancient view that held that the heavenly bodies obeyed one set of laws and objects on Earth obeyed another. The success of Newton's insight that the entire universe was governed by uniform laws made possible the modern scientific view that most, if not all, physical phenomena can be understood by applying scientific laws.

Newton well understood his debt to previous investigators. He is noted for saying, "If I have seen farther, it is because I stand on the shoulders of giants." Yet Newton's ideas so changed our view of the world that it is difficult to compare his achievements with those who went before him. In the following excerpt, the Harvard historian of science I. Bernard Cohen and Tufts University professor of the philosophy of science George E. Smith outline the

I. Bernard Cohen and George E. Smith, *The Cambridge Companion to Newton*. Cambridge, UK: Cambridge University Press, 2002. Copyright © 2002 by Cambridge University Press. Reproduced by permission.

story of Newton's early life and show how questions from colleagues led him to his insight into the nature of gravity.

Newton lived into his eighty-fifth year, from 1642 to 1727, the year after the third edition of the *Principia* appeared. His life may be divided into four segments, the first ending in 1661 when he entered Trinity College, Cambridge, as an undergraduate, and the second extending to the publication of the *Principia* in 1687. The third period is marked by the renown that the *Principia* brought him; it concludes with his becoming disenchanted with Cambridge in the early 1690s and his permanent move to London and the Mint in 1696. In the final period, Newton remained intellectually active in London, though his achievements of legend occurred mostly during his Cambridge years, stretching from his early twenties to his early fifties.

Newton's Youth

Newton's pre-Cambridge youth spans the period from the start of the Civil War to the restoration of Charles II.[1] He was born into a Puritan family in Woolsthorpe, a tiny village near [the English town of] Grantham, on Christmas Day 1642 (in the Julian calendar, old style), a little short of twelve months after [Italian astronomer] Galileo had died. Newton's father, who had died the previous October, was a farmer. Three years after Newton's birth, his mother Hannah married a well-to-do preacher, 63-year-old Barnabas Smith, rector of North Witham. She moved to her new husband's residence, leaving young Isaac behind, to be raised by his aged maternal grandparents. Hannah returned to Woolsthorpe and the family farm in 1653, after Smith died, with three new children in tow. Two years later Isaac was sent to boarding school in Grantham, returning to Woolsthorpe in 1659. The family expected that he would manage his father's

---

1. The English Civil War (1642–1651) resulted in a brief period of parliamentary rule, followed by the dictatorship of Oliver Cromwell (1653–1658). The monarchy was restored in 1660.

farm. It soon became evident, however, that he was not cut out to be a farmer. The headmaster of the Grantham school and Hannah's brother, who had received an M.A. from Cambridge, then persuaded her that Isaac should prepare for the university; and in 1661 he entered Trinity College as an undergraduate.

Newton's years at Trinity College, as a student and Fellow and then as a professor, appear to have been spent predominantly in solitary intellectual pursuits. As an undergraduate he read the works of Aristotle and later commentators and some scientific works such as [German astronomer Johannes] Kepler on optics. At some point within his first two years as a student, he began reading widely on his own, supplementing the classical education Cambridge was providing with more contemporary writings of such figures as [French philosopher René] Descartes.

Rapid Progress in Mathematics

Cambridge then had on its faculty one of the leading British mathematicians, Isaac Barrow, whose lectures he attended. Newton, however, largely taught himself mathematics through extensive reading of recent publications, most notably the second edition of [Dutch mathematics professor Frans] van Schooten's Latin translation, with added commentary, of Descartes's *Géométrie*. Within an incredibly short period, less than two years, Newton mastered the subject of mathematics, progressing from a beginning student of university mathematics to being, *de facto*, the leading mathematician in the world. He reached this status during 1665–6, a time when the university was closed because of the great plague and he had returned to the family farm in Woolsthorpe. It was during this period that Newton developed the basic results of the differential and integral calculus, including the fundamental theorem relating the two. No later than this time, he also made his experiments on refraction and color that similarly put him at the forefront in optics. His notebooks from the mid-1660s show him also working out answers to questions about motion, most notably uniform circular motion, questions that were undoubtedly provoked by his encountering the ideas of Galileo and especially Descartes (from whom, among much else, he learned the law of inertia). It was during this early period that Newton independently discovered the v^2/r rule for uniform circular motion,[2] a few years before [Dutch mathematician] Christiaan Huygens published it in his renowned *Horologium Oscillatorium.*

On his return to Cambridge following the plague year, Newton was elected a Fellow of Trinity College, receiving his M.A. in 1668. The requirement of a fellowship in those days included a formal statement of allegiance to the principles of the Church of England. Before fulfilling this requirement, Newton initiated an intense study of theology, especially the implications of the doctrine of the Trinity. He ended up by rejecting this doctrine as a distortion of Christianity. At this time, Newton was appointed to the Lucasian Professorship of Mathematics, which was financed by private rather than state funds—the basis for Newton not being examined on his beliefs concerning the Trinity and the religious principles of the Church of England.

Newton Studies Alchemy

During these years, Newton continued his work in mathematics and optics, and he became immersed in chemical and alchemical research and experiments. He wrote a tract, "De analysi," or "On Analysis by Infinite Series," in which he presented his key discoveries in the calculus. This work was circulated among British mathematicians and, notably, a copy was sent to the publisher John Collins in London. It was undoubtedly because of this tract that Barrow recommended the youthful Newton to succeed him as Lucasian Professor of Mathematics. Newton occupied this chair from 1669 until he formally resigned in 1701, five years after moving to London.

Newton's sole formal publication before the *Principia* was a series of letters on the theory of light and colors, including the

2. The force "felt" by an object traveling around a circle at a constant speed is proportional to the square of its velocity (v^2) divided by the radius of the circle (r).

invention of a reflecting telescope, published in the *Philosophical Transactions of the Royal Society* from 1672 to 1676. He was so embittered by the controversies that were engendered by these publications that he vowed to publish no further discoveries from his research in natural philosophy. The publication of these optical letters and his circulating of tracts in mathematics gave Newton a reputation as a major scientist in Britain and abroad. His formal publications, however, were merely the tip of an iceberg. Newton's professorship required him to deposit in the University Library a copy of his lectures. Among these are his Optical Lectures of 1670–2, which, as [historian of science] Alan Shapiro has shown, present an enormous range of experiments bolstering and complementing those described in his publications. There are also Lectures on Algebra from 1673 to 1683. These registered lectures are ambitious to a point that one has trouble seeing how the students could have handled the material. These lectures too, however, represent but a fraction of Newton's intellectual efforts during the 1670s. For example, his private papers show much more extensive successful research in mathematics during this decade than the lectures reflect, and he continued his research in chemistry, alchemy, biblical chronology, prophecy, and theology, as well as occasional physics.

An Initial Breakthrough

In late 1679, in an effort to reinvigorate the activities of the Royal Society, [experimental scientist] Robert Hooke wrote to Newton posing various research issues, with the goal of stimulating Newton to renew his active association with the Society. During the ensuing exchange of letters, Hooke told Newton of his "hypothesis" that curved or orbital motion could be analyzed by supposing two components: an inertial tangential motion and an accelerated motion directed toward a center of force. He also raised the question of the precise trajectory described by a body under an inverse-square force directed toward a central point in space. During the course of this brief correspondence, Newton discovered the relation between inverse-square centripetal forces and Keplerian motion that comprises the initial stepping stone of the *Principia*.

Yet he communicated this to no one. Moreover, whatever further conclusions he reached at the time, universal gravity was not one of them, for in 1681 he concluded that comets do not generally button-hook around the Sun.

In the summer of 1684 [British astronomer] Edmond Halley visited Newton in Cambridge in order to ask him a question that the London savants could not answer: what curved path results from an inverse-square force? Newton is reported to have replied without any hesitation: the curve produced by an inverse-square force is an ellipse. He promised Halley to send the proof on to London. Halley received a tract, Newton's "De motu corporum in gyrum [On the Motion of Bodies in Orbit]," in November. He was so impressed by the magnitude of Newton's achievement that he hastened to Cambridge for a second visit. On arrival, he learned that Newton, evidently stimulated by Halley's first visit, was continuing research on orbital motion. Newton gave Halley permission to register his tract with the Royal Society while awaiting further results. Such were the beginnings of the *Principia*.

It was agreed that Newton's book would be published by the Royal Society. Halley was to supervise the actual publication. The manuscript of Book 1 of the *Principia* arrived in London in spring of 1686, prompting a controversy with Hooke, who claimed priority for the concept of an inverse-square solar force. Halley managed to keep Newton working in spite of the controversy, finally receiving Book 2 in March 1687 and Book 3 in April.

Adulation and Opposition

Publication of the *Principia* in 1687, which ended Newton's life of comparative isolation, led to adulation in Britain and intense opposition to his theory of gravity elsewhere. He was elected to represent Cambridge University in Parliament in 1689 (and again in 1701). He continued experimental research in chemistry, writing his principal alchemical essays in the early 1690s, and in optics, exploring diffraction phenomena and laying out but not finishing a book on optics. He also initiated work on a radically restructured second edition of the *Principia*, an effort he abandoned when he suffered some sort of mental breakdown in 1693. He had been pursuing positions in London before the breakdown, and his efforts were finally rewarded when he was appointed warden of the Mint in 1696, and Master of it in 1699. This nine-year period between when Newton was thrust into prominence and when he departed from Cambridge, while intense in more ways than one, yielded only manuscripts, and no new publications. Clearly these years were marked by turmoil.

Newton's subsequent thirty years in London contrast sharply with his thirty-plus years of comparatively solitary research in Cambridge. He was elected President of the Royal Society in 1703, a post he held until his death, and he was knighted in 1705. Catherine Barton, the extraordinarily vivacious teenage daughter of his half-sister, moved in with him, gaining great prominence in London social circles; she continued to reside with him until he died, even after she married John Conduitt (who succeeded Newton as Master of the Mint) in 1717.

The first decade of the new century saw him publishing the first edition of his *Opticks*, a work written in English rather than in Latin. An appendix to the *Opticks* contained two earlier tracts in mathematics, one of which exhibited Newton's dot-notation for differentials. There was also an edition of Newton's lectures in algebra and a Latin edition of the *Opticks* (1706). During the last years of the decade he began work in earnest on a second edition of the *Principia*, which was finally published in 1713. Although this edition was not radically re-structured, 397 of its 494 pages involved changes from the first edition—sometimes mere changes in wording, but in places a complete rewriting or the addition of new material. One important feature of the second edition was the concluding Scholium Generale with its slogan, "Hypotheses non fingo." As [historian of science] Alexandre Koyré determined, Newton meant "I do not feign hypotheses." He did not invent fictions in order to provide scientific explanation.

Dispute over the Calculus

Continental [European] natural philosophers found it difficult to accept Newton's concept of a force of universal gravity.

Thus [German philosopher and mathematician Gottfried] Leibniz, like Huygens and others, was strongly opposed to Newton's theory of gravity from the time it first appeared. Leibniz's response was to publish an alternative account of Keplerian motion in 1689, followed by his more important papers in dynamics. The relationship between the two did not turn nasty, however, until one of Newton's followers, John Keill, declared in 1709 that Leibniz had stolen the calculus from Newton. . . . It was complicated by the fact that Leibniz had been in England and had visited John Collins in the early 1680s, before publishing his own fundamental results in calculus. Furthermore, Newton had not then published his work on the calculus, instead only circulating his ideas in manuscript form. The priority dispute also spilled over into open disputes about the theory of gravity and its philosophical and theological implications. . . . Of course, Newton's calculus differed in key respects from Leibniz's, and we are now aware that the two men made their breakthroughs independently. Today we know that Newton was first in inventing the calculus, but that Leibniz was first in publishing it and then forming a group working on its further development and dissemination.

Newton remained intellectually engaged during the last ten years of his life, though less in science and mathematics than in theology, chronology, and prophecy. Further editions of his *Opticks* appeared in 1717/18 (and posthumously in 1730). Newton also produced a third edition of the *Principia*, appearing in 1726, when he was 83 years old. It does not differ in essentials from the second edition; the main change was some new text based on recent data. Though his theory of gravity remained still largely unaccepted on the Continent, there can be no question but that Newton had himself achieved the status of legend throughout the educated world. He died on 20 March 1727.

Franklin's Theory of Electricity Proves There Is an Element of Chance in Discovery

Thomas S. Kuhn

Thomas S. Kuhn is one of the foremost philosophers of science. He wrote his most famous work, *The Structure of Scientific Revolutions*, while he was a graduate student in physics. Kuhn's work fundamentally changed the view of how scientists as a community work to increase the knowledge of nature.

Before Kuhn, the view was generally that science was a fairly straightforward series of hypotheses, experiments, and results. Kuhn's work showed that in reality the early stages of science are marked by nearly random fact gathering. Facts are collected but have little meaning when they are merely listed in so-called natural histories or encyclopedias. Science begins to advance when competing theories about a subset of facts are put forward. These theories are tested experimentally, and some are found more fruitful (i.e., they advance understanding) than others. At times theories are completely wrong, but the experiments devised to test the theories lead researchers in a profitable direction.

Kuhn's real insight was that once a series of experiments shows a fruitful area of research, most scientists follow what Kuhn calls the paradigm of that area. Most experiments conducted are similar to the major ones that established the area. Scientists at this point are mainly concerned with explaining small discrepancies between the theory behind the paradigm and actual observation. It is assumed that better experiments can clear up any such problems. However, at certain times (though more commonly at the early stages of the history of a science), enough observed discrepancies build up for there to be a *paradigm shift*, a radical new theory that leads to different types of experiments and fundamentally different views of nature.

In the following excerpt, Kuhn explains how Benjamin Franklin's theory of electricity—that electrcity was the result of objects having different charges, positive or negative, in close vicinity or connected by a conductor—explained more about electrical phenomena than rival theories that concentrated on friction and attraction or electricity's fluidity. Because Franklin's theory was successful in explaining more, it pointed the way for further research and rapid progress in the study of electricity.

The history of electrical research in the first half of the eighteenth century provides a concrete and known example of the way a science develops before it acquires its first universally received paradigm. During that period there were almost as many views about the nature of electricity as there were important electrical experimenters, men like Hauksbee, Gray, Desaguliers, Du Fay, Nollett, Watson, Franklin,[1] and others. All their numerous concepts of electricity had something in common—they were partially derived from one or another version of the mechanico-corpuscular philosophy[2] that guided all scientific research of the day. In addition, all were components of real scientific theories, of theories that had been drawn in part from experiment and observation and that partially determined the choice and interpretation of additional problems undertaken in research. Yet though all the experiments were electrical and though most of the experimenters read each other's works, their theories had no more than a family resemblance.

One early group of theories, following seventeenth-century practice, regarded attraction and frictional genera-

---

1. Francis Hauksbee, Stephen Gray, Jean Desaguliers, Charles-François Du Fay, Jean-Antoine Nollett, William Watson, and Benjamin Franklin were all early investigators of electricity.   2. the belief that all physical phenomena could be explained by the mass, shape, and position of small elementary particles called corpuscles

tion as the fundamental electrical phenomena. This group tended to treat repulsion as a secondary effect due to some sort of mechanical rebounding and also to postpone for as long as possible both discussion and systematic research on Gray's newly discovered effect, electrical conduction. Other "electricians" (the term is their own) took attraction and repulsion to be equally elementary manifestations of electricity and modified their theories and research accordingly. (Actually, this group is remarkably small—even Franklin's theory never quite accounted for the mutual repulsion of two negatively charged bodies.) But they had as much difficulty as the first group in accounting simultaneously for any but the simplest conduction effects. Those effects, however, provided the starting point for still a third group, one which tended to speak of electricity as a "fluid" that could run through conductors rather than as an "effluvium" that emanated from non-conductors. This group, in its turn, had difficulty reconciling its theory with a number of attractive and repulsive effects. Only through the work of Franklin and his immediate successors did a theory arise that could account with something like equal facility for very nearly all these effects and that therefore could and did provide a subsequent generation of "electricians" with a common paradigm for its research.

Excluding those fields, like mathematics and astronomy, in which the first firm paradigms date from prehistory and also those, like biochemistry, that arose by division and recombination of specialties already matured, the situations outlined above are historically typical. Though it involves my continuing to employ the unfortunate simplification that tags an extended historical episode with a single and somewhat arbitrarily chosen name (e.g., Newton or Franklin), I suggest that similar fundamental disagreements characterized, for example, the study of motion before Aristotle and of statics before Archimedes, the study of heat before [Joseph] Black, of chemistry before [Robert] Boyle and [Hermann] Boerhaave, and of historical geology before [James] Hutton. In parts of biology—the study of heredity, for example—the first universally received paradigms are still more recent; and it remains an open question what parts of social science have yet acquired such paradigms at all. History suggests that the road to a firm research consensus is extraordinarily arduous.

Early Fact-Gathering Is Nearly Random

History also suggests, however, some reasons for the difficulties encountered on that road. In the absence of a paradigm or some candidate for paradigm, all of the facts that could possibly pertain to the development of a given science are likely to seem equally relevant. As a result, early fact-gathering is a far more nearly random activity than the one that subsequent scientific development makes familiar. Furthermore, in the absence of a reason for seeking some particular form of more recondite [hidden] information, early fact-gathering is usually restricted to the wealth of data that lie ready to hand. The resulting pool of facts contains those accessible to casual observation and experiment together with some of the more esoteric data retrievable from established crafts like medicine, calendar making, and metallurgy. Because the crafts are one readily accessible source of facts that could not have been casually discovered, technology has often played a vital role in the emergence of new sciences.

Theory and Method Necessary

But though this sort of fact-collecting has been essential to the origin of many significant sciences, anyone who examines, for example, [ancient Roman scholar] Pliny's encyclopedic writings or the Baconian [written by philosopher of science Francis Bacon] natural histories of the seventeenth century will discover that it produces a morass. One somehow hesitates to call the literature that results scientific. The Baconian "histories" of heat, color, wind, mining, and so on, are filled with information, some of it recondite. But they juxtapose facts that will later prove revealing (e.g., heating by mixture) with others (e.g., the warmth of dung heaps) that will for some time remain too complex to be integrated with theory at all. In addition, since any description must be partial, the typical natural history often omits from its immensely circumstantial accounts just those details that later scientists will find sources of important illumination. Almost none of the early "histories" of electricity, for example, mention that chaff, attracted to a rubbed glass rod, bounces off again. That effect seemed mechanical, not electrical. Moreover, since the casual fact-gatherer seldom possesses the time or the tools to be critical, the natural histories often juxtapose descriptions like the above with others, say, heating by antiperistasis (or by cooling), that we are now quite unable to confirm. Only very occasionally, as in the cases of ancient statics, dynamics, and geometrical optics, do facts collected with so little guidance from pre-established theory speak with sufficient clarity to permit the emergence of a first paradigm.

This is the situation that creates the schools characteristic of the early stages of a science's development. No natural history can be interpreted in the absence of at least some implicit body of intertwined theoretical and methodological belief that permits selection, evaluation, and criticism. If that body of belief is not already implicit in the collection of facts—in which case more than "mere facts" are at hand—it must be externally supplied, perhaps by a current metaphysic, by another science, or by personal and historical accident. No wonder, then, that in the early stages of the development of any science different men confronting the same range of phenomena, but not usually all the same particular phenomena, describe and interpret them in different ways. What is surprising, and perhaps also unique in its degree to the fields we call science, is that such initial divergences should ever largely disappear.

The Triumph of Franklin's Paradigm

For they do disappear to a very considerable extent and then apparently once and for all. Furthermore, their disappearance is usually caused by the triumph of one of the pre-paradigm schools, which, because of its own characteristic beliefs and preconceptions, emphasized only some special part of the too sizable and inchoate pool of information. Those electricians who thought electricity a fluid and therefore gave particular emphasis to conduction provide an excellent case in point. Led by this belief, which could scarcely cope with the known multiplicity of attractive and repulsive effects, several of them conceived the idea of bottling the electrical fluid. The immediate fruit of their efforts was the Leyden jar,[3] a device which might never have been discovered by a man exploring nature casually or at random, but which was in fact independently developed by at least two investigators in the early 1740's. Almost from the start of his electrical researches, Franklin was particularly concerned to explain that strange and, in the event, particularly revealing piece of special apparatus. His success in doing so provided the most effective of the arguments that made his theory a paradigm, though one that was still unable to account for quite all the known cases of electrical repulsion. To be accepted as a paradigm, a theory must seem better than its competitors, but it need not, and in fact never does, explain all the facts with which it can be confronted.

What the fluid theory of electricity did for the subgroup that held it, the Franklinian paradigm later did for the entire group of electricians. It suggested which experiments would be worth performing and which, because directed to secondary or to overly complex manifestations of electricity, would not. Only the paradigm did the job far more effectively, partly because the end of interschool debate ended the constant reiteration of fundamentals and partly because the confidence that they were on the right track encouraged scientists to undertake more precise, esoteric, and consuming sorts of work. Freed from the concern with any and all electrical phenomena, the united group of electricians could pursue selected phenomena in far more detail, designing much special equipment for the task and employing it more stubbornly and systematically than electricians had ever done before. Both fact collection and theory articulation became highly directed activities. The effectiveness and efficiency of electrical research increased accordingly, providing evidence for a societal version of Francis Bacon's acute methodological dictum: "Truth emerges more readily from error than from confusion."

---

3. A Leyden jar "stores" static electricity. It consists of a cylinder lined inside and out with metal foil, capped by a (usually) metal ball. The device can be charged by rubbing the ball. Electric charge builds up until a spark results.

The Royal Society of London Promotes Early Science

Raymond Phineas Stearns

Raymond Phineas Stearns was a historian of science at the University of Illinois. Here he explains one of the keys to the success of the scientific revolution—the founding of the Royal Society of London, an association of men interested in the new experimental and mathematical science.

The Royal Society was founded along the lines of philosopher Francis Bacon's ideas. He believed that knowledge was advanced by conducting numerous experiments and then drawing general conclusions from the data produced by the experiments. Science should be broken into fields, or disciplines, in order to organize the conduct of these experiments. An organization like the Royal Society would allow men (no women were members in this era) to discuss findings in their specialized areas. This discussion would lead to the unification of knowledge and the synthesis of new ideas about how nature worked.

Stearns outlines how the Royal Society was formed. With limited support from the English king, Charles II, the men were able to meet in London or its surroundings with the king's blessing. However, they received no financial support and had to rely on member contributions. This may have been a blessing in disguise; the English society, unlike its government-subsidized French equivalent, was not subject to a high level of royal interference. Some members, however, did try to use the society's public activities to increase their private fortunes.

The immediate facts in the origin of the Royal Society are clear and well substantiated. On November 28, 1660, only a few months after the restoration of the Stuart monarchy, a group of men interested in the new science met at Gresham College, London, to hear a lecture by [architect] Christopher Wren. [Oxford scholar] Dr. [John] Wilkins was in the chair. After the meeting Dr. Wilkins joined with eleven other persons present at the occasion to propose the foundation of a "College for the promoting of Physico-Mathematicall Experimental Learning." The members felt that they could improve their regular meetings "according to the manner of other Countries, where there were voluntary associations of men into academies for the advancement of various parts of learning, so they might do something answerable here for the promoting of Experimental Philosophy." So they agreed to continue weekly meetings and for the future to charge each member a ten-shilling admission fee as well as a weekly assessment of one shilling to defray the costs of experiments and other expenses. They also drew up a tentative list of forty-one names of individuals to be invited to join the association. At this point, in fact if not in name, the Royal Society of London had its beginnings.

The King's Support

A week later (December 5), 112 persons signed the "Obligation" (as it came to be called) to "consent and agree that we will meet together weekly (if not hindered by necessary occasions) to consult and debate concerning the promoting of Experimental Learning. . . ." They also agreed to pay the admission fee and the weekly shilling assessed at the previous meeting. [Society member] Sir Robert Moray reported to the assembly that the King had been informed of their plans to form a voluntary association, approved of them, and indicated his readiness to encourage them. The assembly then pushed forward to perfect a temporary constitution for the association, to appoint a committee to arrange for experiments to be conducted at future meetings, and to enter into a scientific correspondence with interested, like-minded, and able persons both at home and abroad. The following week (December 12), temporary officers were set up (President, Treasurer, and "Register," or Secretary), and membership rules were discussed. No one, save those with the rank of baron or above, was to be admitted without scrutiny. Election was to be by ballot, two-thirds of the members present must approve or the election was invalid, and twenty-one members were to constitute a quorum. No new member was to be elected on the same day that his name was proposed. Future meetings, at least for the time being, would be held at Gresham College or, during the time of the college's vacation, in William Ball's room in the Middle Temple. Two servants were also employed, an amanuensis [copyist] to assist the Secretary and an "operator" to assist in the conduct of experiments.

Charters, Statutes, and Objectives

In the course of the following year, a variety of experiments were performed at the association's meetings, membership was somewhat expanded, scientific correspondence was initiated, plans were drafted to test, by empirical means, the scientific validity of a number of classical works hitherto given wide credence (such as [Roman writer] Virgil's *Georgics*), and committees were appointed "to consider of proper Questions to be enquired of in the remotest parts of the world." During this time, too, [writer and naturalist] John Evelyn suggested the name (the Royal Society) for the association, and Sir Robert Moray, carefully selected as one in good standing with the King, successfully negotiated a royal charter, issued as of July 15, 1662. By its terms the King expressed a desire "to extend not only the boundaries of the Empire, but also the very arts and sciences," especially those philosophical studies "which by actual experiments attempt either to shape out a new philosophy or to perfect the old." To this end, the King granted corporate existence to the Royal Society, "whose studies are to be applied to further promoting by the authority of experiments the sciences of natural things and of useful arts." In addition to corporate status, the charter also extended to the Society various privileges including the ordering of its own internal affairs, the right to meet in London or within a radius of ten miles of the city, the right to correspond abroad on scientific matters, and the imprimatur, or privilege to print items relating to the work of the Society. A second charter, issued in 1663, tidied up several administrative matters, altered the Society's legal title to "the Royal Society of London for Promoting Natural Knowledge," and declared the King to be founder and patron. A third charter (1669) corrected some legal omissions of the second charter and reasserted the purposes of the Society in the same words. By these documents the Royal Society acquired legal status and the prestige which was associated with royal approval.

Seeking Complete Understanding of Nature

In the meantime, the Society drew up, in 1663, its original statutes. They proclaimed: "The business of the Society in their ordinary Meetings shall be, to order, take account, consider, and discourse of philosophical experiments and observations; to read, hear, and discourse upon letters, reports, and other papers, containing philosophical matters; as also to view, and discourse upon, rarities of nature and art; and thereupon to consider what may be deduced from them, or any of them; and how far they, or any of them, may be improved for use or discovery." There were limitations set, however. The Society was specifically designed to promote "Physico-Mathematicall Experimental Learning," and it refused to meddle with "Divinity, Metaphysics, Moralls, Politicks, Grammar, Rhetorick or Logick." The Society set out to "examine all systems, Theories, principles, Hypotheses, Elements, Histories & Experiments of things Natural, Mathematicall & Mechanicall invented, recorded, or practised by any Considerable Author, Ancient or Modern, in order to the compiling of a Compleat system of Solid Philosophy, for explicating all phenomena produced by Nature or Art, & rendering a rational account of the causes of things." It would own no "hypothesis, system, or doctrine of the principles of Natural Philosophy . . . till by mature debate & clear arguments, chiefly such as are deduced from legitimate experiments, the truth of such positions be demonstrated invincibly." The time of the assembly was "to be employed in proposing and making experiments, discoursing of the truth, manner, grounds & use thereof; reading & discoursing upon Letters, reports, and other papers concerning philosophicall & mechanicall matters; Viewing and discoursing of curiosities of Nature and Art; and doing such other things as the Council or the President alone shall appoint." The limitations doubtless helped the Society to avoid sterile controversies and to steer clear of many of the rocks upon which similar organizations foundered. By this token, also, they enabled the Society more rapidly to advance experimental learning in the years ahead. But at the same time, they may well have contributed to that unhappy separation of science and morals which many scholars find deplorable in the present day.

Freedom from Royal Dictate

The Royal Society, as chartered, was a self-governing and self-perpetuating body. Every year, on St. Andrew's Day (November 30), the Fellows of the Society elected their own officers by ballot. The officers consisted of a President, Vice-President, Treasurer, two Secretaries, and a Council of twenty-one members. The President and Council constituted the governing body of the Society, attending to all questions of policy, business, and finances. The latter, especially in the early years, was often troublesome. Although the King was generous in the privileges granted by the charters, he did not endow the Society with viable lands or other resources from the royal purse, and the Society, unlike the French Academy of Sciences founded by Louis XIV only a few months later (1662), had no access to state funds and was left to its own private resources. At the outset, these consisted principally of the admission fees of Fellows and the weekly assessments of one shilling each. As time passed, these sums were increased by action of the Council, which also encouraged wealthy Fellows and other well-wishers to make gifts to the Society. But endowments accrued slowly, and until well into the eighteenth century the Society's funds were often inadequate to meet its needs, especially for the publication of scientific treatises. However, the Society's lack of access to the royal purse largely left it free from royal dictation, and in this respect the Royal Society was better off than its French counterpart. With the exercise of judicious policies as set by the President and Council, the Society was free to set its own course without royal interference.

It is evident from the records of the Royal Society that its objectives were broadly Baconian[1] in nature. But for the realization of the Baconian ideal—to promote the development of a new experimental philosophy looking toward the enunciation of scientific laws underlying natural phenomena—some of the greatest barriers lay within the Society itself. There was an ever-present strain of utilitarianism in the objectives of the Royal Society. This was evident in many of the English forerunners of the Society, even in the works of Francis Bacon himself. It was referred to in the charters, which coupled the "useful arts" with the object of "further promoting by the authority of experiments the science of natural things." It was given concrete expression by [chemist] Robert Boyle's book, *Some Considerations Touching the Usefulness of Experimental Natural Philosophy* (London, 1663, followed by a second part in 1671). And it permeated the minds of many of the Fellows from the Society's beginning. The danger lay, as Bacon had foreseen, in "the little cells of human wit" content with one of the foundation stones of the larger edifice of science which Bacon envisaged. Not all of the men elected into the fellowship of the Royal Society comprehended the Society's larger objectives or were able to sustain that objective constantly before their eyes. In consequence, while the larger "wits" of the Society pursued the long-term philosophical ends of Bacon's works, some Fellows, together with forces outside the Society, sought the more proximate end of private advantage.

Public Science and Private Advantage

As the Society officially sought to have "all the proposals that shall be made concerning Mechanical Inventions be referred to the Council of this Society, to be by them Exam-

---

1. the idea of philosopher Francis Bacon that science should be broken down into subfields, but that subfield specialists should communicate to unify their knowledge with that of specialists in other areas

ined, whether they be new, true, and usefull," it was forced from time to time to fend off applications for its approval sought for private advantage. In 1663 Sir William Petty brought his double-bottomed ship to the Society for formal approval, and the Council, after entertaining "the sense of the Society thereupon," ordered "that the Matter of Navigation, being a State-Concern, was not proper to be managed by the Society; And that Sir William Petty, for his private satisfaction, may, when he pleases, have the sense (if he hath not already) of particular Members of the Society, concerning his new Invention." Later the same year, in a debate on whaling occasioned by a report on the whaling industry by a representative of the Greenland Company, the Society was led by a motion from Sir Robert Moray to consider "whether there might not be devised an Engin fit to strike the Whales with more ease and surnesse, and at a greater distance," and it was ordered that "Dr. Wilkins and [experimental scientist] Mr. [Robert] Hook should think upon such an Engin that might be cheap and easy to be managed." In the 1670's the importunities of John Beale of Yeovil, Somerset, a valued correspondent of the Society and an agricultural reformer of substance, to meddle in policies to improve English cider-making and free England from its dependence upon French wines, went beyond the real interests and powers of the Society. In 1693 the Society mistakenly gave a testimonial to John Marshall, a glass-grinder, for a new method of grinding glasses and soon found itself embroiled with all the glass grinders of London.

The Mysterious Art of Alchemy Intrigues Early Scientists

Lawrence M. Principe

Robert Boyle and Isaac Newton were two of the top early scientists. Boyle, known as the Father of Chemistry, is renowned for his careful experiments that proved that Earth was surrounded by a sea of air. He discovered air pressure and developed a way to accurately measure this pressure. Newton was the brilliant English physicist and mathematician who mathematically described the force of gravity and was able to use his discovery to explain the orbits of the planets.

Given their accomplishments in what is considered real science, it is surprising that they would be involved in the mysterious world of alchemy. This secret practice was devoted to finding the philosopher's stone, a substance that could supposedly, among other things, change base metals into gold. Alchemy was full of mysterious ideas. For example, chemical substances were given the names of Roman gods, and sulfur was represented as a dragon.

This may sound very strange today, but in the late 1600s and early 1700s, the most advanced experimental scientists were avid collectors of alchemical knowledge. Newton compiled large collections of alchemical texts. Boyle eagerly sought out alchemical "adepts" (*adepti*) who were skilled in manipulating chemicals. According to the chemist and historian of science Lawrence M. Principe, a professor at Johns Hopkins University, Newton's and Boyle's interest in alchemy shows that during the early modern period the now disreputable practice was considered a serious source of knowledge. Newton and Boyle concealed their knowledge of the occult subject because they were true believers in its power; alchemical knowledge was potentially dangerous in the wrong hands.

It is clear that at present there is a growing interest in alchemy. This new attention to a subject long dismissed out of hand as a field for serious scholarly inquiry is in large part due to the successful linkage of alchemy with prominent figures of early modern science, especially Sir Isaac Newton. Once the extent of Newton's involvement with traditional alchemy was made manifest by the labors of [historians of science] B.J.T. Dobbs, Karin Figala, Richard S. Westfall, and others, alchemy could no longer be uncomplicatedly rejected as mere fraud or gullibility without impugning Newton himself. Thus, whereas Newton's status as the rationalist par excellence initially made his alchemical involvement seem unbelievable, that status helped to rehabilitate the much-maligned subject of alchemy.

Alchemy Attracts Top Early Scientists

Since the revelation of Newton's alchemical interests, other figures of the early modern period have begun to reveal their own alchemical dimensions. Most notable among these is Robert Boyle. Recent studies demonstrate that the "Father of Chemistry" was equally a son of traditional alchemy. Far from repudiating traditional alchemy, as is commonly believed, Boyle pursued it with great avidity. He strove, for example, to discover the secret preparation of the transmutatory Philosophers' Stone, of whose real existence and powers he was certain. Significantly, Boyle's interest in and devotion to alchemy actually increased over the course of his career rather than being repudiated as a youthful whim. These findings in the case of Boyle strongly reaffirm the conclusions regarding the importance of alchemy in the early modern period, which were drawn from earlier investigations of Newton. . . .

In regard to alchemy, Boyle and Newton seem to have much in common. Both are major Scientific Revolution figures who devoted huge amounts of time to alchemical pursuits. But although both serve as arguments in favor of the continued appeal of alchemy, that general similarity may obscure some telling differences that can provide a richer, more nuanced view of the late seventeenth-century status of alchemy as well as of the intellectual complexions of these two great thinkers. I shall first examine the respective strategies Boyle and Newton used to uncover the secrets of alchemy, and then compare the expectations and motivations that each held in regard to his alchemy.

Approaches to Alchemy

Seekers after the secrets of alchemy can approach the subject through three kinds of sources—the written record left by past *adepti*, direct communication with living sources, and laboratory investigation. Various alchemical seekers employed these three methods in varying proportions, and Newton and Boyle were no exceptions. But the differences in the relative emphases accorded to these sources of knowledge by Boyle and Newton reveal some intriguing differences not only in their own philosophical dispositions, but also in the varied ways in which alchemy could be viewed and deployed in the early modern period.

The reader of Newton's alchemical manuscripts is struck at once by the preponderance of material that is not of Newtonian origin, a fact commented upon by many historians of science. By far the greater part of Newton's alchemical output is in the form of transcriptions, translations, extracts, collations, and compendia of various alchemical authorities. In contrast, among the Boyle papers there are few such items. Most of the alchemical tracts that occur in the Boyle archive are in fact gifts from their authors or copies made by scribes outside of Boyle's employ, rather than copies made specifically by or for Boyle. While this dearth of transcriptions relative to the Newton papers may be quite simply explained by invoking differences in study habits between the two men—Boyle's sickliness and consequent inability to write for himself, or Boyle's greater wealth enabling him to purchase books and manuscripts more readily—the difference regarding collations and compendia cannot be so readily explained away. The making of concordances and compilations characteristic of Newton's alchemical studies is unknown in Boyle's.

A clear example of Newton's work in this regard is the massive *Index chemicus* [*Chemical Index*], a topical index on which he labored for decades (ca. 1680–1700). In its final form, the *Index* contains 879 headings and exceeds one hundred pages and twenty thousand words in length. This long-term exercise was Newton's attempt to gather together in one place the parsimonious, widely scattered revelations of alchemical truths provided by various authors, and to piece these bits together in the hopes of elucidating a greater part of the great alchemical mystery. Another example of such endeavor is seen in the manuscripts of concatenated extracts, such as the "Praxis" manuscript (written in the late 1690s), which in spite of its title gives very little indication of any practical operations, but is instead a series of quotations from numerous alchemical authors laid together. This type of composition—or rather compilation—occurs frequently in such alchemical collections as the *Theatrum chemicum* [*Chemical Theater*], and owes its origin to the alchemical belief that "all authors say one [the same] thing," a credo that Newton himself must have adopted. . . .

Boyle Consults with Alchemical "Adepts"

Boyle was certainly familiar with alchemical texts as well, as his references to them in both published and unpublished works make clear. Yet Boyle seems never to have invested texts with the same degree of importance as did Newton. Boyle's emphasis in his study of alchemy was on nonwritten sources—either results from his own laboratories or reports brought to him of the experiments and experiences of others. Moreover, throughout his life he made it abundantly clear that he valued and invited communication with alchemical *adepti*. In the preface to the *Sceptical Chymist* (1661), Boyle remarks on how he would be "willingly and thankfully" instructed by the *adepti* regarding the nature and generation of metals; this desire is expressed even more forcefully in the preface to the *Producibleness of Chymical Principles* (1680). Additionally, I have elsewhere argued that Boyle's famous but previously problematic paper in the *Philosophical Transactions* on an "incalescent" mercury is in fact a plea for direct advice from alchemical *adepti* regarding the method of employing this mercury to produce the Philosophers' Stone.

Boyle was not disappointed in his hopes of gaining alchemical communications; travelers and correspondents brought him a wealth of information from across Europe and beyond. Boyle himself mentions many such interviews in both published and unpublished papers. Indeed, in the incalescent mercury paper he remarks how in order to learn about philosophical mercuries, he "purposely enquir'd of several prying Alchymists, that have spent much labour, and many Trials . . . and have of late years travelled into many parts of Europe to pry into the Secrets of other Seekers of Metalline Transmutations." In some cases, a traveling adept or his disciple visited Boyle and answered various of Boyle's questions, and sometimes presented him with a small sample of a precious alchemical rarity. The most dramatic of such interviews are those in which traveling *adepti* demonstrate projective transmutation before Boyle himself; a detailed first-person account of the most gripping of these transmutations witnessed by Boyle has been published. These events were almost certainly more influential than anything else in shaping and promoting Boyle's alchemical beliefs and activities.

A curious fragment among the Boyle papers may represent original notes from just such an interview. These sheets, judging by their small size and format, are the remnant of a disbound memorandum book of the kind that survives intact elsewhere in the archive. They are noteworthy also because they are in Boyle's own hand—which is rare in the archive—suggesting that the original volume was something he may have carried around with him. There amid memoranda . . . are several pages of hastily penciled notes as incoherent as they are incomprehensible. These seem to be memoranda jotted down after or during a series of alchemical conversations, one of which is dated as "15 August" of an unspecified year. The interpretation of this document as interview notes is greatly strengthened by two observations. First, there are bracketed sections such as "due proportion of gold [q. an commune]" where Boyle seems to be reminding himself to "question whether common" gold or not at the next opportunity. Similarly, there are references to anecdotes like those likely to occur in a conversation; for example, "half a coccos kindled and nearly killed him." Second, a fair copy of these scrawled notes exists elsewhere in the archive. In the hand of Boyle's amanuensis [secretary or scribe] Robin Bacon, these notes are copied out in a neater format, and considerably expanded. . . .

Newton and Boyle Believe in Alchemy's Power

Returning to Newton, we find little evidence of his going out of his way to access oral alchemical knowledge or manifesting any interest in meeting reputed *adepti*. The few instances of it are scattered and brief—for example, a few bits of correspondence from [scientist and friend of Newton] Fatio de Duillier and Newton's notorious exchange with [English philosopher] John Locke regarding the extraction of alchemical processes from the papers of the recently deceased Boyle. One other exception is Newton's apparent contact with the shadowy Cleidophorus Mystagogus, alias William Yarworth. But these are the exceptions rather than the rule, and in any event are briefer and doubtless far less significant to Newton than Boyle's encounters were to Boyle. Indeed, Newton wrote disparagingly of Boyle's circle of alchemical correspondents, informants, and collaborators—as well as of Boyle himself—and declined repeatedly to participate in such communication. A mutilated letter of 1689 to Fatio states that "Mr Boyle has divers times offered to communicate & correspond with me in these matters but I ever declined it because of his [*word cut from paper*] & conversing with all sorts of people & being in my opinion too open and too desirous of fame."

Newton's condemnation of Boyle's putative "openness" recalls his letter to [secretary of the Royal Society] Henry Oldenburg after the publication of the paper on incalescent mercury. In that missive Newton urges that Boyle "preserve high silence" in this matter, for fear of "immense damage to the world." Although Boyle sought alchemical advice regarding the use of this mercury, he certainly agreed with Newton in regard to secrecy, for he refused to answer questions about this mercury, and the next time he mentioned it in print he averred that "for the sake of Mankind, I resolve not to teach the preparation." Indeed, Newton learned directly how unnecessary his advice was, for after Boyle "revealed" a related prize secret to both John Locke and Newton, Newton later complained that Boyle had "reserved a part of it from my knowledge . . . what he has told me is imperfect & useless with knowing more than I do." Thus Newton had to quiz Locke to see if Boyle had divulged more of the process to him. Both Boyle and Newton understood the importance of maintaining alchemical secrecy. . . . As we can see by their own words, Boyle and Newton were not at all embarrassed, but were instead in fearful awe of the immense power of alchemy.

Chapter 4

The Legacy of Science

Turning | Points
IN WORLD HISTORY

The Enlightenment and Science Had Long-Lasting Effects on Society

Brian L. Silver

One of the earliest reactions to the scientific revolution and its philosophical counterpart, the Enlightenment, was from the Romantic movement of the early 1800's. Science was closely associated with the Enlightenment, a period in European history dating roughly from the end of the 1600s until the upheaval of the French Revolution in the 1790s. Enlightenment thinkers believed that the principles of reason could apply to human beings as well as to nature and sought to reshape society according to the principles of rationality.

Unfortunately, the reality of the early industrial revolution did not match the dreams of the Enlightenment philosophers. The technology that was the fruit of the scientific revolution—for example, mechanized factories—dislocated thousands of small artisans. Peasants were also displaced by "rationalization farming"; land that had once been held for common use was enclosed for the purposes of scientific agricultural production. These changes resulted in the growth of urban slums and the despoliation of the countryside.

A group of poets, authors, and philosophers rebelled against what they saw as the inhumanity of scientific and enlightenment thought, which they blamed for the turmoil of early industrialization. Poets such as William Blake and Percy Shelley claimed that science had reduced the universe to a mechanism. Science broke things into parts in order to investigate them; the Romantics sought to restore the unity of nature in its entirety. Unfortunately, the Romantics' rejection of science often led to extremes of mysticism and irrationality. Surprisingly, the movement was so influential that it even affected the thought of nineteenth-century scientists.

Brian L. Silver describes the Romantics' thought in a selection taken from his work *The Ascent of Science*. Silver was professor of chemistry at the Techion, Israel's technical institute. He died shortly before his book was published.

At the end of the eighteenth century, rationality was being downgraded all over Europe. The Romantics ruled the intellectual roost. At a dinner given in 1817 by the second-rate English painter Benjamin Haydon, and attended by [William] Wordsworth, [John] Keats, and other writers, it is said that the toast was "Newton's health, and confusion to mathematics."

Was the Enlightenment dream of a Utopia ushered in by science killed by the Industrial Revolution, which was born between 1780 and 1820? Is it simplistic to suppose that many saw the social ravages of industrialization and felt that science, mistakenly identified with technology, had deluded man into a false belief in the Garden of Eden? One who definitely saw things this way was [English poet] William Blake's friend, the painter Samuel Palmer, who looked at the expanding and ugly urban industrial landscape and cried out, "If so-called science bids us give up our faith, surely we have a right to ask for something better in return!" And the claim of the French Revolution that it would put scientific principles into practice rang hollow in the ghastly reality of the guillotine. The culmination of the Enlightenment, the great intellectual revolt of rational secularism, had ended in the slaughter of the Reign of Terror.

The status of science was visibly eroded during these years. [Scottish historian] Thomas Carlyle dismissed the scientist's claim to have revealed nature's secrets: "Scientists have been nowhere but where we also are; have seen some handbreaths deeper than we see, into the Deep that is infinite, without bottom as without shore." Typically of the times, the poets [Percy

Bysshe] Shelley, [Samuel Taylor] Coleridge, and Keats (who
was a pharmacist by training) had all been attracted to science
in their youth and dabbled with scientific experiments. (Coleridge attended the lectures of the great chemist Sir Humphry
Davy in order, so he said, to improve his stock of metaphors.)
But the nature that appeared in their mature poetry was much
closer to the unspoiled nature of [French philosopher Jean-
Jacques] Rousseau than the matter-in-motion of the Royal
Society.

Was it by chance that the great flowering of Romantic poetry in England occurred in the years when the status of science declined? Wordsworth, in the year of the French Revolution, wrote,

> Enough of Science and of Art;
> Close up these barren leaves;
> Come forth, and bring with you a heart
> That watches and receives.

Those barren leaves doubtless included the pages of [Isaac
Newton's] *Principia*.

Galileo and Newton, Boyle and Lavoisier, Hooke and
Huygens,[1] had begun the demystification of the natural
world. But, as the eighteenth century progressed, many
thought that things precious had been lost in that great ad-
venture, not least the mystery of existence. [English essayist
Thomas] De Quincey would have said that imagination had
died; Blake branded science the tree of death.

The scientific revolution had had little patience with what
was seen as unclear thinking. When Boyle wrote of atoms in
The Sceptical Chymist, he cited the mystic Pythagoras [an ancient Greek philosopher], but in the end he stressed that it
was the prosaic evidence of the senses and the cold operation
of reason that were the final arbiters. The day of the balance
and the ruler, of the microscope and the telescope, had arrived. In [French writer] Voltaire's Europe there could be no
return to the days when the sixteenth-century alchemist and

---

1. Italian astronomer Galileo Galilei, English physicist Isaac Newton, English
chemist Robert Boyle, French chemist Antoine Lavoisier, English experimenter
Robert Hooke, and Dutch optical scientist Christiaan Huygens.

physician Paracelsus saw God as an alchemist and the cosmos as a chemical distillation. After the seventeenth century, no self-respecting natural philosopher would dream of saying, as did Paracelsus, "Man is a Sun and a Moon and a Heaven filled with stars." Nature had been kidnapped by the professors.

The models to which the Enlightenment had looked had been cast in the stern mold of the Roman Republicans. *Enthusiasm* was a dirty word in the vocabulary of [English philosopher John] Locke and Voltaire: it smacked of religious excess. The Scottish philosopher Adam Smith wrote, in his classic book, *An Inquiry into the Nature and Causes of the Wealth of Nations* (1776): "Science is the great antidote to the poison of enthusiasm and superstition." But the imagination, and the supposed intuitive ability of man to understand the universe, could not be ignored for long.

There arose a new skepticism that, in contrast to that of sixteenth- and seventeenth-century Europe, was directed not at the fossilized teaching of the Church and the ancients but at the claims of science and reason and their now hollow-sounding promises of progress and justice. If science appeared to many to literally have taken the magic out of life, it had, by way of recompense, promised to rescue man from the daily round of work and disease and deliver a "glorious and paradisiacal" world, as prophesied by [English linguist and scientist] Joseph Priestley. By the turn of the century it was clear that it hadn't.

The poet William Cowper saw practical science "building factories with blood," and the Industrial Revolution's image was immortalized in Blake's condemning phrase: "those dark Satanic mills" although he was possibly referring symbolically to Newton's mechanics rather than to real machinery. Scientists will point out, rightly, that to discover iron is not to make swords. The discoveries of science in the sixteenth and seventeenth centuries were in the main not directly connected with the technology that blackened the Midlands of England. The creation of machines for weaving was the work of inventive engineers, not scientists. But few in the late eighteenth and early nineteenth century saw it that way. For them the natural philosophers had brought misery.

Demolishing Reason

When the demolition team came to remove reason from its pedestal and replace it with imagination, poets were in the forefront. Wordsworth had once hoped that the "impassioned countenance of the sciences" would shine on the soul of the poet, but in the end it seemed to him that the mechanical, rational cosmos of Newton had substituted a "universe of death" for the true universe, "which moves with light and life instinct, actual divine, and true." He had pinpointed the loneliness of the mechanical universe.

The Enlightenment concluded that we are responsible for our own destinies, but few were prepared to be alone in the godless universe of [philosopher Paul Henri] d'Holbach, that "dead" universe which was the apparently inescapable end point of the natural philosopher's probings. Few would accept [French encyclopedist Denis] Diderot's compensation for losing the after-world: "What posterity is for the philosopher, the other world is for the religious man." For HMS [*homme moyen sensuel*, the French concept of average man] this offers cold comfort, and even in the Age of Reason, humanity clung to things irrational, steering clear of the depressing conclusion that all is matter and mechanics. Thus, in the eighteenth century we find apparent devotees of reason displaying intense interest in phrenology and in such shady characters as [psychiatrist Franz] Mesmer (whence mesmerism), an admirer of Paracelsus and the proposer of "animal magnetism." Although a committee, set up at the request of Louis XVI and including [Antoine] Lavoisier and Benjamin Franklin, returned a negative report on the medical benefits of Mesmer's "cures," he still attracted attention and patients. They *wanted* to believe in him. Even more successful was Count Cagliostro (real name Guiseppe Balsamo), who, at the height of the prestige of the philosophes [French Enlightenment philosophers], told fortunes by gazing into water and speaking to the dead. Communication with the dead has a more obvious appeal than the silence of the galaxies. In the face of the cold comfort offered by reason, the appeal of immortality is irresistible. In this respect the Enlightenment threw little light into the nineteenth century. In

1874, William Crookes, a notable British physicist who dabbled in spiritualism, studied the evidence for the existence of Katie King, the spirit attendant on the medium Florence Cook. Crookes came to the conclusion that Katie was genuine. He was subsequently, but one hopes not consequently, knighted and elected to the presidency of both the Royal Society and the British Association.[2] As late as the early 1900s, another prominent British physicist, Sir Oliver Lodge, was completely taken in by the tricks of spiritualist mediums. Had he approached the phenomena with the eye and mind of a scientist, he would have detected the frauds, but he wanted to believe—so he did. The same need provides a good income for TV evangelists and psychics.

Although reason trembled as the eighteenth century progressed, it did not fall. But if it was far too late in man's intellectual history to bury reason, at least it could be rebuked for its arrogance and put in its place, which in a way is what Romanticism did. In fairness to the philosophes, they had given what they generally called "passion," or "the passions," a place of central, sometimes dominant, importance in their scheme of things. Diderot wrote to his mistress Sophie Volland, "I forgive everything that is inspired by passion," and it would be a mistake to interpret that as lover's language, as an inspection of Diderot's writings will show. Indeed many of the philosophes' statements sound as though they come from the mouths of the Romantics. The philosophes had a more balanced attitude to "imagination" and science than the Romantics. They rarely denied the place of the arts, nor the absolutely essential place of the imagination in the creative process.

It is a mistake, made by Blake and the Romantics, to see the philosophes and the other heroes of the Enlightenment as extremists in a war between reason and imagination. Much of their attractiveness comes from their recognition that, in general, the excesses of both reason and passion are equally to be avoided.

---

2. The Royal Society and the British Association are prestigious academic organizations.

Romanticism and *Naturphilosophie* [German for "natural philosophy"] were themselves doomed after 1830, ironically from the very expansion of industrial power that they so loathed. A prosperous upper middle class grew up in England and Germany, its wealth usually based on industry. Science was now seen, in the guise of technology, to be producing welcome results in the real world, while the philosophers, especially the German variety, merely turned out obscure and impotent tomes. The middle-class became increasingly materialistic and politically conscious, and in the nineteenth century science would regain its prestige, sometimes for the wrong reasons.

The Enlightenment: A Different Perspective

In recognizing the long-range liberating role of the Enlightenment, we should realize its limitations. It was not a mass movement. At its peak it involved only a few tens of thousands of people, mostly rich or middle-class. The Enlightenment and Newton meant little or nothing to the average man. As [German philosopher Immanuel] Kant said, he was living in an Age of Enlightenment, but the age was unenlightened. The "radical" leaders of the Enlightenment believed in universal education, where "universal" almost always meant the professional and merchant classes, not the proletariat. Only [the marquis de] Condorcet, of the Enlightenment's French luminaries, believed that women should have equal status to men, although Diderot blamed men's historical dominance of women for their "inferiority." D'Holbach declared that women's weaker organs prevented them from attaining genius. Rousseau, despite a nod toward equal educational opportunities for women, still proclaimed that women had no originality and recommended that they concentrate on pleasing men. The editors of the *Encyclopédie* had no qualms about including illustrations of factories employing child labor.

It would be difficult to prove the thesis that the Enlightenment seriously damaged religion at the time. The philosophes and a significant number of English intellectuals may have been deist or atheist, but the general population knew little of these things. In fact, many of the clergy were among those who bought the *Encyclopédie*, and some of the philosophes saw reason as, in principle, compatible with theology. In England in particular, the clergy saw science as a legitimate interest that offered no threat to belief.

The "radicals" of the Enlightenment left a permanent mark on Western culture and on man's concept of his role, rights, and potential, but they were not revolutionaries in the image of Lenin or Che Guevara. They were writers and talkers, not guerillas, although some of them, like Voltaire, Rousseau, and Condorcet, suffered or risked exile or imprisonment for their views. Some of them might have preferred a secular state, but few were democrats, and there is little evidence to show that they foresaw or desired the bloody revolution that was to come. They never created a party or a popular movement. All the "big names" except Condorcet died by the 1780s, so that the movement died socially before the Revolution. Marie-Jean-Antoine Nicolas de Caritat, marquis de Condorcet, perhaps the wisest of the philosophes, died in 1794 in a prison cell, persecuted by those who had perverted the principles of the Enlightenment. Perhaps, in his last days, he recalled Diderot's resigned lament, "The philosopher may have to wait. He may find that he can only speak forcefully from the depth of his tomb."

Results of the Enlightenment

The Enlightenment had its triumphs. We no longer, in the West, officially burn heretics or rack and then strangle servant girls who bewitch children, as happened in Switzerland as late as 1782. We can still echo Condorcet's cry for "reason, toleration and humanity."

Perhaps the best epitaph for the Age of Reason was written by [American political writer] Tom Paine when he claimed that he was "contending for the rights of the living and against their being willed away, and controlled, and contracted for, by the manuscript-assumed authority of the dead."

In retrospect, the Enlightenment's near-total belief in reason and science as a universal and almost imminent panacea now appears as naive optimism. And yet the seventeenth-century scientific revolution and the eighteenth-century Enlightenment liberated us, giving us the confidence to use our reason and the confidence to doubt it. The Enlightenment gave us the right to question and the right to doubt, even the existence of God. It gave us the courage to challenge the wisdom of the ancients, no matter how sonorous the prose in which it was couched, nor how established the hierarchy of its priests. Kant, who saw the Enlightenment as a revolt against superstition, suggested for it a quote from [Roman poet] Horace *Sapere aude! Dare to know!* We dare.

There was, however, a price to pay. The Enlightenment gave man a lonely dignity, a home in a mechanistic cosmos in which God had a doubtful status. For those who accept this fate, it may be, as the materialist [Thomas] Hobbes said, that "there is no such thing as perpetual tranquility of mind while we live here." Three centuries later he was echoed by [existentialist writer Albert] Camus, who, accepting the absurdity of the cosmos, advises us to pull back on our bowstrings and face the enemy: "There can be no contentment but in proceeding."

As for Romanticism, thankfully it still speaks to us, a reminder of the individual mind. In book 5 of the *Prelude*, Wordsworth tells of a dreamer who meets an Arab fleeing from a tidal wave that will swallow up the world. The Arab carries a shell and a stone, and explains that both are in reality books: the stone is Euclid's *Elements of Geometry*. The shell is "something of more worth": "An Ode, in passion uttered."

Science Enables Western Europe to Dominate the Globe

Herbert Butterfield

Herbert Butterfield was a professor of modern history at Cambridge University in England. In this excerpt, he briefly outlines both the origin and the importance of the scientific revolution for western Europe (and by extension for the Americas).

According to Butterfield, the Mediterranean had long been the center of intellectual progress. Indeed, during the Middle Ages, the eastern Mediterranean and lands farther east were far ahead of Western Europe in terms of scientific knowledge. Yet repeated attacks by invaders from Central Asia—the Mongols, Turks, and others—took its toll on the advanced civilization of the East.

Meanwhile, scholars in western Europe had been slowly rediscovering and relearning the science of the ancient Greeks. In addition, they were beginning to go beyond that science to make discoveries of their own. Reinforced by Eastern scholars fleeing the fall of Constantinople to the Ottoman Turks (1453), Western scholarship joined with both the technical knowledge possessed by craftsmen and a spirit of experimentation to spawn real advances in science.

Soon it was evident that this new way of thinking about the world could lead to great material advances. More importantly, science seemed to be unique in that it was self-sustaining; it showed no signs of slowing down its growth. Science came to organize the whole Western view of the world, so much so that "Westernization" came to mean the adoption of the scientific view of the world.

Until a comparatively recent date—that is to say, until the sixteenth or the seventeenth century—such civilisation as existed in our whole portion of the globe had been centred for thousands of years in the Mediterranean, and during the Christian era had been composed largely out of Græco-Roman and ancient Hebrew ingredients. Even at the Renaissance, Italy still held the intellectual leadership in Europe, and, even after this, Spanish culture had still to come to its climax, Spanish kings ruled over one of the great empires of history, and Spain had the ascendancy in the Counter-Reformation [the Catholic reaction to Protestantism, 1560–1648]. Until a period not long before the Renaissance, the intellectual leadership of such civilisation as existed in this quarter of the globe had remained with the lands in the eastern half of the Mediterranean or in empires that stretched farther still into what we call the Middle East. While our Anglo-Saxon forefathers were semi-barbarian, Constantinople [now Istanbul], and Baghdad were fabulously wealthy cities, contemptuous of the backwardness of the Christian West.

How Western Europe Came to Lead the World

In these circumstances it requires to be explained why the West should have come to hold the leadership in this part of the world; and, considering the Græco-Roman character of European culture in general, it is necessary to account for the division of the continent and to show why there should ever have arisen anything which we could call the civilisation of the West. Explanations are not difficult to find. Even when the Roman Empire surrounded the whole of the Mediterranean, there had been tension between East and West—a tension greatly increased when a second capital of the Empire had been founded and the oriental influences were able to gather themselves together and focus their influence on the city of Constantinople. In the subsequent period—the age of the Barbarian Invasions—the differences were increased when Constantinople held out against attacks and preserved the continuity of classical culture, while, as we have seen, the West was so reduced that it had to spend centuries recapturing and reappropriating it—gathering the fragments together again and incorporating them into its own peculiar view of life. The religious cleavage between Rome and Byzantium [Constantinople] in the middle ages (when differences of religion seemed to penetrate into every department of thought) accentuated the discrepancies between Latin and Greek and led to divergent lines of development—in the West, for example, the friction between Church and State gave a tremendous stimulus to the progress of society and the rise of political thought. The West developed independently, then, but, though it may have been more dynamic, it was still for a long time backward. Even in the fifteenth century—in the period of the high Renaissance—the Italians were ready to sit at the feet of exiled teachers from Constantinople and to welcome them as men like Einstein were welcomed not very long ago in England or America. By this time, however, visitors from the Byzantine Empire were expressing their wonder at the technological advances in the West.

Invaders from Asia

An important factor in the decline of the East and the rise of Western leadership, however, was one which has been unduly overlooked in our historical teaching, for it has played a decisive part in the shaping of the map of Europe, as well as in the story of European civilisation itself. From the fourth to the twentieth century one of the most remarkable aspects of the story—the most impressive conflict that spans fifteen hundred years—is the conflict between Europe and Asia, a conflict in which down to the time of [English scientist Isaac] Newton's *Principia* it was the Asiatics who were on the aggressive. From the fourth to the seventeenth century—when they still expected to reach the Rhine—the greatest menace to any culture at all in Europe were the hordes of successive invaders from the heart of Asia, coming generally by a route to the north of the Black Sea (a region which remained therefore a sort of no-man's-land almost down to the time of the French Revolution), but coming later south of the Caspian Sea and into Asia Minor and the Mediterranean region. Beginning with the Huns, and continuing with the Avars, the Bulgars, the Magyars, the Petchenegs, the Cumans, etc., these hordes—generally Turkish or Mongol in character—sometimes succeeded one another so quickly that one group was thrust forward into Europe by the pressure of others in the rear, or a chain of them would be jostling one another in a westerly direction—all of which culminated in the Mongol invasions of the thirteenth century, and the conquests of the Ottoman Turks after that.

Downfall of Eastern Mediterranean Civilisation

These Asiatic invaders had something to do with the downfall of Rome and the western empire over fifteen hundred years ago; they overthrew Constantinople, the second Rome, in 1453; and for centuries they virtually enslaved Russia and dominated Moscow, which later came to stand in the position of a third Rome. It was they who hung as a constant shadow over the East and eventually turned the eastern Mediterranean lands into desert; and they put an end to the glory of Baghdad. Because of their activity over so many centuries it was the western half of Europe that emerged into modern history as the effective heir and legatee of the Græco-Roman civilisation. From the tenth century A.D. these Asiatics—though for centuries they had tormented us and carried their depredations as far as the Atlantic coast—were never able to break into the West again or to do more than besiege Vienna. The tenth century represents something like a restoration of stability, therefore—the time from which Western civilisation makes its remarkable advance. One aspect of the period that comes to its culmination in the Renaissance is the emergence of western Europe to a position of independence and, indeed, of conscious cultural leadership.

A primary aspect of the Renaissance, however, as we have seen, is the fact that it completes and brings to its climax the long process by which the thought of antiquity was being recovered and assimilated in the middle ages. It even carries to what at times is a ludicrous extreme the spirit of an exaggerated subservience to antiquity, the spirit that helped to turn Latin into a dead language. Ideas may have appeared in new combinations, but we cannot say that essentially new ingredients were introduced into our civilisation at the Renaissance.

We cannot say that here were intellectual changes calculated to transform the character and structure of our society or civilisation. Even the secularisation of thought which was locally achieved in certain circles at this time was not unprecedented and was a hot-house growth, soon to be overwhelmed by the fanaticism of the [Protestant] Reformation and the Counter-Reformation. During much of the seventeenth century itself we can hardly fail to be struck, for example, by the power of religion both in thought and in politics.

Scientific Revolution Makes Renaissance Pale by Comparison

People have talked sometimes as though nothing very new happened in the seventeenth century either, since natural science itself came to the modern world as a legacy from ancient Greece. More than once in the course of our survey we ourselves have even been left with the impression that the scientific revolution could not take place—that significant developments were held up for considerable periods—until a further draft had been made upon the thought of antiquity and a certain minimum of Greek science had been recovered. Against all this, however, it might be said that the course of the seventeenth century, as we have studied it, represents one of the great episodes in human experience, which ought to be placed—along with the exile of the ancient Jews or the building-up of the universal empires of Alexander the Great and of ancient Rome—amongst the epic adventures that have helped to make the human race what it is. It represents one of those periods when new things are brought into the world and into history out of men's own creative activity, and their own wrestlings with truth. There does not seem to be any sign that the ancient world, before its heritage had been dispersed, was moving towards anything like the scientific revolution, or that the Byzantine Empire, in spite of the continuity of its classical tradition, would ever have taken hold of ancient thought and so remoulded it by a great transforming power. The scientific revolution we must regard, therefore, as a creative product of the West—depending on a complicated set of conditions which existed only in western Europe, depending partly also perhaps on a certain dynamic quality in the life and the history of this half of the continent. And not only was a new factor introduced into history at this time amongst other factors, but it proved to be so capable of growth, and so many-sided in its operations, that it consciously assumed a directing rôle from the very first, and, so to speak, began to take control of the other factors—just as Christianity in the middle ages had come to preside over everything else, percolating into every corner of life and thought. And when we speak of Western civilisation being carried to an oriental country like Japan in recent generations, we do not mean Græco-Roman philosophy and humanist ideals, we do not mean the Christianising of Japan, we mean the science, the modes of thought and all that apparatus of civilisation which were beginning to change the face of the West in the latter half of the seventeenth century.

The Use of Science Raises Ethical and Practical Dilemmas

Robert N. Proctor

Robert N. Proctor is a professor of the history of science at the University of Pennsylvania. He specializes in studying the history of medicine in the twentieth century. His specialty gives him an excellent background for a critique of modern science.

According to Proctor, science and technology have always brought social problems. Some of these problems were economic. During the Great Depression, for example, even some scientists wanted to halt the development of machines that were replacing workers in factories. Science also creates problems regarding the unethical use of scientific knowledge, as when psychologists used the clinical knowledge they had gained to help sell movie-theater popcorn and soft drinks using subliminal messages.

Proctor also holds that science's responsibility for some of the greatest advances in the last century has been significantly overstated. For example, historians have shown that the great increase in life expectancy has been due more to public health, sanitation, and nutritional measures than to any sort of miracle drugs developed in laboratories.

As one might imagine, concerns about the negative impact of science on society are often voiced in times of economic crisis. In the 1930s, many blamed the Great Depression on the failure of scientists and engineers to consider the human impact of their work. L. Magruder Passano, a professor of mathematics at MIT [Massachusetts Institute of Technology] wrote to *Science* magazine in 1935 suggesting that the chief aim of scientific research was "to enable those who already receive an undue share of the wealth produced by industry and research, to appropriate a share still larger." Harvey Cushing, a professor of surgery at Yale, complained that "the average man" had begun to feel that "scientific research and the labor-saving inventions which grow out of it are chiefly responsible for the hard times and unemployment and uneven distribution of property" made so apparent in the Depression. When [British industrialist] Sir Josiah Stamp and others called for a moratorium on science and invention, what they were really worried about was the displacement of men by machines—one of the primary causes, in their view, of the Great Depression. One reason [pharmacologist] Theodore Koppanyi in the 1940s opposed the founding of the National Science Foundation was his concern that there was already enough science being done. His solution appears to be unique in the history of science criticism, recommending as he did that the government follow the example of the Agricultural Adjustment Administration and pay people *not* to do research!

Military Use of Science

The concerns of Koppanyi sound curiously anachronistic today. More familiar are the kinds of doubts raised by postwar atomic scientists worried that they had unleashed "a monster" into the world. After the detonation of atomic bombs over Hiroshima and Nagasaki, project leader [atomic scientist] J.R. Oppenheimer summed up the doubts of several of his colleagues when he stated that scientists "had come to know sin." Scientists organized to try and halt the rapidly growing arms race; in 1945 the *Bulletin of the Atomic Scientists* began to mark time until "mid-night," when final nuclear war would begin. The sense of shame felt by physical scientists spread to other fields: psychologists began to question the ethics of using subliminal techniques to sell products (by inserting into movies 1/3000-second messages exhorting viewers to "Eat Popcorn" or "Drink Coca-Cola"); [psychology professor] Arthur Bachrach drew an explicit parallel between the moral responsibilities faced by psychologists armed with such techniques and those of physicists who built the bomb.

Physics is not the only area for which World War II represents a turning point in the ethics of science. Human experimentation became a postwar concern especially in the wake of the 1946–47 Nuremberg trials, where German physicians accused of crimes against humanity were shown to have performed cruel and often fatal experiments on prisoners in Nazi concentration camps. The Nuremberg Code that emerged from the physicians' trial was supposed to codify a set of standards for the ethical treatment of human subjects, including informed consent, the use of humans only as a last resort, and the avoidance of any experiment that might bring about the death or permanent injury of the subject.

In subsequent years, however, the code would be violated time and again, even in the country of its authors. In 1949, for example, officials at the Hanford Nuclear Reservation in southeast Washington released some 27,000 curies of radioactive xenon-133 and iodine-131 into the atmosphere as part of an experiment to determine dispersal patterns for radio-active isotopes. Details of the so-called Green Run remain classified, but it is suspected that the experiment (in which 8,000 square miles were contaminated with more than one thousand times the radiation released at Three Mile Island) was part of an effort to discover the location of Soviet plutonium plants. Residents of local communities were not informed until 1986, when an environmentalist group obtained documentation on the experiments from the Department of Energy under the Freedom of Information Act.

Experiments on Humans

There are other examples. In the 1960s the U.S. Army and Central Intelligence Agency gave LSD [lysergic acid diethylamide, a hallucinogenic drug] to several unsuspecting persons as part of a project to explore the effects of the drug; at least one person died from trauma caused by the experience. In the notorious Tuskegee Syphilis Experiment, 400 black men from Alabama suffering from the advanced stages of syphilis were allowed to go untreated for as long as forty years (1932–1972) as part of a U.S. Public Health Service experiment to chart the course of the disease. It was not until

1972 that the experiment was halted, after a reporter for the Associated Press broke the story. There are the infamous Willowbrook experiments, where retarded children were deliberately infected with hepatitis in order to test the effects of an experimental vaccine; there are the secret radiation experiments conducted in the 1950s by the Atomic Energy Commission to determine the health effects of ingested uranium. There are the secret germ-warfare tests the U.S. Army conducted by spraying bacteria into New York subways and populated areas around San Francisco—experiments described by one critic as "science gone mad."

These and other examples were in blatant violation of the principles of the Nuremberg Code. Ironically, the code never has been recognized as having legal standing. When a soldier victim of an LSD study sued the U.S. Army, the case went all the way to the Supreme Court. In 1987, in the case of *Stanley vs. the United States*, the court voted 5 to 4 against the soldier; the decision made it clear that the government could not be held legally or even financially responsible to the standards articulated in the Nuremberg Code. Disturbing also is the fact that many Americans were apparently willing even to help administer such experiments if ordered to do so by scientific authorities. The psychologist Stanley Milgram in a series of pathbreaking studies in the early 1960s demonstrated the extremes to which people would go in administering pain to experimental subjects on orders of scientists urging that "the experiment must go on."

Critiques of Science Increase in the 1960s

The 1960s was a watershed in science criticism. As many orthodox academic philosophers remained content to formalize the laws of science, critics began to question the logic of scientific "rationality" itself, condemning what they saw as reason propelled by its own inner logic, or the ideal of science as the best way of knowing, or the use of science as an instrument of social control. [Philosopher] Herbert Marcuse's *One-Dimensional Man* excoriated the society in which peace meant readiness for war; Rachel Carson's *Silent Spring* warned that chemical agriculture was killing butterflies and birds. Some began to question whether tobacco and chemical executives really *belonged* on the boards of national cancer research institutions. Others asked if it was right and proper that Madison Avenue [New York City address of most advertising agencies] advertising should be the second largest employer of Ph.D. psychologists, the C.I.A. the largest employer of Ph.D. historians, the National Security Agency the world's largest employer of mathematicians.

Some have tended to lump together all opponents of science under the general rubric of "antiscience," or those who simply fear any tampering with nature, ([environmental activist] Jeremy Rifkin's work has often been cast in this light—sometimes fairly, sometimes not). But not all of those who criticize science are "antiscience" in principle, or prefer the Stone Age to the present, or deny that "life itself would be impossible without chemicals" (the slogan of an Allied Chemical media campaign in 1981–82). In recent years, the romantic critique of science has been superseded by more complex critiques based not on longings for an earlier and simpler age but rather on broadening participation in science or redirecting science toward environmental responsibility, international cooperation, or other social goals. Criticism in some cases has led to the establishment of entirely new academic disciplines: environmental toxicology, restoration ecology, technological assessment, bioethics, conservation biology, ecological economics, environmental ethics, geophysiology, and so forth.

In recent years the critique of science has been especially pronounced in four areas: medicine, agriculture, biological determinism, and the militarization of science. These areas are not neatly separate from one another, because many new problems (pesticide pollution, for example) and new techniques (plasmid cloning, for example) have eroded the boundaries that once separated, say, agriculture and medicine. The same gene-insertion techniques used to produce human insulin (to treat diabetes) are being used today to produce bovine [cattle] growth hormone (for use in agriculture) and biowarfare agents (for use by the military). A biotechnology firm may produce pharmaceuticals and genetically altered seeds along with bacteria that eat up oil spills. A military agency may fund research on global warming, high-definition TV, or the environmental effects of nuclear war. Critics of militarization may base their critique on environmentalist or feminist principles; the same groups protesting biological determinism may also object to the commercialization of university laboratories or the environmental hazards brought about by petrochemical agriculture.

Dilemmas in Medical Research

Medicine has become a field of endless controversy—not just because nearly everyone's interests are at stake, but also because advances in the science in question may be only tenuously linked to advances in human welfare. Concerns about human experimentation, rights to refuse treatment (or to die), the use of fetal tissue or animals for research, and new forms of transplants or fertilization and birthing have all raised doubts about what it means for medical science to advance. One broad set of concerns has to do with the nature and scale of medical intervention. Have physicians overestimated the value of "heroic" medical techniques? When does the prolongation of life no longer serve the best interests of a patient? Do patients have the right to choose the type of treatment they want—what about "alternative" cancer treatments, for example, many of which are now illegal? Can a physician be sued for failing to perform amniocentesis or other genetic tests? When does the cost of a procedure exceed its benefit? And who should bear those costs? Can aborted fetal tissues be used to treat Parkinson's disease or juvenile diabetes? How must animals be treated in medical research? Should animals be used to test ballistic effects and new cosmetics?

A related set of concerns centers on the question of whether medicine really is the key to health. [Professor of social medicine] Thomas McKeown in the 1970s showed that the rise in life expectancy over the last two centuries in industrial nations owed less to improvements in medicine (the discovery of the pathogens causing measles and whooping cough, for example, or the subsequent development of vaccines) than to improvements in sanitary conditions and diet, including separation of sewage and drinking water. [Scientist] D.P. Burkitt argued that increased consumption of dietary fiber was likely to do far more to eliminate colon cancer than innovations in chemotherapy or surgery; [scientist] Samuel Epstein postulated that industrial pollution, rather than a failure of medical technique, was the likely cause for the growing incidence of many cancers. Many of these criticisms emerged out of recognition that policy priorities were skewed toward the cure of disease rather than its prevention. Thus critics were not surprised when [President] Richard Nixon's much heralded "war on cancer" (launched in 1971) proved to be a losing one, as cure rates remained little changed while incidence rates actually increased for many cancers. In the Soviet Union, the average life span of adult males actually began to decline in the late 1960s and early seventies, to the point that the Soviet government stopped publishing vital statistics. Critics observing such trends argued that for most people most of the time, human health has less to do with medicine than with diet, exercise, and the cleanliness and safety of the home and workplace. [Radical social theorist] Ivan Illich in 1975 went so far as to suggest that doctors do as much to injure health as to help it.

The Unique Social Role of the Scientist

Barry Commoner

Barry Commoner is a biologist and environmental scientist-turned-political activist. He was among the pioneers of the environmental movement. In 1980 he ran for president of the United States on the Citizens' Party ticket.

In the following selection, Commoner explains the unique role the scientist has to play in debates over science and technology. Commoner holds that part of the job of the scientist is to communicate his or her expertise to the general public. This will allow the public to participate in informed debate over such matters as nuclear weapons testing or insecticide use. Commoner's view contradicts that of many scientists who believe that, as technical experts, they should be in charge of policy regarding technical innovation.

In addition, Commoner believes that scientists must shake off their atomistic view of the world, for the technology they develop is not limited to isolated laboratories but affects entire natural systems. Wise use of scientific knowledge, he argues, requires that technology be viewed as part of the natural system in which it will be used.

For a long time the issue of the scientist's social responsibility was discussed only in occasional seminars, but now it has become an important, frequently discussed issue for many scientists. The consequences of scientific development have dominated the political life of this country and of the world. For example, when the public complains about the enormous burden of the military budget, we should remember that the

Barry Commoner, "The Ecological Crisis," *The Social Responsibility of the Scientist*, edited by Martin Brown. New York: The Free Press, 1971. Copyright © 1971 by The Free Press. Reproduced by permission of the author.

costly armament is largely an achievement of modern science and technology. Every scientist now knows that almost anything he learns may quickly be converted to a military or commercial use. The gap between scientific discoveries and their application has become very narrow. Scientists can no longer evade the social, political, economic, and moral consequences of what they do in the laboratory.

What is required, then, is that we understand why the progress of science has led to the grave social issues which plague society, and to determine what role the scientist should play in resolving these issues.

I believe that the system of science and technology, as practiced in the United States and in all other developed countries, is in many ways unsound and unfit as a guide to the nature of man and the world in which he lives. We live in nature; society operates in nature, and our ability to exist in the natural world depends on our knowledge of it. Science should provide that knowledge and technology guide our application of it. But we are failing in these aims. In New York harbor the sewage bacterial count has risen a hundredfold in the last decade [the 1960s], even though marked improvements in the extent of sewage treatment have been made. Apparently there is something wrong with the technology of sewage treatment, which after all was designed to get *rid* of bacteria.

This is an example of a very general problem; increasing environmental pollution is evidence that our technology is, in important ways, incompetent. Behind this incompetence is an intrinsic weakness in science. Let us consider the sewage disposal problem as an example.

Sewage Treatment as an Example of Failed Technology

Sewage consists of waste materials, including bacteria (which can spread disease) and organic matter. Organic matter plays a role in a biological cycle which occurs in water and in soil. In surface water, organic matter is broken down by bacteria; the products are nitrate, phosphate, and carbon dioxide, inorganic materials. In the process, the microorganisms consume oxygen. These are nutrients for another group of organisms, the algae. These organisms take up the inorganic materials and reconvert them to organic matter. Algae are eaten by fish, which convert the algal organic matter into their own organic substance. As the fish produce wastes, or when they die, organic matter is released to the water and the cycle is complete. This cycle once offered what seemed like a good way to dispose of organic wastes: Let it flow through pipes into a lake or a river. Microorganisms decay the waste and the resulting inorganic matter (nitrate, for example) goes down the river, into the sea, and away.

This system of sewage disposal works fine as long as human population density around lakes and rivers remains relatively small. But when large amounts of organic material are poured into the waterways, the natural cycle breaks down. The oxygen content of water is limited by the low solubility of oxygen in water. If enough organic matter is added to the water, the bacteria working on it become so active that they consume all the available oxygen, and the bacteria asphyxiate themselves and die. The whole system breaks down; the water becomes foul.

This problem was solved by sanitary engineers when they domesticated the bacteria. Domestication is a very interesting process. In domestication an organism doesn't change its biological functions, but it performs those functions in a place convenient for man. When sewage treatment plants were developed, the bacteria of decay were allowed to function in a convenient place—a sewage treatment pond. The pond was aerated to provide enough oxygen for the bacteria to function. Such a treatment plant is able to convert the organic matter to inorganic materials, which can then be released into surface waters without imposing a burden on their oxygen content. Most of the biological oxygen demand of the sewage is removed.

Technological Failure

But this technological achievement, which is fundamental to the process of urbanization in the U.S., has already proven to be a disastrous failure. Why? Since such sewage treatment plants are capable of handling large amounts of sewage, they release inordinate amounts of inorganic materials into the surface water. But this excess of nutrients causes the algae to grow intensively, forming thick layers. The top layer absorbs the sunlight and the algae on the bottom are deprived of the wavelengths they require. The overall result is that large overgrowths of algae, called "algal blooms," grow up quickly, then die. And when the algae die they release organic matter to the water, again stressing its oxygen content. The end result is, again, the disruption of the natural cycle.

Lake Erie [one of the Great Lakes] has become, in a sense, a huge underwater cesspool. Some 40 feet of organic matter, originating partly in raw sewage and partly in organic matter regenerated by the algae, has been deposited on the bottom of the lake in some places. The reason why this organic matter hasn't caused catastrophic trouble is that there is a thin layer of iron oxide which binds the muck on the bottom and doesn't let it get into the lake. But the iron oxide is in an oxidized form, and every summer when the oxygen content of the water tends to go to zero in the water, the iron oxide changes its chemical composition to a reduced form which is no longer capable of sealing off the bottom deposit. This Pandora's Box of accumulated biological oxygen demand opens to some degree every summer. There is a danger that at some point huge masses of accumulated organic matter may suddenly be released in the lake. If this happens all of the oxygen-using organisms of the lake will die.

A balance sheet has been drawn up for Lake Erie, for the amount of nitrogen and phosphorus entering and leaving the lake. It has been found that much of the nitrate and phosphate—inorganic products of sewage treatment—entering the lake remains in it. This means that the technology of sewage disposal around Lake Erie is a failure. . . .

The Atomism of Modern Science

If modern technology has failed, there must be something wrong as well with our science, which generates technology. Modern science operates well as long as the system of interest is not complex. We can understand the physical relationship between two particles, but add a third particle and the problem becomes extraordinarily difficult. Modern science has only poor methods for dealing with systems that are characterized by complex interactions. A living thing, or a single living cell, is such a system. Modern biology is dominated by the view that the most successful way to understand a biological system is to reduce it to molecular ones. Molecular biology is regarded as the cutting edge of modern biological research. But there is no way of achieving a "molecular biology" of a complex, circular process such as that operating in a sewage treatment pond, or in natural waters. What is decisive is the interaction among the separate parts—whether organisms in an ecosystem or molecules within a single cell. As a result, such studies are not regarded as part of advanced science, and become instead "applied science"—supposedly beneath the dignity of a "pure scientist" to consider. But sewage is relevant to the human condition—which depends on real, complex things. Nature is composed of living things, not enzymes. In nature, enzymes exist only as parts or products of living things. The tendency to atomize reality is a fundamental fault of modern science. It generates technology which fails to accommodate to the complex reality of nature.

This atomistic approach is characteristic of our technology. For example, [economist] John Kenneth Galbraith explains in *The New Industrial State* that the large corporations, the large manufacturers, have perfected the techniques of mass production and management to such an extent that they appear to run the society. But, Galbraith points out, there is no science or technology for producing a whole car; there is only a science and technology for engine blocks, paint, glass, or rubber. This kind of atomized technology is certainly a successful way to produce automobiles. But the approach fails as soon as the automobile leaves the factory and comes into contact with the environment. The automobile then becomes an instrument for producing lung cancer through the asbestos flaked off the brake linings, and emphysema from the noxious gases and particles it releases into the air. It contributes to algal overgrowths because it puts out nitrogen oxides which in the air may be converted to nitrates. . . . All this came about because the automobile was regarded as a compilation of parts, rather than as an agent in environmental processes.

Differing Views on the Social Role of the Scientist

If there are serious signs that science and technology are incompetent in understanding and reacting with natural systems, how are we in the scientific community to deal with this problem? One position is that our social system must be bent to accommodate the inherent competence of science. For example, Professor Immanuel Mesthene of Harvard proposes that in order to deal with modern technology we need a new political ethos.

To be able to vote intelligently and participate in democracy, the citizen must understand various relationships between nature and science. To talk about superhighways versus rapid transit, he must know about smog. To talk about the Nuclear Test Ban Treaty, he must know about strontium 90 and iodine 131.[1] To talk about bond issues for sewage, he must know about the nitrogen cycle. But most citizens lack this understanding. Therefore, Mesthene suggests that we need to take the control of policies from the public and turn it over to specialists, experts who do understand the technical background of such modern problems.

I reject this view. One reason is that it is antidemocratic. A second reason is that there is a better alternative. If the public is uninformed on technical matters it is only because scientists have not fulfilled their obligation to inform the public. When armed with technical information, the public is perfectly competent to make political decisions.

Some scientists take the position that there is no relationship between science and society. They believe that science exists in and of itself, as a kind of religion; that it has its own self-justification, as a personal, intellectual pursuit. However, scientists are, after all, people born into a society and educated by it. As they grow up they become (some more, some less) subject to effects of social forces. . . .

---

1. Strontium 90 and iodine 131 are two radioactive isotopes that are created by the explosion of nuclear weapons.

The Unique Social Role of the Scientist

The issues of nuclear war, insecticides, public transportation, and sewage disposal are not just scientific issues; they are moral, social, and economic issues. They should be decided by the public as a whole. But the public cannot exercise its conscience on these matters unless it knows the scientific facts. In the old days, morality worked on the basis of simple Newtonian mechanics. That is, hitting somebody with a rock would hurt him so much that the moral issue of throwing rocks at your neighbor was clear. The hurt that rock-throwing can cause is obvious; no scientist is needed to explain it. But scientists who understand the subtle laws of ecology are needed to tell people how using insecticides on Mississippi Valley farms will kill the catfish and wipe out the Cajun fishing industry in Louisiana. The issues resulting from the failures of science and technology are social, political, and moral ones; the scientist's job is to get the relevant information before the public, so that a democratic decision can be made.

There *is* a relation between science and society. The unique responsibility of a scientist is not to determine how his knowledge shall be used, because that determination does not involve his unique capabilities as a scientist. It involves only his moral position as a person. He ought to acknowledge that every person has the same right to a moral position as he does.

I believe that the scientist has a unique responsibility. He is the custodian of the knowledge that everyone needs to exercise his own conscience. If the scientist doesn't get the information to the public, the public is being cut off from the exercise of its morality.

Humanity is living under the shadow of a nuclear war. A nuclear holocaust would destroy our society. This is the gravest moral crisis in the history of the world. Yet we all live with it, tolerate it. If most people in the United States *understood* the facts of nuclear warfare, I am convinced that we would disarm. Unfortunately, the public has been protected from its own conscience by the failure of the scientific community to get the facts before the public.

When the public is informed, action comes quickly. When,

much to everybody's surprise, 80 Senators voted to approve the Nuclear Test Ban Treaty, a careful analysis was made of the factors influencing the vote. The study found that the Senators had received a lot of mail from mothers who feared the dangers of fallout. What influenced the Senators most was that the mothers who wrote the letters knew how to spell "strontium 90." They knew the facts, and the Senators feared facing not simply enraged women, but informed enraged women. The force behind this informed public was education by the scientists of the community. After all, it was the scientists who first knew how to spell "strontium 90."

The unique role of the scientist, then, is to inform the public about the failures in science and technology, and to give the public a chance to let its conscience operate on the huge and potentially disastrous social problems that have been generated by the progress of modern science and technology.

Science Will Continue to Enrich the Nation and the World

Lewis M. Branscomb

In the early 1960s a center of science and technology sprang up almost spontaneously in the small town of Boulder, Colorado. In those days, money for scientific research was plentiful. The public was supportive of science, as were politicians and business leaders. There was little of the bureacracy that researchers must deal with today. The conditions were ideal for clusters of scientific and technological expertise to form in such out-of-the-way places.

The Harvard-based physicist Lewis M. Branscomb, who currently is a cochair of the National Academies Committee on Science and Technology for Countering Terrorism, recounts those early days in Boulder with nostalgia. Branscomb is still optimistic about the possibilities of science in the United States and beyond. Despite some misgivings on the part of intellectuals and the public, Branscomb believes that science continues to improve our daily lives. Science can thrive, however, only if the nation continues to invest money and talent in research.

During one of those sometimes-turbulent years in the early 1970s, University of Colorado sociology professor Howard Higman asked me to fill in at the last minute on a panel during the university's World Affairs Week. I said, "Sure, what's the subject?" "Technolatry," he said, leaving me to go to the discussion and find out what it meant.

Well, I soon found out. My fellow panelists, an unemployed poet, a political radical, and a literature professor gave me to understand that, whatever "technolatry" was, it was something I was guilty of. I soon appreciated that "technolatry" is the idolatry of science and technology.

I pleaded not guilty, noting that in the computer industry we pray *for* the computer, not *to* it. But I've been thinking about that discussion, and I'm ready to change my plea to "nolo contendere [no contest]."

Science Fuels a Revolution in Rising Expectations

The pace of technological change receives much public attention. But the most fundamental revolution that has overtaken mankind in the modern era is a revolution of rising expectations all around the world.

History tells us that misery has always been the lot of the majority of mankind. For the whole history of the human race, few ever expected it to be any different. Today the leaders of developing countries are well aware of the value of the knowledge, the science, and the technology possessed by the industrialized nations. Our American history demonstrates what a former colony can do with its own resources when it reaches out to older countries for help in building up indigenous technical capability.

Now we have grown beyond the level of minimum satisfaction of our material needs. But developing countries know, as we do, that while self-sufficiency is probably an unrealistic goal, every nation could have a rising standard of living consistent with sound principles of ecology and with the energy and food resources which the Earth is capable of sustaining. A number of developing countries—the so-called newly industrializing countries—are demonstrating that this is achievable in practice.

This proof of the possibility of a better life for mankind provides stark contrast to the reality of conflict and misery that are still the lot of most of humanity. But, at last, human beings have begun to set the right goals for themselves, and we should not get too discouraged if it takes several decades to realize this extraordinary vision of human expectations for an increasing number of nations on Earth.

Unhappily, the depth of this conviction is scarcely matched in any country by an equal degree of understanding of how science should be nourished, technology generated, and the skills of well-trained people mobilized for these noble goals. And I insist they are noble—and I won't attempt to deal with the Luddite argument that capability in science and technology should be suppressed simply because people do foolish things with it. After all, I've already confessed to being a technophile. I will, of course, cheer for [mathematician and author] Freeman Dyson's argument for good taste in technology.

Probably, the Japanese and Germans have the most impressive records for deliberate goal setting and implementation planning—at the national level—for science, technology, and education. I want to discuss some of the major issues under debate in the United States in the field of science and technology policy.

The Growth of a "Science City"

First, let me note that when times are good and everyone is optimistic about the future, we Americans get along very nicely without comprehensive goals and plans. When times are confused, a good fraction of the really important decisions for the future have more to do with a few people of vision than all the committees, agencies, and exhortations.

Consider how this wonderful town of Boulder, Colorado, the Akademe-Gorodok [Russian for "academic town"] of the U.S.A., came to have such a concentration of diverse scientific institutions. It would have been very rational for the federal government to decide to build a science city 30 miles from a major metropolis in the nation's central mountains, as the Soviet Union did. The Japanese built one too, northwest of Tokyo. But our science city didn't come about as the result of a central government decision. It all began with the accident of fate that Donald Menzel was born in the high-mountain mining town of Climax, Colorado, and had the audacity to want to be a great astronomer at Harvard University.

When Prof. Menzel set out to establish a high altitude observing station for study of the solar corona he naturally thought of Climax as a logical location. He then hired one of Harvard astronomy's more promising graduates, Walter Orr Roberts, to move to Climax to establish and run the observing station. The pioneering nature of this venture is attested to by the experience of Walt Roberts' new bride Janet. She refused to abandon Climax—and her husband—despite the rigors of homemaking at high altitude. To her new bride's request for cake recipes that would work at 11,000 feet altitude, she received the following reply: "Dear Madame, we regret to inform you that there are no such recipes for the good and sufficient reason that no one lives at an altitude of 11,000 feet."

Boulder's scientific and technical focus also owes a lot to Colorado physics professor Edward U. Condon, and his beloved little yellow house on Tenth Street. When he was the Director of the National Bureau of Standards in Washington DC, he maneuvered the Congress into selecting Boulder for the location of the Bureau's new Radio Standards Laboratory and Central Radio Propagation Laboratory. The latter evolved into the Environmental Science Services Administration (ESSA), which in turn evolved into the National Oceanic and Atmospheric Administration.

Scientific Libidos

In the early 1960s, the University of Colorado in Boulder breathed the heady aroma of national recognition for excellence, which stimulated a lot of scientific libidos. Quigg Newton, former Denver Mayor, was President of the University of Colorado, and the National Science Foundation was encouraging "centers of excellence" in the nation's emerging research universities. Boulder Astrophysicists Richard Thomas and John Jefferies and the Atomic Physics research group I headed in NBS Washington connived with the Chairman of the University's physics department, Wesley Brittin, to form the Joint Institute for Laboratory Astrophysics (JILA). Walter Roberts traded in the High Altitude Observatory on a bigger, splashier model, the National Center for Atmospheric Research. Ball Brothers, the midwest firm famous for its home-canning fruit jars, established a major space research satellite design, production and operations business. The Coors Beer Company established a high-tech ceramics business. [Computer companies] Hewlett-Packard and IBM moved laboratories and plants to the Boulder area.

In those days everybody studied atmospheres in one way or another. Every vision had its little research club; Boulder became an alphabet soup of institutional acronyms. Dr. Alan Kolb, a plasma physicist then at the Naval Research Laboratory, used to ask each person he met in Boulder, "Which club do you belong to?"

Those of you who lived that history know it couldn't have happened as a planned act. We all had royal battles. But the constraints were lower then—there was a place where each could find a niche—and everyone believed in the value of whatever we were fighting for.

Science Is the Goose That Laid the Golden Egg

I am sure you all know the Aesop fable of the goose that laid golden eggs. The goose of a vital science and technology capability is not dead in the United States. The goose is only confused and seems to be losing self-confidence.

I sometimes find myself baffled by the premature obituaries for American science, technology, our competitiveness in world markets, indeed our role as a constructive leader in the partnership of nations. The computer industry is thriving as never before, growing five times faster than free-world economies as a whole. Competition is fierce; prices are plunging as wave after wave of microelectronic technology produces a productivity explosion. The demand for hiring computer scientists and electrical, mechanical, and chemical engineers exceeds the supply to the point that hundreds of tenure-track positions stand unfilled. While I realize that the computer and communications industries are almost unique, if our society takes a complacent attitude toward science and technology long enough, even our leadership industries will suffer. I find myself saying, "The goose is not dying; it is just exhausted from laying so many golden eggs. Why not try feeding it instead of kicking it around?"

Some of this confusion results from the difficulties of historical readjustment. From a brief, but extraordinary, period in the 1960s and 1970s, when American scientific preeminence was unchallenged, we come to the 1980s, when the whole relationship of science to technology and the economy is under debate and review. The goose must feel that it lives in the barnyard of the proverbial farmer who kept pulling up the plants and looking at their roots to understand why they were not growing faster.

To those who believe you can continue to extract golden eggs from the goose without keeping it alive and feeding it well, I would say, "there is no free lunch." To those who believe that every interested group or nation should demand a larger and larger piece of the world's technological assets, without contributing in like measure, I would answer, "The pie served at that lunch does not have to be cut in ever smaller slivers. The pie can be baked bigger and bigger."

Can we afford the investments needed to get the economic pie growing again?

Flourishing science and a robust technology will ultimately pay for themselves, *if* our nation commits itself to excellence in science and technology, each driving the other in a vigorous interrelationship, and *if* technology is pressed vigorously by the private sector, in a publicly encouraged drive for competitive economic performance worldwide.

Appendix of Documents

Document 1: Aristotle Classifies

The ancient Greek philosopher Aristotle was at his most scientific, in the modern sense of the word, when studying biology. Here he describes the various categories of animals, classifying them according to whether they live in groups or alone, whether they are carnivorous or vegetarian, etc. Such description and classification was a precursor of modern science.

The following differences are manifest in [animals'] modes of living and in their actions. Some are gregarious, some are solitary, whether they be furnished with feet or wings or be fitted for a life in the water; and some partake of both characters, the solitary and the gregarious. And of the gregarious, some are disposed to combine for social purposes, others to live each for its own self.

Gregarious creatures are, among birds, such as the pigeon, the crane, and the swan; and, by the way, no bird furnished with crooked talons is gregarious. Of creatures that live in water many kinds of fishes are gregarious, such as the so-called migrants, the tunny, the pelamys, and the bonito.

Man, by the way, presents a mixture of the two characters, the gregarious and the solitary.

Social creatures are such as have some one common object in view; and this property is not common to all creatures that are gregarious. Such social creatures are man, the bee, the wasp, the ant, and the crane.

Again, of these social creatures some submit to a ruler, others are subject to no governance: as, for instance, the crane and the several sorts of bee submit to a ruler, whereas ants and numerous other creatures are every one his own master.

And again, both of gregarious and of solitary animals, some are attached to a fixed home and others are erratic or nomad.

Also, some are carnivorous, some graminivorous, some omnivorous: whilst some feed on a peculiar diet, as for instance the bees and the spiders, for the bee lives on honey and certain other sweets, and the spider lives by catching flies; and some creatures live on fish. Again, some creatures catch their food, others treasure it up; whereas others do not so.

Some creatures provide themselves with a dwelling, others go without one: of the former kind are the mole, the mouse, the ant, the bee; of the latter kind are many insects and quadrupeds. Further, in respect to locality of dwelling-place, some creatures dwell under ground, as the lizard and the snake; others live on the surface of the ground, as the horse and the dog. [Some make to themselves holes, others do not so.]

Some are nocturnal, as the owl and the bat; others live in the daylight.

Moreover, some creatures are tame and some are wild: some are at all times tame, as man and the mule; others are at all times savage, as the leopard and the wolf; and some creatures can be rapidly tamed, as the elephant.

Again, we may regard animals in another light. For, whenever a race of animals is found domesticated, the same is always to be found in a wild condition; as we find to be the case with horses, kine, swine, [men,] sheep, goats, and dogs.

The Works of Aristotle. (J.A. Smith and W.D. Ross eds). Volume IV, *Historia Animalium*, trans. D'Arcy Wentworth Thompson. Oxford: Clarendon Press, 1910.

Document 2: Bacon Compares Mathematical Reasoning with Experimentation

The English monk Roger Bacon was an experimental scientist whose thinking was far in advance of his time. In this writing from A.D. 1268, Bacon argues that proof, both through reasoning and through experience, is necessary to advance knowledge.

Having laid down the main points of the wisdom of the Latins as regards language, mathematics and optics, I wish now to review the principles of wisdom from the point of view of experimental science, because without experiment it is impossible to know anything thoroughly.

There are two ways of acquiring knowledge, one through reason, the other by experiment. Argument reaches a conclusion and compels us to admit it, but it neither makes us certain nor so annihilates doubt that the mind rests calm in the intuition of truth, unless it finds this certitude by way of experience. Thus many have arguments toward attainable facts, but because they have not experienced them, they overlook them and neither avoid a harmful nor follow a beneficial course. Even if a man that has never seen fire, proves by good reasoning that fire burns, and devours and destroys things, nevertheless the mind of one hearing his arguments would never be convinced, nor would he avoid fire until he puts his hand or some combustible thing into it in order to prove by experiment what the argument taught. But after the fact of combustion is experienced, the mind is satisfied and lies calm in the certainty of truth. Hence argument is not enough, but experience is.

This is evident even in mathematics, where demonstration is the surest. The mind of a man that receives that clearest of demonstrations concerning the equilateral triangle without experiment will never stick to the conclusion nor act upon it till confirmed by experiment by means of the intersection of two circles from either section of which two lines are drawn to the ends of a given line. Then one receives the conclusion without doubt. What Aristotle says of the demonstration by the syllogism being able to give knowledge, can be understood if it is accompanied by experience, but not of the bare demonstration. What he says in the first book of the Metaphysics, that those knowing the reason and cause are wiser than the experienced, he speaks concerning the experienced who know the bare fact only without the cause. But I speak here of the experienced that know the reason and cause through their experience. And such are perfect in their knowledge, as Aristotle wishes to be in the sixth book of the Ethics, whose simple statements are to be believed as if they carried demonstration, as he says in that very place. . . .

And because this experimental science is a study entirely unknown by the common people, I cannot convince them of its utility, unless its virtue and characteristics are shown. This alone enables us to find out surely what can be done through nature, what through the application of art, what through fraud, what is the purport and what is mere dream in chance, conjuration, invocations, imprecations, magical sacrifices and what there is in them; so that all falsity may be lifted and the truths we alone of the art retained. This alone teaches us to examine all the insane ideas of the magicians in order not to confirm but to avoid them, just as logic criticizes the art of sophistry. This science has three great purposes in regard to the other sciences: the first is that one may criticize by experiment the noble conclusions of all the other sciences, for the other sciences know that their principles come from experiment, but the conclusions through arguments drawn from the principles discovered, if they care to have the result of their conclusions precise and complete. It is necessary that they have this through the aid of this noble science. It is true that mathematics reaches conclusions in accordance with universal experience about figures and numbers, which indeed apply to all sciences and to this experience, because no science can be known without mathematics. If we would attain to experiments precise, complete and made certain in accordance with the proper method, it is necessary to undertake an examination of the science itself, which is called experimental on our authority.

Roger Bacon, *On Experimental Science*, The Library of Original Sources (Milwaukee: University Research Extension Co., 1901), pp. 369–76.

Document 3: Copernicus Describes the Apparent Motions of the Sun

In the Middle Ages, scholars believed that the sun traveled around the earth. In the following extract from his Commentariolus *(written sometime between 1507–1515), Copernicus describes the earth's motions; its revolutions around the sun, its daily rotation on its axis, and the "wobble" from the tilt or "declination" of its axis. These motions of the earth are what cause the apparent motions of the sun. This was the fundamental insight that started the scientific revolution.*

The Apparent Motions of the Sun

The earth has three motions. First, it revolves annually in a great circle about the sun in the order of the [zodiacal] signs, always describing equal arcs in equal times; the distance from the center of the circle to the center of the sun is ½₅ of the radius of the circle. The radius is assumed to have a length imperceptible in comparison with the height of the firmament; consequently the sun appears to revolve with this motion, as if the earth lay in the center of the universe. However, this appearance is caused by the motion not of the sun but of the earth, so that, for example, when the earth is in the sign of Capricornus, the sun is seen diametrically opposite in Cancer, and so on. On account of the previously mentioned distance of the sun from the center of the circle, this apparent motion of the sun is not uniform, the maximum inequality being 2⅙°. The line drawn from the sun through the center of the circle is invariably directed toward a point of the firmament about 10° west of the more brilliant of the two bright stars in the head of Gemini; therefore when the earth is opposite this point, and the center of the circle lies between them, the sun is seen at its greatest distance from the earth. In this circle, then, the earth revolves together with whatever else is included within the lunar sphere.

The second motion, which is peculiar to the earth, is the daily rotation on the poles in the order of the signs, that is, from west to east. On account of this rotation the entire universe appears to revolve with enormous speed. Thus does the earth rotate together with its circumjacent waters and encircling atmosphere.

The third is the motion in declination. For the axis of the daily rotation is not parallel to the axis of the great circle, but is inclined to it at an angle that intercepts a portion of a circumference, in our time about 23½°. Therefore, while the center of the earth always remains in the plane of the ecliptic, that is, in the circumference of the great circle, the poles of the earth rotate, both of them describing small circles about centers equidistant from the axis of the great circle. The period of this motion is not quite a year and is nearly equal to the annual revolution on the great circle. But the axis of the great circle is invariably directed toward the points of the firmament which are called the poles of the ecliptic. In like manner the motion in declination, combined with the annual motion in their joint effect upon the poles of the daily rotation, would keep these poles constantly fixed at the same points of the heavens, if the periods of both motions were exactly equal. Now with the long passage of time it has become clear that this inclination of the earth to the firmament changes. Hence it is the common opinion that the firmament has several motions in conformity with a law not yet sufficiently understood. But the motion of the earth can explain all these changes in a less surprising way. I am not concerned to state what the path of the poles is. I am aware that, in lesser matters, a magnetized iron needle always points in the same direction. It has nevertheless seemed a better view to ascribe the changes to a sphere, whose motion governs the movements of the poles. This sphere must doubtless be sublunar [i.e., earthly].

Nicolas Copernicus, *Three Copernican Treatises*, Edward Rosen (trans) 2nd Edition. New York: Dover Publications, 1958, pp. 61–65.

Document 4: Galileo's Elegant Explanation of Motion

Galileo refutes the argument that lighter objects (e.g., a wooden ball) accelerate faster than heavier objects (e.g., a lead ball). Instead, Galileo comes close to discovering the law of inertia (formulated later by Isaac Newton), whereby heavier objects start to move more slowly, but also tend to move for longer periods of time.

Why, at the beginning of their natural motion, bodies that are less heavy move more swiftly than heavier ones.

This problem, surely, is no less attractive than difficult. Other writers, too, have tried to explain its solution, e.g., Averroes and his followers. But, in my opinion, they labored in vain laying down certain unattractive hypotheses. For they hold that air is heavy in its own region, from which it follows that things which have more air are heavier in the region of air—and this is also Aristotle's opinion. Thus [they say] a wooden sphere, for example, since it has more air in it than a leaden one, has three heavy elements, air, water, and earth; while the leaden one, since it has less air in it, has, as it were, only two heavy elements: the result of this is that the wooden sphere falls [in air] more swiftly than the leaden. And not content with this, they also say that rare lead is heavier than dense iron in air for the reason that there are more parts of air in rare lead than in dense iron. No one will fail to see how many and how serious are the difficulties that this solution involves.

In the first place, who does not know that air is neither heavy nor light in its own region, and that, as a consequence, it moves neither upward nor downward? . . .

Secondly, if the velocity of the [natural] motion of a body depends on its weight, as everyone holds, and if the leaden sphere has earth and water in place of the portions of air that are in the wooden sphere, and if earth and water are heavier than air, as we can readily believe, then will not the lead be heavier and fall more swiftly? And as for what they say about iron and lead, to show that air adds to the weight, if lead is heavier because it has more air, then wood will be heavier than both iron and lead, since it has more air than either of them.

Thirdly, if the great quantity of air which is in wood makes the wood move more swiftly, then it will always [and not merely in the beginning] move more swiftly, so long as it is in the air. But experience shows us the opposite. For it is true that wood moves more swiftly than lead in the beginning of its motion; but a little later the motion of the lead is so accelerated that it leaves the wood behind it. And if they are both let fall from a high tower, the lead moves far out in front. This is something I have often tested. Therefore we must try to derive a sounder explanation on the basis of sounder hypotheses.

Oh, how readily are true explanations derived from true principles! If it is true, as we said, that bodies, when they begin their motion from a state of rest, begin it with an impressed force in the opposite direction equal to their weight, then the bodies that are heavier will begin their motion charged with a greater contrary force. But if heavier bodies must destroy more of the force that impels them in the opposite direction [to their natural motion] than must lighter bodies, then it surely follows that heavier bodies move more slowly since they are subject to greater resistance. And, on the other hand, if this is true, it follows that the heavier bodies must fall faster, once they have destroyed so much of the contrary resistance that they are no longer hindered by as much as the lighter bodies are. And experience again definitely confirms this.

Galileo Galilei, *"On Motion" and "On Mechanics,"* I.B. Drabkin (trans). Madison: University of Wisconsin Press, 1960, pp. 106–109.

Document 5: Galileo Claims that Venus Orbits the Sun

In this excerpt, Galileo answers a letter in which "Apelles" (the pseudonym of Christoph Scheiner, a Catholic priest and astronomer) claims that sunspots will allow a method of determining whether Venus orbits the sun. "Nonsense," says Galileo in this 1613 letter. By directly observing Venus with a telescope, the astronomer can distinguish "phases" of Venus which are like the phases of the moon; new, quarter, half, full. Just as the moon's apparent phases are caused by its orbit around the earth, Venus's phases are caused by its rotation around the sun. This was an important proof of the Copernican (sun-centered) system.

Apelles suggests that sunspot observations afford a method by which he can determine whether Venus and Mercury revolve about the sun or between the earth and the sun. I am astonished that nothing has reached his ears—or if anything has, that he has not capitalized upon it—of a very elegant, palpable, and convenient method of determining this, discovered by me about two years ago and communicated to so many people that by now it has become notorious. This is the fact that Venus changes shape precisely as does the moon; and if Apelles will now look through his telescope he will see Venus to be perfectly circular in shape and very small (though indeed it was smaller yet when it [recently] emerged as evening star). He may then go on observing it, and he will see that as it reaches its maximum departure from the sun it will be semicircular. Thence it will pass into a horned shape, gradually becoming thinner as it once more approaches the sun. Around conjunction it will appear as does the moon when two or three days old, but the size of its visible circle will have much increased. Indeed, when Venus emerges [from behind the sun] to appear as evening star, its apparent diameter is only one-sixth as great as at its evening disappearance [in front of the sun] or its emergence as morning star [several days thereafter], and hence its disk appears forty times as large on the latter occasions.

These things leave no room for doubt about the orbit of Venus. With absolute necessity we shall conclude, in agreement with the

theories of the Pythagoreans and of Copernicus, that Venus revolves about the sun just as do all the other planets. Hence it is not
necessary to wait for transits and occultations of Venus to make certain of so obvious a conclusion. No longer need we employ arguments that allow any answer, however feeble, from persons whose
philosophy is badly upset by this new arrangement of the universe.
For these opponents, unless constrained by some stronger argument, would say that Venus either shines with its own light or is of
a substance that may be penetrated by the sun's rays, so that it may
be lighted not only on its surface but also throughout its depth.
They take heart to shield themselves with this argument because
there have not been wanting philosophers and mathematicians who
have actually believed this—meaning no offense to Apelles, who
says otherwise. Indeed, Copernicus himself was forced to admit the
possibility and even the necessity of one of these two ideas, as otherwise he could give no reason for Venus failing to appear horned
when beneath the sun. As a matter of fact nothing else could be said
before the telescope came along to show us that Venus is naturally
and actually dark like the moon, and like the moon has phases.

Galileo Galilei, *Discovery and Opinions of Galileo*, (trans) Stilman Drake. Garden City, New York:
Doubleday and Company, 1957, pp. 93–94.

Document 6: Galileo's Statement Before the Inquisition

*In 1633 Galileo was called to Rome to testify before the Inquistion, a
group of Catholic priests charged with stamping out heretical beliefs.
Here he defends himself against the charge of heresy.*

Called, there appeared personally at Rome in the Palace of the
Holy Office, in the usual quarters of the Reverend Fathers Com-
missaries, in the presence of the Reverend Father Vincenzo Mac-
ulano, Commissary General, and the Reverend Doctor Carlo Sin-
ceri, Fiscal Procurator of the Holy Office, etc., Galileo, son of the
late Vincenzo Galilei, Florentine, seventy years of age, who,
sworn to testify the truth, was asked by the Doctor: . . .

Q: Do you know or can you guess the cause that this order was
given to you?

A: I imagine that the cause of my having been ordered to come
before the Holy Office is to give an account of my recently printed
book; and I suppose this because of the order given to the printer
and to me, a few days before I was ordered to come to Rome, not
to issue any more of those books, and similarly because the printer
was ordered by the Father Inquisitor that he send the original

manuscript of my book to the Holy Office at Rome.

Q: Explicitly what is in the book you imagine was the reason for the order that you come to the City?

A: It is a book written in dialogue, and it treats of the system of the world, or rather, the two chief systems, that is, the arrangements of the heavens and of the elements.

Q: Why and at what time did you write the said book, and where?

A: As to the place, I composed it at Florence, [starting] about ten or twelve years ago, and I was occupied on it about six or eight years, though not continuously.

Q: Tell whether you were at Rome another time, particularly in 1616, and for what occasion.

A: I was in Rome in 1616, and afterward I was here in [1624,] the second year of the pontificate of His Holiness Urban VIII, and last I was here three years ago, on the occasion of my wish to have my book printed. The occasion for which I was at Rome in the year 1616 was that, hearing questions raised about the opinion of Nicholas Copernicus concerning the motion of the earth and stability of the sun and the order of the celestial spheres, in order to assure myself against holding any but holy and Catholic opinions, I came to hear what must be held concerning this matter.

Q: Did you come because you were called, and if so, for what reason were you called, and where and with whom did you treat of the said matter?

A: In 1616 I came to Rome of my own accord, without being called, and for the reason I told you; and in Rome I treated of this business with some Cardinals who governed the Holy Office at that time, in particular with Cardinals Bellarmine, Araceli, San Eusebio, Bonzi, and d'Ascoli.

Q: Tell in detail what you treated of with the said cardinals.

A: The occasion of dealing with the said cardinals was that they wished to be informed of the doctrine of Copernicus, his being a very difficult book to understand for those not of the mathematical and astronomical profession; and in particular they wanted to know the arrangement of the celestial orbs under the Copernican hypothesis, etc.

Q: You say you came to Rome to be able to have the truth about the said matter; say also what was the outcome of this business.

A: Concerning the controversy that went on about the said opinion of the stability of the sun and motion of the earth it was determined by the Holy Congregation of the Index that such an opinion, taken absolutely, is repugnant to Holy Scripture, and it is only to be admitted hypothetically, the way in which Copernicus took it.

Q: Were you then notified of the said decision, and by whom?

A: I was notified of the said decision of the Congregation of the Index, and I was notified by Cardinal Bellarmine.

Q: What were you told of the said decision by his Eminence Bellarmine, and did anyone else speak to you about it, and what?

A: Cardinal Bellarmine informed me that the said opinion of Copernicus could be held hypothetically, as Copernicus held it; and his Eminence knew that I held it hypothetically, that is, in the way Copernicus held it, as may be seen from the same cardinal's reply to a letter of Father Paolo Antonio Foscarini, of which I have a copy and in which are these words: "It appears to me that your Reverence and Signor Galileo did wisely to content yourselves to speak hypothetically and not absolutely," and this letter of the said cardinal is under date of 12 April 1615.

Q: What decision was made and then notified to you in the month of February, 1616?

A: In the month of February, 1616, Cardinal Bellarmine told me that since the opinion of Copernicus absolutely taken contradicted the Holy Scriptures it could not be held or defended, but that it might be taken hypothetically and made use of. In conformity with this I have an affidavit of the same Cardinal Bellarmine, made in the month of May, on the 26th, 1616, in which he says that the opinion of Copernicus cannot be held or defended, because of its being against the Holy Scriptures, of which affidavit I present a copy, and here it is.

Stillman Drake, *Galileo at Work*, Chicago: University of Chicago Press, 1978, pp. 344–47.

Document 7: Kepler Praises Galileo

The astronomer Johannes Kepler was a keen observer of celestial phenomena and just as competent in astronomical calculations. He eagerly read Galileo's work on the solar system, The Sidereal Messenger, *and felt moved to write Galileo. In this letter, written about 1610, he praises Galileo's discoveries, but also emphasizes his own work.*

I may perhaps seem rash in accepting your claims so readily with no support from my own experience. But why should I not believe a most learned mathematician, whose very style attests the soundness of his judgment? He has no intention of practicing deception in a bid for vulgar publicity, nor does he pretend to have seen what he has not seen. Because he loves the truth, he does not hesitate to oppose even the most familiar opinions, and to bear the jeers of the crowd with equanimity. Does he not make his writings public, and could he possibly hide any villainy that might be perpetrated? Shall I disparage him, a gentleman of Florence, for the things he has seen? Shall I with my poor vision disparage him with his keen sight? Shall he with his equipment of optical instruments be disparaged by me, who must use my naked eyes because I lack these aids? Shall I not have confidence in him, when he invites everybody to see the same sights, and what is of supreme importance, even offers his own instrument in order to gain support on the strength of observations?

Or would it be a trifling matter for him to mock the family of the Grand Dukes of Tuscany, and to attach the name of the Medici to figments of his imagination, while he promises real planets?

Why is it that I find part of the book verified by my own experience and also by the affirmations of others? Is there any reason why the author should have thought of misleading the world with regard to only four planets?

Three months ago the Most August Emperor raised various questions with me about the spots on the moon. He was convinced that the images of countries and continents are reflected in the moon as though in a mirror. He asserted in particular that Italy with its two adjacent islands seemed to him to be distinctly outlined. He even offered his glass for the examination of these spots on subsequent days, but this was not done. Thus at that very same time, Galileo, when you cherished the abode of Christ our Lord above the mere appellation [of a Galilean], you vied in your favorite occupation with the ruler of Christendom (actuated by the same restless spirit of inquiry into nature).

But this story of the spots in the moon is also quite ancient. It is supported by the authority of Pythagoras and Plutarch, the eminent philosopher who also, if this detail helps the cause, governed Epirus with the power of a proconsul under the Caesars. I say nothing about Mästlin and my treatise on "Optics," published six years ago; these I shall take up later on in their proper place.

Such assertions about the body of the moon are made by others on the basis of mutually self-supporting evidence. Their conclusions agree with the highly illuminating observations which you report on the same subject. Consequently I have no basis for questioning the rest of your book and the four satellites of Jupiter. I should rather wish that I now had a telescope at hand, with which

I might anticipate you in discovering two satellites of Mars (as the relationship seems to me to require) and six or eight satellites of Saturn, with one each perhaps for Venus and Mercury.

For this search, so far as Mars is concerned, the most propitious time will be next October, which will show Mars in opposition to the sun and (except for the year 1608) nearest to the earth, with the error in the predicted position exceeding 3°.

Johannes Kepler, *Kepler's Conversation with Galileo's* Sidereal Messenger, Edward Rosen (trans), New York: Johnson Reprint Corporation, 1965, pp. 12–15.

Document 8: Francis Bacon's Ideal Research Center

In his unfinished novel New Atlantis, *excerpted here, Francis Bacon tells a story of a group of Englishmen shipwrecked on a mysterious island. The island is governed according to the principles of Bacon's scientific ideas. Here, one of the rulers of the island describes the island's laboratories to the outsiders. The description is a prototype of the modern scientific research center, complete with laboratories, space for breeding animals, and even chambers to create artificial weather.*

"God bless thee, my son; I will give thee the greatest jewel I have. For I will impart unto thee, for the love of God and men, a relation of the true state of Salomon's House. Son, to make you know the true state of Salomon's House, I will keep this order. First, I will set forth unto you the end of our foundation. Secondly, the preparations and instruments we have for our works. Thirdly, the several employments and functions whereto our fellows are assigned. And fourthly, the ordinances and rites which we observe.

"The end of our foundation is the knowledge of causes, and secret motions of things; and the enlarging of the bounds of human empire, to the effecting of all things possible.

"The preparations and instruments are these: We have large and deep caves of several depths; the deepest are sunk 600 fathoms; and some of them are digged and made under great hills and mountains; so that if you reckon together the depth of the hill and the depth of the cave, they are, some of them, above three miles deep. For we find that the depth of a hill and the depth of a cave from the flat are the same thing; both remote alike from the sun and heaven's beams, and from the open air. These caves we call the lower region. And we use them for all coagulations, indurations, refrigerations, and conservations of bodies. We use them likewise for the imitation of natural mines and the producing also of new artificial metals, by compositions and materials which we use and lay there for many years. We use them also sometimes (which may seem strange) for curing of some diseases, and for prolongation of life, in some hermits that choose to live there, well accommodated of all things necessary, and indeed live very long; by whom also we learn many things.

"We have burials in several earths, where we put divers cements, as the Chinese do their porcelain. But we have them in greater variety, and some of them more fine. We also have great variety of composts and soils, for the making of the earth fruitful.

"We have high towers, the highest about half a mile in height, and some of them likewise set upon high mountains, so that the vantage of the hill with the tower is in the highest of them three miles at least. And these places we call the upper region, account the air between the high places and the low as a middle region. We use these towers, according to their several heights and situations, for insulation, refrigeration, conservation, and for the view of divers meteors—as winds, rain, snow, hail, and some of the fiery meteors also. And upon them in some places are dwellings of hermits, whom we visit sometimes and instruct what to observe.

"We have great lakes, both salt and fresh, whereof we have use for the fish and fowl. We use them also for burials of some natural bodies, for we find a difference in things buried in earth, or in air below the earth, and things buried in water. We have also pools, of which some do strain fresh water out of salt, and others by art do turn fresh water into salt. We have also some rocks in the midst of the sea, and some bays upon the shore for some works, wherein are required the air and vapor of the sea. We have likewise violent streams and cataracts, which serve us for many motions; and likewise engines for multiplying and enforcing of winds to set also on divers motions.

"We have also a number of artificial wells and fountains, made in imitation of the natural sources and baths, as tincted upon vitriol, sulphur, steel, brass, lead, nitre, and other minerals; and again, we have little wells for infusions of many things, where the waters take the virtue quicker and better than in vessels or basins. And among them we have a water, which we call water of paradise, being by that we do it made very sovereign for health and prolongation of life.

"We have also great and spacious houses, where we imitate and demonstrate meteors—as snow, hail, rain, some artificial rains of bodies and not of water, thunders, lightnings; also generations of bodies in air—as frogs, flies, and divers others.

"We have also certain chambers, which we call chambers of health, where we qualify the air as we think good and proper for the cure of divers diseases and preservation of health.

"We have also fair and large baths, of several mixtures, for the cure of diseases, and the restoring of man's body from arefaction [dryness]; and others for the confirming of it in strength of sinews, vital parts, and the very juice and substance of the body.

"We have also large and various orchards and gardens, wherein we do not so much respect beauty as variety of ground and soil, proper for divers trees and herbs, and some very spacious, where trees and berries are set, whereof we make divers kinds of drinks, beside the vineyards. In these we practise likewise all conclusions of grafting, and inoculating, as well of wild-trees as fruit-trees, which produceth many effects. And we make by art, in the same orchards and gardens, trees and flowers, to come earlier or later than their seasons, and to come up and bear more speedily than by their natural course they do. We make them also by art greater much than their nature; and their fruit greater and sweeter, and of differing taste, smell, color, and figure, from their nature. And many of them we so order as that they become of medicinal use.

"We have also means to make divers plants rise by mixtures of earths without seeds, and likewise to make divers new plants, differing from the vulgar, and to make one tree or plant turn into another.

"We have also parks, and enclosures of all sorts, of beasts and birds; which we use not only for view or rareness, but likewise for dissections and trials, that thereby may take light what may be wrought upon the body of man. Wherein we find many strange effects: as continuing life in them, though divers parts, which you account vital, be perished and taken forth; resuscitating of some that seem dead in appearance, and the like. We try also all poisons, and other medicines upon them, as well of chirurgery [surgery] as physic. By art likewise we make them greater or smaller than their kind is, and contrariwise dwarf them and stay their growth; we make them more fruitful and bearing than their kind is, and contrariwise barren and not generative. Also we make them differ in color, shape, activity, many ways. We find means to make commixtures and copulations of divers kinds, which have produced many new kinds, and them not barren, as the general opinion is. We make a number of kinds of serpents, worms, flies, fishes of putrefaction, whereof some are advanced (in effect) to be perfect creatures, like beasts or birds, and have sexes, and do propagate.

Neither do we this by chance, but we know beforehand of what matter and commixture, what kind of those creatures will arise.

"We have also particular pools where we make trials upon fishes, as we have said before of beasts and birds.

"We have also places for breed and generation of those kinds of worms and flies which are of special use; such as are with you your silkworms and bees.

Document 9: True Knowledge Comes from Experience

The French philosopher René Descartes spent his early adult life wandering around Europe, "storing up experiences." He took this course because he was disappointed in his early education, which was based strictly on book learning. In his Discourse on Method *(1637), he explains his idea of how knowledge should be acquired.*

As soon as my age permitted me to leave the supervision of my teachers, I gave up entirely the study of letters. And, resolving to search for no knowledge but that which could be found in myself, or in the great book of the world, I used the rest of my youth to travel, to see courts and armies, to frequent people of differing dispositions and conditions, to store up various experiences, to prove myself in the encounters with which fortune confronted me, and everywhere to reflect upon the things that occurred, so that I could derive some profit from them. For it seemed to me that I might discover much more truth in each man's reasoning about affairs that are important to him, in whose aftermath he will suffer if he has judged badly, than in the thoughts of a man of letters in his study, concerning speculations which produce no effect and are of no consequence to him—except perhaps that the further they are removed from common sense, the more vanity he derives from them, because he will have to use that much more intelligence and craft to try to render them plausible. And I always had an extreme desire to learn to distinguish the true from the false, in order to see clearly in my actions, and walk with confidence in this life.

It is true that while I was doing nothing but considering the mores of other men, I found nothing there to satisfy me, and that I noted almost as much diversity there as I had before among the opinions of philosophers. So that the greatest benefit I derived was that, seeing many things which were commonly accepted and approved by other great peoples, although they seemed extravagant and ridiculous to us, I learned to have no very firm belief in any-thing that had been taught to me only by example and custom; and so I was delivered little by little from many errors, which can obscure our natural light, and render us less capable of listening to reason. But after I had thus spent some years studying the book of the world, and trying to acquire some experience, one day I resolved also to study within myself, and to use all the forces of my mind to choose the roads I should follow. In this I succeeded much better, it seems to me, than if I had never left either my country or my books.

René Descartes, *Discourse on Method, Optics, Geometry, and Meteorology*, Paul J. Olscamp (trans), Indianapolis: Bobbs-Merrill and Co., 1965, pp. 6–10.

Document 10: Boyle's Experiments on Sound in a Vacuum

Robert Boyle was the founder of modern chemistry. In this experiment conducted in 1660 he uses a pump device that he invented to create a vacuum in a glass jar. He uses this vacuum to test whether sound is transmitted by air.

That the air is the medium, whereby sounds are conveyed to the ear, hath been for many ages, and is yet the common doctrine of the schools. But this received opinion hath been of late opposed by some philosophers upon the account of an experiment made by the industrious [Athanasius] Kircher, and other learned men; who have (as they assure us) observed, that if a bell, with a steel clapper, be so fastened to the inside of a tube, that upon the making the experiment *de vacuo* [in a vacuum] with that tube, the bell remained suspended in the deserted space at the upper end of the tube: and if also a vigorous load-stone be applied on the outside of the tube to the bell, it will attract the clapper, which, upon the removal of the load-stone falling back, will strike against the opposite side of the bell, and thereby produce a very audible sound; whence divers have concluded, that it is not the air, but some more subtle body, that is the medium of sounds. But because we conceived, that, to invalidate such a consequence from this ingenious experiment, (though the most luciferous that could well be made without some such engine as ours) some things might be speciously enough alledged; we thought fit to make a trial or two, in order to the discovery of what the air doth in conveying of sounds, reserving divers other experiments triable in our engine concerning sounds, till we can obtain more leisure to prosecute them. Conceiving it then the best way to make our trial with such a noise, as might not be loud enough to make it difficult to discern slighter variations in it, but rather might be, both lasting (that we might take notice by what degrees it decreased) and so small, that it could not grow much weaker without becoming imperceptible; we took a watch, whose case we opened, that the contained air might have free egress into that of the receiver. And this watch was suspended in the cavity of the vessel only by a pack-thread, as the unlikeliest thing to convey a sound to the top of the receiver; and then closing up the vessel with melted plaister, we listened near the sides of it, and plainly enough heard the noise made by the balance. [Boyle clearly recognized the importance of controlling the conditions in an experiment. The method of supporting the source of the noise at first sight appears irrelevant. On further reflection, however, it is clear that the sound might be transmitted through this support. If so, a thread seemed less likely to convey sound than a metal or wooden support. To make sure that a watch so suspended by a thread in air could still be heard, Boyle proceeded to determine whether he could hear the watch *before* he pumped out the air.] Those also of us, that watched for that circumstance, observed, that the noise seemed to come directly in a streight line from the watch unto the ear. And it was observable to this purpose, that we found a manifest disparity of noise, by holding our ears near the sides of the receiver, and near the cover of it: which difference seemed to proceed from that of the texture of the glass, from the structure of the cover (and the cement) through which the sound was propagated from the watch to the ear. But let us prosecute our experiment [that is, let us start pumping the air out of the receiver in which the watch is suspended by a thread]. The pump after this being employed, it seemed, that from time to time the sound grew fainter and fainter; so that when the receiver was emptied as much as it used to be for the foregoing experiments, neither we, nor some strangers, that chanced to be then in the room, could, by applying our ears to the very sides, hear any noise from within; though we could easily perceive, that by the moving of the hand, which marked the second minutes, and by that of the balance, that the watch neither stood still, nor remarkably varied from its wonted motion. And to satisfy ourselves farther, that it was indeed the absence of the air about the watch, that hindered us from hearing it, we let in the external air at the stop-cock; and then though we turned the key and stopt the valve, yet we could plainly hear the noise made by the balance, though we held our ears sometimes at two foot distance from the outside of the receiver; and this experiment being reiterated into another place, succeeded after the like manner. Which seems to prove, that whether or no the air be the only, it is at least the principal medium of sounds.

"Boyle's Experiments on Air as a Medium for Transmitting Sound," in *Harvard Case Histories in Experimental Science*, James Bryant Conant et al., editors Cambridge, MA: Harvard University Press, 1957, pp. 30–32.

Document 11: Advice on Conducting Experiments

Robert Boyle was one of the first geniuses of experimentation, a so-called virtuoso. His use of apparatus and measurement pointed the way for future scientists. His writings describe his experiments in detail so others could repeat them; repetition of scientific findings would become a core requirement for scientific proof. In this excerpt from New Experiments Physico-Mechanical, *the First Continuation (1669) he gives some advice on scientific technique to his readers.*

About the Making of Mercurial and other Gauges, whereby to Estimate How the Receiver is Exhausted

Because the air being invisible, it is not always easy to know whether it be sufficiently pumped out of the receiver that was to be exhausted, we thought it would be very convenient to have some instrument within the receiver that might serve for a gauge or standard, whereby to judge whether or no it were sufficiently exhausted.

To this purpose divers expedients were thought on, and some of them put in practice; which, though not equally commodious, may yet all of them be usefully employed, one on this occasion, and another on that.

The first (if I misremember not) that I proposed was a bladder (which may be greater or less, according to the size of the vessel it is to serve for) to be very strongly tied at the neck, after having had only so much air left in the folds of it as may serve to blow up the bladder to its full dimensions, when the receiver is very well exhausted, and not before. But though . . . I yet make use of small bladders on certain occasions, in which they are peculiarly convenient, yet in many cases they do, when the glasses are well exhausted, take up too much room in them, and hinder the objects included in the receiver from being observed from all sides of it.

Another sort of gauge was made with quicksilver poured into a very short pipe, which was afterwards inverted into a little glass of stagnant quicksilver, according to the manner of the Torricellian experiment. For this pipe being but a very few inches long the mercury in it would not begin to descend till a very great proportion of air was pumped out of the receiver; because till then the spring of the remaining air would be strong enough to be able to keep up so short a cylinder of mercury. And this kind of gauge is no bad one. But because, to omit some other little inconveniences, it cannot easily be suspended (which in divers experiments it is fit the gauge should be) and the mercury in it is apt to be too much shaken by the motion of the engine, there was another kind of gauge by some ingenious man (whoever he were) substituted in its place, consisting of a kind of siphon whose shorter leg hath belonging to it a large bubble of glass, most commonly made use of at an illustrious meeting of virtuosi. . . .

But none of the gauges I had formerly used, nor even this last, having the conveniences that some of my experiments require, I was fain to devise another, which is that I most make use of, as having advantages, some or other of which each of the gauges already mentioned wants. . . .

To make the gauge we are speaking of, take a very slender and cylindrical pipe of glass of six, eight, ten, or more inches in length, and not so big as a goose-quill (but such as we employ for the stems of sealed weather-glasses) and having at the flame of a lamp melted it, but not too near the middle, to make of it by bending it a siphon, whose two legs are to be not only parallel to one another, but as little distant anywhere from one another as conveniently may be. In one (which is usually the longer of these legs) there is to be left at the top either half an inch or a whole inch, or more or less than either (according to the length of the gauge or the scope of the experimenter) of air in its natural state, neither rarefied nor condensed; the rest of the longer leg, and as great a part of the shorter as shall be thought fit, being to be filled with quicksilver. This done there may be marks placed at the outside of the longer or sealed leg, whereby to measure the expansion of the air included in the same leg; and these marks may be either little glass knobs about the bigness of pins heads, fastened by the help of a lamp at certain distances to the longer leg of the siphon, or else the divisions of an inch made on a list of paper and pasted on, either to the siphon itself, or to the slender frame which on some occasions we fasten the gauge to.

This instrument being conveyed into a receiver (which for expedition sake we choose as small as will serve the turn) the air is to be very diligently pumped out, and then notice is to be taken to what part of the gauge the mercury is depressed, that we may know, when we shall afterwards see the mercury driven so far, that the receiver the gauge is placed in, is well exhausted.

"Some Considerations of Experimental Technique," in Marie Boas Hall, *Robert Boyle on Natural Philosophy: An Essay with Selections from His Writings*. Bloomington: Indiana University Press, 1965, pp. 385–89.

Document 12: Newton's Discovery of the Spectrum of Light

Isaac Newton experimented with prisms (pieces of solid glass cut into triangle shapes) in order to discover the nature of light. In the three experiments published in his Opticks *in 1704 but probably first carried out in the early 1670s, he discovers that sunlight forms a spectrum (or rainbow-colored image) when passed through a prism. He carefully notes the size of the image and how it is stretched by the prism, and he notes the angle each color of light makes with the prism. In this way, he proves by experiment that different colors of light bend at different angles when they pass through a prism.*

The Light of the Sun consists of Rays differently Refrangible.

The PROOF by Experiments.

Exper. 3.

In a very dark Chamber, at a round Hole, about one third Part of an Inch broad, made in the Shut of a Window, I placed a Glass Prism, whereby the Beam of the Sun's Light, which came in at that Hole, might be refracted upwards toward the opposite Wall of the Chamber, and there form a colour'd Image of the Sun. The Axis of the Prism (that is, the Line passing through the middle of the Prism from one end of it to the other end parallel to the edge of the Refracting Angle) was in this and the following Experiments perpendicular to the incident Rays. About this Axis I turned the Prism slowly, and saw the refracted Light on the Wall, or coloured Image of the Sun, first to descend, and then to ascend. Between the Descent and Ascent, when the Image seemed Stationary, I stopp'd the Prism, and fix'd it in that Posture, that it should be moved no more. For in that Posture the Refractions of the Light at the two Sides of the refracting Angle, that is, at the Entrance of the Rays into the Prism, and at their going out of it, were equal to one another. . . . The Prism therefore being placed in this Posture, I let the refracted Light fall perpendicularly upon a Sheet of white Paper at the opposite Wall of the Chamber, and observed the Figure and Dimensions of the Solar Image formed on the Paper by that Light. This Image was Oblong and not Oval, but terminated with two Rectilinear and Parallel Sides, and two Semicircular Ends. On its Sides it was bounded pretty distinctly, but on its Ends very confusedly and indistinctly, the Light there decaying and vanishing by degrees. The Breadth of this Image answered to the Sun's Diameter, and was about two Inches and the eighth Part of an Inch, including the Penumbra. For the Image was eighteen Feet and an half distant from the Prism, and at this distance that Breadth, if diminished by the Diameter of the Hole in the Window-shut, that is by a quarter of an Inch, subtended an Angle at the Prism of about half a Degree, which is the Sun's apparent Diameter. But the Length of the Image was about ten Inches and a quarter, and the Length of the Rectilinear Sides about eight Inches; and the refracting Angle of the Prism, whereby so great a Length was made, was 64 degrees. With a less Angle the Length of the Image was less, the Breadth remaining the same. If the Prism was turned about its Axis that way which made the Rays emerge more obliquely out of the second refracting Surface of the Prism, the Image soon became an Inch or two longer, or more; and if the Prism was turned about the contrary way, so as to make the Rays fall more obliquely on the first refracting Surface, the Image soon became an Inch or two shorter. And therefore in trying this Experiment, I was as curious as I could be in placing the Prism by the above-mention'd Rule exactly in such a Posture, that the Refractions of the Rays at their Emergence out of the Prism might be equal to that at their Incidence on it. This Prism had some Veins running along within the Glass from one end to the other, which scattered some of the Sun's Light irregularly, but had no sensible Effect in increasing the Length of the coloured Spectrum.

Isaac Newton, *Opticks*. New York: Dover Publications, 1952, pp. 26–35.

Document 13: Newton's Dispute with Huygens

Isaac Newton engaged in a running dispute with the Dutch astronomer and optics expert Christiaan Huygens. Newton had written that white sunlight could be separated by a prism into all the colors of the rainbow (red, orange, yellow, green, blue, violet). Huygens doubted that white light was composed of as many colors as Newton claimed. Newton responds to the criticism here in a letter of 1673, written to the Royal Society of London's secretary, Henry Oldenburg.

It seems to me that M. Hugens takes an improper way of examining the nature of colours whilst he proceeds upon compounding those that are already compounded, as he doth in the former part of his letter. Perhaps he would sooner satisfy himself by resolving light into colours as far as may be done by Art, and then by examining the properties of those colours apart, and afterwards by trying the effects of reconjoyning two or more or all of those, & lastly by separating them again to examin wt changes that reconjunction had wrought in them. This will prove a tedious & difficult task to do it as it ought to be done but I could not be satisfied till I had gone through it. However I onely propound it, and leave every man to his own method.

As to the contents of his letter I conceive my former answer to the Quære about the number of colours is sufficient, wch was to this effect, that all colours cannot practically be derived out of Yellow & Blew, & consequently that those Hypotheses are fals wch imply they may. If you ask wt colours cannot be derived out of Yellow & Blew, I answer none of those wch I defined to be originall and if he can show by experiment how they may I will acknowledg my self in an error. Nor is it easier to frame an Hypothesis by assuming onely two originall colours rather then an indefinite variety, unless it be easier to suppose that there are but two figures sizes & degrees of velocity or force of the æthereal corpuscles or pulses rather then an indefinite variety, wch certainly would be a very harsh supposition. No man wonders at the indefinite variety of waves of the sea or of sands on the Shore, but were they all of but two sizes it would be a very puzzeling phænomenon. And I should think it as unaccountable if the severall parts or corpuscles of which a shining body consists, wch must be supposed of various figures sizes and motions, should impress but two sorts of motion on the adjacent æthereall Medium, or any other way beget but two sorts of rays. But to examin how colours may be thus explained Hypothetically is besides my purpose. I never intended to show wherein consists the nature and difference of colours, but onely to show that *de facto* they are originall & immutable qualities of the rays wch exhibit them, & to leave it to others to explicate by Mechanicall Hypotheses the nature & difference of those qualities; wch I take to be no very difficult matter. But I would not be understood as if their difference consisted in the different refrangibility of those rays. For that different refrangibility conduces to their production no otherwise then by separating the rays whose qualities they are. Whence it is that the same rays exhibit the same colours when separated by any other meanes; as by their different reflexibility; a quality not yet discoursed of.

Isaac Newton, *The Correspondence of Isaac Newton*, Vol 1 1661–1675. H.W. Turnbull editor. Cambridge, UK: Cambridge University Press, 1959, pp. 264–65.

Document 14: Newton's Three Laws of Motion

Isaac Newton's famous three laws of motion created the modern science of mechanics. Newton starts his Principia Mathematica *(1697) with these three axioms, or starting points. In them, he develops a system that unites the motion of the planets with the motion of falling objects here on earth.*

AXIOMS, OR
LAWS OF MOTION
LAW I

Every body continues in its state of rest, or of uniform motion in a right line, unless it is compelled to change that state by forces impressed upon it.

PROJECTILES continue in their motions, so far as they are not retarded by the resistance of the air, or impelled downwards by the force of gravity. A top, whose parts by their cohesion are continually drawn aside from rectilinear motions, does not cease its rotation, otherwise than as it is retarded by the air. The greater bodies of the planets and comets, meeting with less resistance in freer spaces, preserve their motions both progressive and circular for a much longer time.

LAW II

The change of motion is proportional to the motive force impressed; and is made in the direction of the right line in which that force is impressed.

If any force generates a motion, a double force will generate double the motion, a triple force triple the motion, whether that force be impressed altogether and at once, or gradually and successively. And this motion (being always directed the same way with the generating force), if the body moved before, is added to or subtracted from the former motion, according as they directly conspire with or are directly contrary to each other; or obliquely joined, when they are oblique, so as to produce a new motion compounded from the determination of both.

LAW III

To every action there is always opposed an equal reaction: or, the mutual actions of two bodies upon each other are always equal, and directed to contrary parts.

Whatever draws or presses another is as much drawn or pressed by that other. If you press a stone with your finger, the finger is also pressed by the stone. If a horse draws a stone tied to a rope, the horse (if I may so say) will be equally drawn back towards the stone; for the distended rope, by the same endeavor to relax or unbend itself, will draw the horse as much towards the stone as it does the stone towards the horse, and will obstruct the progress of the one as much as it advances that of the other. If a body impinge upon another, and by its force change the motion of the other, that body also (because of the equality of the mutual pressure) will undergo an equal change, in its own motion, towards the contrary part. The changes made by these actions are equal, not in the velocities but in the motions of bodies; that is to say, if the bodies are not hindered by any other impediments. For, because the motions are equally changed, the changes of the velocities made towards contrary parts are inversely proportional to the bodies. This law takes place also in attractions, as will be proved in the next Scholium.

Isaac Newton, "Axioms, or Laws of Motion," in *Mathematical Principles of Natural Philosophy and His System of the World*, Vol 1. (trans) Andrew Motte (1729) (rev) Florian Cajori, Berkeley: University of California Press, 1966, pp. 13–14.

Document 15: A Rival Challenges Newton's Claim to the Discovery of the Law of Gravity

A rival scientist, Robert Hooke, claimed that he was the first to have discovered the law of gravity. Hooke was a great experimenter but did not have the mathematical skills that Newton had. It is likely, therefore, that Newton did in fact first work out the mathematics of gravity. In a letter of 1686, the astronomer Edmond Halley compliments Newton on his discovery, but also warns Newton of the controversy.

"Sir,

"Your incomparable treatise, entitled Philosophiæ Naturalis Principia Mathematica, was by Dr. Vincent presented to the Royal Society on the 28th past; and they were so very sensible of the great honour you do them by your dedication, that they immediately ordered you their most hearty thanks, and that a council should be summoned to consider about the printing thereof; but by reason of the president's attendance upon the King, and the absence of our vice-presidents, whom the good weather has drawn out of town, there has not since been any authentic council to resolve what to do in the matter: so that on Wednesday last the Society, in their meeting, judging that so excellent a work ought not to have its publication any longer delayed, resolved to print it at their own charge in a large quarto of a fair letter; and that this their resolution should be signified to you, and your opinion therein be desired, that so it might be gone about with all speed. I am intrusted to look after the printing it, and will take care that it shall be performed as well as possible; only I would first have your directions in what you shall think necessary for the embellishing thereof, and particularly whether you think it not better, that the schemes should be enlarged, which is the opinion of some here: but what you signify as your desire shall be punctually observed.

"There is one thing more that I ought to inform you of, viz. that Mr. Hooke has some pretensions upon the invention of the rule of the decrease of gravity being reciprocally as the squares of the distances from the centre. He says you had the notion from him, though he owns the demonstration of the curves generated thereby to be wholly your own. How much of this is so, you know best, as likewise what you have to do in this matter; only Mr. Hooke seems to expect you should make some mention of him in the preface, which tis possible you may see reason to prefix. I must beg your pardon, that tis I that send you this ungrateful account; but I thought it my duty to let you know it, that so you might act accordingly, being in myself fully satisfied, that nothing but the greatest candour imaginable is to be expected from a person, who has of all men the least need to borrow reputation.

David Brewster, *Memoirs of the Life, Writings and Discoveries of Sir Isaac Newton*, Vol I. New York: Johnson Reprint Corporation. 1965, pp. 438–39.

Document 17: Early Scientists Question an Englishman in the Middle East

Henry Oldenburg was the secretary of the Royal Society of London, the first and most influential of the scientific associations. As such, he frequently wrote letters to foreigners or Englishmen abroad about all manner of things. Here in a letter of 1668, Oldenburg asks for information from an English doctor in Aleppo (in what is now Syria).

You will easily gather from this, learned Sir, what we wish you and others like you to continue to do. For we wish you to investigate prudently and attentively all things in the Earth, below the Earth, and in the heavens; the air, meteors, and the stars; rivers, seas, lakes; animals, vegetables, and minerals. Nothing should be left unexplored, and wherever you turn you should register your observations and experiments faithfully and accurately; and, when it seems good to you, freely transmit your contribution to this Royal Society, for which we prophesy an enduring future, God willing, because of the strength and genius of its foundation, and a continuing welcome for the labors of experts of all sorts in any corner of the Earth. Among them they keep public Registers; it is the duty of the two secretaries, under solemn oath, to enter in them all those matters which are furnished, observed, and communicated by the Fellows of the Society, or by the philosophers and wise or expert men of other nations, as a perpetual record devoted to the honor of those individuals whose talents and industry deserve it. Therefore when you ask in your letter, excellent Sir, to be informed how you may fit your work for our Society, here is set out for you the procedure of our Foundation, and here is a quite open field in which you along with many others can exercise your abilities and endowments to enrich the life of mankind. You may learn more completely of other aspects of our foundation from the *History of the Royal Society*, recently compiled in elegant language and published by Thomas Sprat.

It remains for me to set before you now those points of detail which come to mind at present as requiring your elucidation, if you will be so good:

1. What figured stones, or shells, etc. have been cast up in your parts by earthquakes? If there are any, we earnestly ask you to send us some samples of them.

2. Whether Mount Sinai is known ever to have been a volcano?

3. And whether there be any volcanoes in your parts, or near by?

4. Whether there are any indications, from which one may deduce that the Dead Sea vents itself anywhere, or has subterranean channels? And what minerals or earths are found near that Sea? If there are any, we beg you to send us some samples.

5. An accurate description of that sea is sought: What is the nature of it waters? What is their [specific] gravity? What bodies float in them, and what sink? What is the degree of their salinity and of what kind is the salt? Would it be worthwhile for some skilled Christians living near the Dead Sea or other inquisitive travelers to it, at your instigation, to examine the waters of the Dead Sea thoroughly, either by distillation or by evaporation, etc. and to send some quantity of the extracted salt to us?

6. Whether Aleppo be so much subject to shaking palsies, as some report?

7. What is the method of training pigeons to carry letters? How much distance do they normally cover in each hour? Does that custom of using pigeons to carry letters still prevail?

8. What is the most probable cause of the unhealthiness of the air at Alexandretta or Scanderoon?

9. Whether the frequent use of coffee ever causes apoplexy or paralysis?

10. Whether the steel of Damascus is a simple or compound metal? If simple, is its excellence due to the nature of the metal or

to the skill of the smiths in tempering it in a particular way? Also, where is the mine from which the the metal used for making that steel is dug?

11. What art do the Arabs use in feeding and training those remarkable horses of world-wide fame?

12. Whether Locusts are as common in your parts as formerly, and whether any remedy has been discovered that will prevent their foul swarming, or drive them away?

13. We desire you to send over some of those insects called *orba orbain*, which can be done conveniently either by putting them in burnt wine (called *Brandy*) or, which is much better, in rectified spirit of wine, well sealed in a glass.

14. Whether medicinal trees or shrubs are found in the Syrian mountains?

Henry Oldenburg, "Letter to Thomas Harpur," in *The Correspondence of Henry Oldenburg* (ed and trans A. Ruppert Hall and Marie Boas Hall) Volume IV, Madison: University of Wisconsin Press, 1967. pp. 422–24.

Glossary

alchemy: The mystical study of the "transmutation" of elements, especially of lead or other base metals into gold. The techniques of alchemy were used by early chemists.

arc: The distance of travel along a curve. This term is often used in describing planetary positions.

Aristotle (384–322 B.C.): Greek philosopher who emphasized empirical observation over the abstract philosophy of his teacher Plato. Aristotle's *Physics* heavily influenced the scholarly thought of the Middle Ages.

astrolabe: An instrument used to determine the position of the stars on any given date.

Francis Bacon (1561–1626): Early philosopher of science whose works explained inductive reasoning, the pursuit of knowledge through the compilation of numerous observations.

Roger Bacon (1214–1294): A monk whose ideas about the necessity of experimentation and observation anticipated the scientific revolution.

ballistics: The study of projectiles, such as cannonballs, in flight. This applied science led to developments in the theoretical study of motion.

Robert Boyle (1627–1691): English scientist known as the "Father of Chemistry." Boyle's wealth, inherited from his father, financed his laboratory and experiments, as well as the work of other scientists.

Tycho Brahe (1546–1601): Danish astronomer who improved the accuracy of astronomical observations, allowing more precise calculations of the motions of the planets.

conic sections: The shapes made by the intersection of a plane and a cone at various angles. Two of the shapes, the parabola and the ellipse, are important for understanding motion under the influence of gravity.

Nicolaus Copernicus (1473–1543): Polish astronomer whose heliocentric model of the universe led to the scientific revolution.

deduction: Reasoning based on logical argument from a few first principles, or axioms. Newtonian physics is deductive in that it is based on three laws.

deferent: In the Ptolemaic system, the large circular orbit along which planets or the center of their epicycles were thought to travel.

degree: 1/360th of the circumference of a circle.

ellipse: One of the conic sections; the oval shape that describes the planets' orbits.

empirical: Based on observation, either with unaided human senses or with the aid of instruments.

English Revolution (1640–1660): The period of political upheaval in England that culminated in the overthrow and beheading of King Charles I. The revolution took place during the beginnings of English science.

epicycle: In the Ptolemaic system, a small circular orbit along which planets were thought to travel.

Galileo Galilei (1564–1642): Italian astronomer and mathematician whose use of the telescope in astronomy confirmed the truth of the Copernican system.

geocentric: Earth-centered. The Ptolemaic system was a geocentric system; the sun, moon, and planets were believed to revolve around Earth, which was thought to be the center of the solar system.

heliocentric: Sun-centered. The Copernican system was radical because it was heliocentric.

Christiaan Huygens (1629–1695): A Dutch scientist and rival of Isaac Newton.

induction: Scientific reasoning based on insight gained from numerous observations of either nature (as in astronomy) or experiments (as in chemistry).

Johannes Kepler (1571–1630): German astronomer who determined that planets travel in elliptical orbits; he also discovered that the speed of travel of a planet is related to its distance from the sun.

mechanics: The study of objects in motion.

minute: 1/60th of a degree.

Isaac Newton (1642–1727): Perhaps the greatest scientist of the scientific revolution. Newton's laws united the study of motion on Earth, such as ballistics, with the study of the motions of the planets.

Henry Oldenburg (1618–1677): The secretary of the Royal Society. He helped communicate scientific ideas between England and Europe.

Paracelsus (1493–1541): Swiss physician and alchemist whose teachings influenced scientific chemistry and medicine.

paradigm: A framework of thought in which scientists normally work.

paradigm shift: A rapid and radical change in the direction of a given science caused by an accumulation of evidence that cannot be accounted for by the existing scientific paradigm.

philosopher's stone: A mythical substance sought by the alchemists that was believed to have the power to turn lead into gold.

prism: A clear object, generally glass, cut into a triangular shape.

Ptolemy (ca. 85–ca. 165): Greek astronomer who was considered the authority on heavenly motion until the Copernican revolution.

quadrant: An instrument used to measure the angle at which various heavenly objects appear in the sky.

refraction: The bending of light when it passes through glass or another transparent medium.

Renaissance (ca. 1350–1550): The period of history after the Middle Ages said to be a time of "rebirth" of the spirit of humanism and inquiry that characterized the ancient world.

Restoration (1660–1700): The period in English history after the English Revolution when the monarchy was restored. English science began to develop rapidly in this period under the patronage of King Charles II.

Royal Society: A society founded in 1660 to promote the "new experimental science."

spectrum: The colors of the rainbow. White light can be "decomposed" into a spectrum by a prism.

Chronology

B.C.

530
The ancient Greek mathematician Pythagoras works out the formulas for the relationships between lengths of strings (as in a violin) and musical pitch.

ca. 440
Democritus proposes the concept of the atom.

360–323
Aristotle conducts "philosophical" investigations using empirical techniques.

ca. 240
Eratosthenes calculates the circumference of Earth.

A.D.

127–141
Claudius Ptolemy devises his geocentric system of astronomy.

1247–1257
Roger Bacon introduces alchemy and optics to Oxford University in England.

1514
Polish astronomer Nicolaus Copernicus circulates the *Commentariolus.*

1543
Copernicus publishes *De revolutionibus orbium coelestium* (*The Revolutions of the Heavenly Spheres*). He dies shortly thereafter.

1572
Danish astronomer Tycho Brahe observes a supernova in the constellation Cassiopeia. The star appears and then fades, thus challenging the belief in the unchanging nature of the heavens.

1583
Galileo Galilei discovers by experiment that the oscillations of a swinging pendulum take the same amount of time regardless of their amplitude.

1586

Galileo publishes work on experiments with the motion of bodies along inclined planes under the influence of gravity. His experiments allow him to "slow down" gravity's effect, allowing more accurate measures than experiments with free-falling objects.

1591

Galileo conducts his famous experiments on gravity. According to legend, he drops two weights, one ten times heavier than the other, from the Leaning Tower of Pisa. They both hit the ground at nearly the same time, proving wrong Aristotle's theory that heavier objects fall more quickly than lighter objects.

1596

German astronomer Johannes Kepler publishes *Mysterium Cosmographicum*, a mystical interpretation of the Copernican system.

1600

Kepler becomes Tycho's assistant in Tycho's observatory near Prague, Bohemia (now the Czech Republic).

1604

Kepler and many other astronomers witness the outburst of a supernova in the constellation Serpens. At its peak, it is as bright as Venus and then fades away over the next year. It is the last supernova seen in the Milky Way galaxy.

1605

Francis Bacon publishes *The Advancement of Learning*, in which he urges collaboration between the inductive and experimental methods of proof, as opposed to Scholasticism's a priori method.

1609

Galileo constructs his telescope; over time, he improves the magnification of the telescope from four to thirty times. Kepler publishes Tycho Brahe's calculation of the orbit of Mars, revealing his first and second laws of planetary motion.

1610

Galileo discovers Jupiter's four largest moons. The discovery is further proof that the Ptolemaic system is wrong and is published in *The Starry Messenger*.

1613

Galileo publishes his work on sunspots, and again, the medieval view that the heavenly bodies are "perfect" and unchanging is challenged.

1619

Kepler publishes *De cometis* (*On Comets*) and *Harmoniae mundi* (*The Harmonies of the World*); these contain his third law of planetary motion, which relates the size of the orbit to the time it takes for the planet to orbit the sun. On November 10, French mathematician René Descartes has three dreams that he considers critical inspiration for his work in analytic geometry.

1620

Francis Bacon publishes the *Novum Organum*, a milestone in the philosophy of science. Bacon argues that scientists must communicate their discoveries to each other, even when working in different fields.

1632

Galileo publishes *Dialogue Concerning the Two World Systems*, supporting Copernicus's view that the planets circle the sun.

1633

Galileo is prosecuted by the Inquisition in Rome and recants his views.

1635

The *Académie Française* is founded.

1637

Descartes publishes the *Discourse on Method*. Descartes's work sets out principles of reasoning deductively; that is, from a few first principles to a logical conclusion.

1638

Galileo publishes *Dialogues Concerning Two New Sciences*.

1642

Galileo dies. Isaac Newton is born.

1646

English scientists including Robert Boyle meet as the Invisible College to discuss natural philosophy. This secretive body will be superseded by the more open Royal Society.

1655

Dutch mathematician Christiaan Huygens develops a new method for grinding telescope lenses, making a more powerful telescope, with which he discovers one moon of Saturn and the rings of Saturn. His findings are published in 1659 in *Systema Saturnium*.

1659

Boyle develops an air pump for creating vacuums; confirms Galileo's view that bodies fall in a vacuum at the same rate, regardless of weight; and discovers that sound does not travel in a vacuum.

1660

Boyle publishes *New Experiments Physico-Mechanical Touching the Spring of the Air*, in which he states his laws of gases. The Royal Society of England is founded; three years later it gets a royal charter to further its mission of improving experimental science and communication among scientists.

1665

Newton graduates from Cambridge University.

1666

Newton develops calculus ("fluxions"); this invention was necessary to apply mathematics to the motions of the planets. Boyle publishes *Origin of Form and Qualities;* this treatise on chemistry is wrong on several points, but Boyle's experimental techniques point the way toward the future.

1672

Newton sends a brief exposition of his theory of colors to the Royal Society in London, which republishes it in the Royal Society's *Philosophical Transactions*, leading to criticism of Newton.

1679

English scientist Robert Hooke writes Newton suggesting that planets would travel in a straight line except for a constant diversion from this movement around a central point of attraction. Newton does not reply. Later, Hooke claims that he was the inspiration for Newton's theories of gravity and planetary motion.

1687

Newton publishes *Philosophiae Naturalis Principia Mathematica* (*Mathematical Principles of Natural Philosophy*), setting out his three laws of motion.

1688

Newton constructs the first reflecting telescope. This telescope, based on the idea that beams of light are concentrated by a concave mirror, avoids the distortions of color caused by lenses used in refracting telescopes.

1690

English philosopher John Locke publishes his *Essay Concerning Human Understanding*, which gives philosophical grounding for empirical science.

1704

Newton publishes *Opticks*. He starts with clearly stated axioms, or first principles, and derives a logical argument from these axioms. He then conducts empirical tests of the conclusions reached by logical argument.

1727

Isaac Newton dies. He is buried at Westminster Abbey in London.

For Further Research

Books

Wilbur Applebaum, *Encyclopedia of the Scientific Revolution: From Copernicus to Newton.* New York: Garland, 2000.

Marie Boas, *The Scientific Renaissance, 1450–1630.* London: Collins, 1962.

Rudolf Carnap, *Philosophical Foundations of Physics: An Introduction to the Philosophy of Science.* New York: Basic Books, 1966.

A.C. Crombie, *Augustine to Galileo.* London: Heinemann, 1979.

Giorgio De Santillana, *The Crime of Galileo.* London: Mercury, 1961.

Brian Easlea, *Witch Hunting, Magic, and the New Philosophy: An Introduction to Debates of the Scientific Revolution, 1450–1750.* Boston: Humanities, 1980.

Galileo Galilei and Maurice A. Finacchiaro, *Galileo on the World Systems: A New Abridged Translation and Guide.* Berkeley and Los Angeles: University of California Press, 1997.

Daniel Garber, *Descartes' Metaphysical Physics.* Chicago: University of Chicago Press, 1992.

Edward Grant, *Science and Religion, 400 B.C. to A.D. 1550: From Aristotle to Copernicus.* Westport, CT: Greenwood, 2004.

Marie Boas Hall, *Promoting Experimental Learning: Experiment and the Royal Society, 1660–1727.* New York: Cambridge University Press, 1991.

———, *Robert Boyle on Natural Philosophy: An Essay with Selections from His Writings.* Bloomington: Indiana University Press, 1965.

Kenneth J. Howell, *God's Two Books: Copernican Cosmology and Biblical Interpretation in Early Modern Science.* Notre Dame, IN: University of Notre Dame Press, 2002.

Lynette Hunter and Sarah M. Hutton, *Women, Science, and Medicine, 1500–1700: Mothers and Sisters of the Royal Society.* Thrupp, Stroud, Gloucestershire, UK: Sutton, 1997.

Margaret C. Jacob, *The Newtonians and the English Revolution, 1689–1720*. Ithaca, NY: Cornell University Press, 1976.

Hugh Francis Kearney, *Origins of the Scientific Revolution*. London: Longmans, 1964.

David C. Lindberg and Robert S. Westman, *Reappraisals of the Scientific Revolution*. Cambridge, UK: Cambridge University Press, 1990.

Carolyn Merchant, *The Death of Nature: Women, Ecology, and the Scientific Revolution*. London: Wildwood House, 1982.

Robert K. Merton, *Science, Technology, and Society in Seventeenth-Century England*. New York: Howard Fertig, 2002.

Isaac Newton, *Newton Texts, Backgrounds, Commentaries*. New York: W.W. Norton, 1995.

Marjorie Hope Nicolson, *Science and Imagination*. Hamden, CT: Archon, 1976.

William R. Shea, *The Magic of Numbers and Motion: The Scientific Career of René Descartes*. Canton, MA: Science History, 1991.

Charles Joseph Singer, *Greek Biology and Greek Medicine*. New York: AMS, 1979.

Charles Joseph Singer and Edgar Ashworth Underwood, *A Short History of Medicine*. Oxford: Clarendon, 1962.

Tom Sorell, *Descartes: A Very Short Introduction*. Oxford: Oxford University Press, 2000.

Richard S. Westfall, *Never at Rest: A Biography of Isaac Newton*. New York: Cambridge University Press, 1980.

Periodicals

Peter Abbs, "Descartes' Dreams," *Critical Survey*, vol. 5, no. 3, 1993.

Brian S. Baigrie, "The Justification of Kepler's Ellipse," *Studies in History and Philosophy of Science*, vol. 21, no. 4, 1990.

Mario Biagioli, "Galileo's System of Patronage," *History of Science*, March 1990.

Esther Cohen, "Towards a History of European Physical Sensibility: Pain in the Later Middle Ages," *Science in Context*, vol. 8, no. 1, 1995.

I. Bernard Cohen, "Scientific Revolution and Creativity in the Enlightenment," *Eighteenth-Century Life*, vol. 7, no. 2, 1982.

Richard Drayton, "Science and the European Empires," *Journal of Imperial and Commonwealth History*, September 1995.

Adrian Johns, "History, Science, and the History of the Book: The Making of Natural Philosophy in Early Modern England," *Publishing History*, vol. 30, 1991.

Alexander Koyre, "The Origin of Modern Science: A New Interpretation," *Diogenes*, Winter 1956.

Lance Morrow, "Isaac Newton (1642–1727)," *Time*, December 31, 1999.

Richard N. Ostling, "Galileo and Other Faithful Scientists," *Time*, December 28, 1992.

Adriaan Peperzak, "Life, Science, and Wisdom According to Descartes," *History of Philosophy Quarterly*, vol. 12, no. 2, 1995.

Katherine Rudolph, "Descartes' Discourse," *Philosophy Today*, Spring 1993.

A. Mark Smith, "Knowing Things Inside Out: The Scientific Revolution from a Medieval Perspective," *American Historical Review*, June 1990.

Edward Sorel, "First Encounters: Blaise Pascal and René Descartes," *Atlantic*, January 1991.

Melvin S. Steinberg, "Genius Is Not Immune to Persistent Misconceptions: Conceptual Difficulties Impeding Isaac Newton and Contemporary Physics Students," *International Journal of Science Education*, vol. 12, no. 3, 1990.

Pirmin Stekeler-Weithofer, "Plato and the Method of Science," *History of Philosophy Quarterly*, vol. 9, no. 4, 1992.

David Topper, "Newton on the Number of Colours in the Spectrum," *Studies in History and Philosophy of Science*, June 1990.

Internet Sources

David Banach, "Timeline of the Scientific Revolution." www.anselm.edu/homepage/dbanach/time1.htm. A philosophy professor's chronology of the scientific revolution. This is a quick way to orient oneself to the chronological order of the events of the period.

Robert A. Hatch, "The Scientific Revolution: Paradigm Lost?"

Scientific Revolution Homepage. http://web.clas.ufl.edu/users/rhatch/pages/03-Sci-Rev/SCI-REV-Home/08sr-htch.htm. An up-to-date, succinct essay by the editor of the Scientific Revolution Homepage.

Lisa Jardine, "Britain and the Rise of Science," 2002. www.bbc.co.uk/history/discovery/revolutions/jardineih_01.shtml. Outlines the social background of the scientific revolution in Britain, arguably the most important country in the early development of science.

Steven Kreis, "The Scientific Revolution, 1642–1730," History Guide Lectures on Early Modern European History, 2002. www.historyguide.org/earlymod/lecture12c.html. A concise lecture on the eighty-eight-year time period roughly coinciding with the life of Isaac Newton. The text contains useful links to other essays and sources at both the History Guide Web site and other sites.

PBS, "Faith and Reason." www.pbs.org/faithandreason/intro/histo-body.html. An essay accompanying the Public Broadcasting System's production *Faith and Reason*, this site highlights the connection between religious belief and science that was an important feature of early scientific thought.

Murray N. Rothbard, "The Mantle of Science," Ludwig von Mises Institute. www.mises.org/rothbard/mantle.asp. Argues that humans and society cannot be understood using the techniques of the natural sciences; social sciences must develop their own theories and methods.

Eric Weisstein, "World of Scientific Biography: Isaac Newton." http://scienceworld.wolfram.com/biography/Newton.html. A good concise biography of Newton, with an emphasis on his achievements in mathematics. The site contains many links to biographies of other scientists and pages about scientific and mathematical concepts.

Richard S. Westfall, "The Scientific Revolution," 1989, Scientific Revolution Homepage. http://web.clas.ufl.edu/users/rhatch/pages/03-Sci-Rev/SCI-REV-Home/05-RSW-Sci-Rev.htm. A great source of summaries and bibliographic information about the most important books concerning the scientific revolution.

Web Sites

Internet Modern History Sourcebook: Scientific Revolution,

www.fordham.edu/halsall/mod/modsbook09.html. The best source for original documents of the scientific revolution. Here you can find links to excerpts from works by Galileo, Copernicus, Newton, and others. Most of the excerpts are preceded by a short introduction that gives critical background information.

Science Timeline, www.sciencetimeline.net. An extremely detailed chronology of important events in science, from ancient times to the present.

The Scientific Revolution, www.historyteacher.net/APEuroCourse/ WebLinks/WebLinks-ScientificRevolution.htm. Maintained by a high school history teacher in New York, this site contains a wealth of links to various topics about the scientific revolution. The linked information will be useful for students studying for the advanced placement examination in European history.

The Scientific Revolution: Copernicus to Newton, http://academic. brooklyn.cuny.edu/history/virtual/core4-4.htm. A good overview of the major events and people of the scientific revolution in the form of a lecture outline (from Brooklyn College's Shaping of the Modern World course). The site also has numerous linked images and some online documents.

The Scientific Revolution (1550–1700), www.sparknotes.com/ history/european/scientificrevolution. This site, sponsored by bookseller Barnes and Noble, offers a concise guide to the scientific revolution. It could be thought of as a Cliff's Notes–style introduction to the scientific revolution.

Scientific Revolution Homepage, http://web.clas.ufl.edu/users/ rhatch/pages/03-Sci-Rev/SCI-REV-Home. Probably the most comprehensive site on the scientific revolution, created by Professor Robert A. Hatch of the University of South Florida.

Index